D0049285

Biblical
Counseling
for
Today

SWINDOLL
LEADERSHIP
LIBRARY

Biblical Counseling for Today

A Handbook for
Those Who Counsel
from Scripture

JEFFREY WATSON

CHARLES R. SWINDOLL, *General Editor*
ROY B. ZUCK, *Managing Editor*

NELSON REFERENCE & ELECTRONIC
A Division of Thomas Nelson Publishers
Since 1798

www.thomasnelson.com

BIBLICAL COUNSELING FOR TODAY
Swindoll Leadership Library

Unless otherwise indicated, Scripture quotations used in this book are from
the *Holy Bible, New International Version* (NIV),
copyright © 1973, 1978, 1984, International Bible Society.
Used by permission of Zondervan Bible Publishers.

Scripture quotations identified NASB are from the *New American Standard Bible,*
copyright © 1960, 1962, 1963, 1971, 1972, 1973, 1975, 1977, 1995
by the Lockman Foundation. Used by permission.

Scripture quotations marked KJV are from the *King James Version* of the Bible.

Scripture quotations marked NKJV are from the *New King James Version*.
Copyright © 1979, 1980, 1982, Thomas Nelson, Inc., Publisher.

Published in association with Dallas Theological Seminary (DTS):

General Editor: Charles R. Swindoll
Managing Editor: Roy B. Zuck

The theological opinions expressed by the authors are not necessarily the official
position of Dallas Theological Seminary.

Library of Congress Cataloging in Publication Data:

Watson, Jeffrey A.
Biblical counseling / Jeffrey A. Watson
Charles R. Swindoll, general editor
Roy B. Zuck, managing editor
p.   cm.—(Swindoll Leadership Library)
Includes bibliographical references and indexes.

ISBN 0-8499-1358-6

1. Counseling. I. Title.
BV652.25.g38 2000
254'5–dc21   99-048665   CIP

Printed in the United States of America
04 05 06 BVG 9 8 7 6 5 4 3

To the "Lois" and "Eunice" of my family, my grandmother and mother, who first whetted my appetite for truth:

Vivian Virginia Lyon McGee (1895–1966)
Doris Merlyn McGee Watson (1922–)

CONTENTS

FOREWORD

To LISTEN TO A GIFTED COUNSELOR impart advice, encouragement, or correction is like watching a skilled painter or sculptor at work. The good counselor knows when to talk and when not to talk. Like the expert sculptor who knows where to chip and chisel, the qualified counselor knows when to prod and where to probe.

For years I have employed gifted counselors in our radio ministry, *Insight for Living*. It is fascinating to watch them at work. They ask penetrating questions. They jot down notes as they listen to life stories or read them in the letters we receive. They pray and seek wisdom from above. All this is done in an effort to provide relief for the one who is suffering. There's no doubting the giftedness of the one who practices biblical and wise counseling with the right motives, always using Scripture as his or her guide.

Let me clear up any doubts you may have at the outset of reading this fine work on counseling. This is a book about counseling from a *biblical* perspective. This is not advice from the world's best thinkers or philosophers. This is a book about imparting advice from the Book of books, the Bible.

Psalm 1 sets forth two paths for the reader. The first path is "the counsel of the wicked," and the second is "the law of the LORD." The two paths couldn't be more divergent. The results of these two ways of life are stunning in their disparity. Those who follow the first path, the advice of the wicked, will become, "like chaff that the wind drives away." On the other hand those who listen to, meditate on, and delight in "the law of the LORD," become "like a tree planted by streams of water." What a difference going to the right counselor makes!

If you counsel, or work with those who do, this book will become an invaluable tool for you. Jeff Watson knows biblical counseling. He's sat in the chair and listened to the stories. He's given the encouragement, the insight, the advice, or warning when needed. And most important of all, Watson uses God's Word as his manual.

A person gifted in counseling holds a tremendously fragile trust in his or her hands. Day after day people come to the counselor's office, pouring out their hearts and souls. After several visits the counselor is asked to come up with a diagnosis, a "prescription," including a plan of action. What should the hurting one *do* to get well? What words does the counselor offer in hope of bringing help?

Let me underscore one of my strongest convictions here. I believe that unless the counselor is a biblical counselor, the words offered are hollow. The advice is like Texas clouds on a hot summer afternoon—full of promise, but in the end there's no relief, not a drop of rain. The counselor who is not imparting advice from a biblical mind-set is using what James calls "earthly wisdom." "Such wisdom does not come down from heaven, but is earthly, unspiritual, 'of the devil'" (James 3:15).

I urge you to let this book become your manual for proper counseling. Write in the margins. Take notes at the tops and bottoms of pages. Underline freely. Whether you are an experienced counselor or a novice, you'll benefit from Watson's insight on how to counsel from the biblical perspective.

—CHARLES R. SWINDOLL
General Editor

PREFACE

THE GOAL OF THIS BOOK is to paint a verbal portrait of a house, a "goodly house" (Deut. 8:12, KJV) called "biblical counseling." Chapter 1 purchases some conceptual ground for this "goodly house." Chapter 2 posts several "No Trespassing" signs around the perimeter of the property. And chapter 3 drives construction stakes into the ground, marking the shape of the all-important foundation to follow.

In chapters 4–6 the construction foreman studies the blueprints for the intended dwelling, placing an order for the raw materials necessary to deliver the job. Following the interactions of Christ (chapter 4), the commands of Scripture (chapter 5), and the actions of the apostles and prophets (chapter 6), three foundational skills for biblical counseling will be laid respectively: helping people tell their story, helping people choose their goal, and helping people practice change.

In chapters 7–10 we raise the building out of the ground, establishing how and why a counselee grants the trust-permit to a biblical counselor. Chapter 7 focuses on the spiritual character of the biblical counselor. Chapter 8 targets the social character of the biblical counselor. Chapter 9 zeroes in on the professional character of the biblical counselor. The concluding chapter offers the reader a final walk-through of our "goodly house," an inspection of biblical counseling in real life.

ACKNOWLEDGMENTS

A<small>N OLD PROVERB SAYS</small>, "Even the journey of a thousand miles be-gins with a single step." So as I retrace my journey from first thoughts to final drafts, let me express thanks to the many who accompanied me along the way: Charlie Dyer, Roy Zuck, Charles Swindoll, David Moberg, Steve Henry, James Lyons, Ron and Carol Satta, Gale and Tannie Glahn, and my beloved wife, Nancy. May pathways blossom for those whose words and example sustained my travels over uneven terrain: Rick Leineweber, Conrad Smith, Frank Wichern, Phil Bena, Lois Anderson, Brett Ayers, Omar Omland, Gerard Egan, Bill McCartney, Laurie Hall, Janice McBride, Jeff Carroll, James Dobson, Clyde Narramore, and Jeffrey Satinover. Al-though the illustrative scenery along the trek is real, the biographical markers in the stories have been changed to protect the privacy of those involved.

PART ONE

Definitions in Biblical Counseling

CHAPTER ONE

Introduction

"Biblical counseling"—a noble adjective married to a nervous noun. The arithmetic is simple but the marriage is rocky. As I pen the modifier "biblical," Christian readers are ready to nod with a silent "amen." But as the computer clicks in the title's other half, "counseling," reactions may vary like the stock market.

BIBLICAL COUNSELING

The Bible, noble partner to our noun, is so dynamic that it permanently altered the life of a young man. Pen in hand, Paul addressed Timothy. "I have been reminded of your sincere faith, which first lived in your grandmother Lois and in your mother Eunice and, I am persuaded, now lives in you also. . . . But as for you, continue in what you have learned and have become convinced of, because you know those from whom you learned it, and how from infancy you have known the holy Scriptures, which are able to make you wise for salvation through faith in Christ Jesus. All Scripture is God-breathed and is useful for teaching, rebuking, correcting and training in righteousness, so that the man of God may be thoroughly equipped for every good work" (2 Tim. 1:5; 3:14–17).

Like a baby guzzling milk from a bottle, Timothy had nursed on the Old Testament Scriptures. Even before the Light had banished darkness from his soul, a godly mother and grandmother were pointing him toward the sunrise of truth. Apparently in this three-generation Jewish family, there had been a genuine reverence for the Old Testament. And Jesus had declared that much "is written about me in the Law of Moses, the Prophets, and the Psalms" (Luke 24:44). By piling the kindling of Scripture around young Timothy's heart, his family had readied him for the Holy Spirit to light the flame of evangelical understanding.

If a time line were created for this regenerate family, it would show at least three stages to their redemptive history. (1) For years the family saturated itself with the words of the Old Testament. (2) Then Lois and Eunice, through the preaching of Paul, met their Messiah, foretold, now crucified and risen. (3) Then Timothy, beloved son and grandson, became a child of God, a brother in the Lord, as Lois, Eunice, and Paul tag-teamed him for the gospel.

If any skeptics were prone to imagine that the Bible might be good enough to make Timothy "wise" about salvation (2 Tim. 3:15) but not good enough to make him "wise" about the world (1 Cor. 2:1–5; 3:19; James 3:13–18), hold on. Timothy was instructed to pass on to others the same truths Paul had shared with Timothy. These "others" would, in turn, pass them on to "others also" (2 Tim. 2:2, KJV). Using the analogy of spiritual kinship, what Paul (the father) was teaching Timothy (the son) was to be taught to others (the grandchildren), who would teach others also (the great-grandchildren). The same scriptural re-creation that had brought Timothy into the world would sustain him throughout his lifetime in the world. That repository of the Old and New Testaments would be useful in a fourfold way, potentially answering for Timothy and his spiritual offspring the most essential questions they could ever ask of God: "All Scripture is God-breathed and is useful for teaching [What is right?], rebuking [What is wrong?], correcting [How do I get right?], and training [How do I stay right?]."

Timothy's written scriptures were so intimately connected to God that Paul described them as "God-breathed" (3:16). As Lois, Eunice, Timothy, or Paul would read the Scriptures, they knew they were reading the very words of God. And still today God talks to His people through His Word, "teaching . . . rebuking . . . correcting . . . and training" them.

Why did God choose to give us a never-erring library of truth? Why did God communicate to us, using more than forty authors in three languages over fifteen centuries? God did this so His people "may be thoroughly equipped for every good work" (3:17).

And this rich treasury of truth is not void of interpersonal wisdom. In the presence of God, who models "truth in love" (Eph. 4:15), Paul commissioned Timothy with a flexible range of interpersonal responsibilities: "I give you this charge: preach the Word; be prepared in season and out of season; correct, rebuke, and encourage—with great patience and careful instruction" (2 Tim. 4:1–2).

BIBLICAL *COUNSELING*

So far, so good. We are grateful for the Christian nods in favor of our noble adjective, *biblical*. But why not stop here? Why must we bring in that difficult marriage partner, counseling? Why shouldn't our churches be content to bolster their Sunday morning ministries with Bible preaching and teaching, sprinkling throughout the week miniature versions of the same? Because the Bible requires more.

Stepping back through the front door of Timothy's childhood home, we are reminded of both the vertical and the horizontal dimensions of ministry. God saved Timothy, regenerating him through Christ as revealed in Scripture. But clearly God also used the interpersonal relationships in Timothy's life—people who would sow the seed, water the plant, and harvest the fruit (1 Cor. 3:6). While we delight in the product of God, we also affirm the process of God: a loving mother and grandmother, family quiet times or trips to the synagogue, evangelistic messages, and apostolic mentoring. The message became incarnate through method.

But we cannot afford to fixate on methods. We cannot seek to decipher Peter's evangelistic method in Acts 2:14–41 with the assumption that it will yield a technique for two-minute sermons, each guaranteed to reap thousands of converts. For ministry in general and counseling in particular, we cannot lower ourselves to an "anything goes" kind of pragmatism, to a philosophy in which the so-called biblical ends justify the all-too-pagan means.

Nonbiblical Counseling?

A pagan "means" poised toward a biblical "end"? Picture a twenty-year-old woman, stressed out in her first year of college studies, suffering night after night with little sleep. Her parents, believing that God wanted her to regain worry-free sleep, recommended she talk to the pastor's wife about school stress. She did. After several conversations her sleep improved noticeably.

There was just one problem: a certain recurring dream. In the dream the young woman and her four sisters were violently attacked. In a bizarre twist, the dream also included the young woman's father standing passively by, rather enjoying the ordeal. Unknown to the parents, the young woman went back to the pastor's wife dozens of times. Using dream analysis and hypnosis, the pastor's wife concluded that the woman had survived a tormented childhood during her elementary-school years. With coaching, the counselee "remembered" wicked assaults, an incestuous pregnancy, and a wire-brush abortion performed by her father.

But the "memories" were in sharp contrast to the facts. First, medical investigation proved that the woman was still a virgin. Second, clinical records showed that her father had undergone a vasectomy before she was even in kindergarten. Third, the four sisters reported no hints of abuse. And fourth, three years after leaving home and quitting therapy, the daughter recanted her once-sincere story. While the parents and daughter are now reconciled, the church and the family are not.

Nonbiblical Counselors?

Not only have some of Christ's soldiers coveted the arsenal of the enemy, but some in His army have longed to imitate heroes under the adversary's flag. Why else would a fourth-year Bible college student deceive his parents, arguing that somebody in the registrar's office "had made a typo"? He was not graduating with a mere diploma, he insisted; he was earning a double-major bachelor's degree in psychology and sociology. His parents had traveled two thousand miles to his graduation; how were they to know? Besides, a bronzed plaque was held in front of their eyes later that summer, "proof" that there had been a graduation-bulletin mishap.

Within a couple of years the young man's resumé had magically sprouted two master's degrees. From there it was a short step for this articulate, credentialed young man to candidate for that conspicuous church in the city. Within months of his call he would present an unbelievably good opportunity to his church board. A friend of his, supposedly working at Yale University, had called with the offer of a full scholarship for him to earn a Ph.D. degree in clinical psychology; the church would not have to pay a thing. If the board would only give their blessing, he could take two years of medical school at the local university; that much would transfer up to Yale, he assured them. If the board could free him up to be in medical school on weekdays, he would need to be in New Haven for only three summers of clinical experiments. With a "love-believes-all-things" naiveté, the board allowed him to apply.

Within three years church members could proudly point to their "Doctor." And as the deception mushroomed, major insurance companies paid for his psychotherapy, a Christian publisher wrote a contract for his first book, and two eminent Christian graduate schools urged him to join their faculties. But as his tenth anniversary with the church drew near, his sin found him out (see Num. 32:23). The church fell apart like a house of cards. Having learned to love "the enticing words of man's wisdom," many in the congregation admitted that their faith had rested in man and not in God.

Magicians, Beware!

For some, it may seem unbelievable to imagine a pastor's wife using dream analysis and hypnosis to probe the heart, which is "deceitful above all things, and desperately wicked" (Jer. 17:9, NKJV). For others, it may seem inconceivable that a pastor could so love the things that are in the world (1 John 2:15) that he would masquerade as an Ivy-League clinical psychologist. But in a world system where the arch deceiver seeks control of every soul on the globe, it is all too common for people to mimic nonbiblical methods or mentors.

Even the children of this world sometimes see through the folly of sailing on ships that have no anchor. In 1995 the New Mexico state legislature sought to set limits on the use of psychology in court.[1] Senate Bill 459 passed both houses of state government, requiring psychiatrists and psychologists when testifying in competency hearings to "wear a cone-shaped hat . . . not less than two feet tall . . . imprinted with stars and lightning bolts." Furthermore these expert witnesses were "to don a white beard . . . and punctuate crucial elements of their testimony by stabbing the air with a wand." At the moment they entered the witness box, the bailiff was instructed "to dim the courtroom lights" and strike twice a Chinese gong. With the help of a little exaggeration, they made their point; the governor vetoed it.

But this battle is not new. This is exactly the quarrel that erupted between the two Simons who stood toe-to-toe in the sands of Samaria.

> Now for some time a man named Simon had practiced sorcery in the city and amazed all the people of Samaria. He boasted that he was someone great, and all the people, both high and low, gave him their attention and exclaimed, "This man is the divine power known as the Great Power." They followed him because he had amazed them for a long time with his magic. . . . [Then] Simon . . . believed and was baptized. . . . He followed Philip everywhere, astonished by the great signs and miracles he saw. When the apostles in Jerusalem . . . sent Peter and John . . . they prayed for them [the Samaritan converts] that they might receive the Holy Spirit. . . . When Simon saw that the Spirit was given at the laying on of the apostles' hands,[2] he offered them money and said, "Give me also this ability so that everyone on whom I lay my hands may receive the Holy Spirit." Peter answered: "May your money perish with you, because you thought you could buy the gift of God with money! You have no part or share in this ministry, because your heart is not right before God. Repent of this wickedness and pray to the Lord. Perhaps he will forgive you for having such a thought in your heart. For I see that you are full of bitterness and captive to sin." Then Simon answered, "Pray to the Lord for me so that nothing you have said may happen to me." (Acts 8:9–24)

One Simon, a fisherman, had received a revelation from on high (Matt. 16:15–19). The other Simon, a magician, had learned his craft from below. The former, famous for his trilogy of proud denials (26:34–35), had discovered the power of humility (1 Pet. 5:5) and honesty (John 21:15–22). The latter, still known for his pride, had built up a following based on deception.

Ancient Pride, Modern Pride

The pride of Simon Magus warns us today about two deceitful thoughts common to the modern therapy movement. One is "We can change people and we don't need God!" The other is "No one can change people, not even God!" In these caricatures God is slandered as irrelevant and impotent.

Some people today reject all notions of therapeutic change. Many are wedded to the deep skepticism of the second slander: "No one can change people, not even God." But Bible believers affirm that people *can* change, based on 2 Corinthians 5:17 ("Therefore, if anyone is in Christ, he is a new creation; the old has gone, the new has come!") and 2 Peter 3:18 ("But grow in the grace and knowledge of our Lord and Savior Jesus Christ"). Because we have seen the power of the gospel, we know that blasphemers can learn to bless (1 Tim. 1:12–17). Because we have witnessed the power of the gospel, we behave as if we are in debt to all kinds of people, ready at all times to give them the gospel, despite all temptations not to (Rom. 1:14–16). With Paul, we sense the need to minister to all kinds of people ("I am obligated"), to preach the gospel to them ("I am eager"), and to expect God to change them ("I am not ashamed").

Those in the therapeutic community who doubt that people can change, with or without God's help, do not expect to see "cures" in their work. At best, they hope that their clients will learn to "manage" their problems. Their therapeutic approach is to tinker around the edges of inconvenient behavior, rarely expecting deep-seated transformation from the inside out.

Surprisingly some who carry the Bible every Sunday are bedfellows to the therapeutic skeptic. Some Christians are firmly convinced that people will not change; but from where does this conviction come? "Can . . . the leopard change its spots?" they ask (Jer. 13:23). Indeed not! But *God* can change their spots (Matt. 19:26). Perhaps the most telltale sign that one has become a change-skeptic is an unwillingness to forgive. After all, how dare God ask us to forgive seventy times seven (18:21–22) when we well know that the person who wronged us will do it again? "After all," we murmur, "people don't change."

Neither of our Simons was a change-skeptic. They both believed in change. However, they raged against each other concerning the source of change. Simon Peter was living proof that deep change comes as a gift from above (James 1:17–18). But Simon the Sorcerer, reaching back into his old life, thought he could buy the power to change people by purchasing secret knowledge about a kind of magic available here below (Acts 8:18–19). Simon the Magician was snared by the first slander: "We can change people and we don't need God! All we need is the right price offered to the right source for religious, insider-trading secrets." Today some new Simons are hoping to buy the right education in some behavioral science, expecting to move God to the periphery, while accomplishing change by another means.

But Simon Peter cursed Simon Magus (8:20) for thinking that God's good gifts could be purchased with anything but the blood of His Son. The old fisherman blistered the old witch doctor with the scorching truth that he was out of sync with God (8:21). Urging him toward repentance (8:22), Peter offered hope that even he might be delivered from the abyss (8:23). You see, Peter believed in change, but change that is sourced in God.

A Nervous Wedding

In olden days weddings were punctuated by the nervous question, "Does anyone here have good reason to believe that these two should not be united as one?" If we were to ask that same question about our marriage between "biblical" and "counseling" today, a discernible mutter would ripple down through the crowd of readers. As we invite objectors to speak up, there is a momentary hush; everyone at the wedding is entertaining a nervous thought. Perhaps one member of the "happy couple" is deceiving the other or maybe the minister has not done his homework.

As in all of life, a good case of nerves indicates some awareness of danger. This was the same kind of nervousness I felt back in the spring of 1973 as my Alitalia Airlines jet banked over Beirut. My camera stopped snapping pictures as I stared at an airport shrouded in black, charred by recent explosions and fire. Within minutes a neat circle of UN Peace-keepers surrounded the aircraft, each with a machine gun slung diagonally across his torso. After their brief sparring match with the wide-eyed Italian crew, I was allowed to debark. The Lebanese civil war had everyone on edge, and once off the plane, I was rushed by an army jeep into the "safety" of the bombed-out terminal.

Unfortunately the career missionary I was replacing, whose wife needed this four-month relief to care for a dying father in the States, was not allowed within a mile of the terminal; things were too dangerous for civilians in there! So much for the welcoming party.

I finally met with the veteran missionary at the sandbagged perimeter, but my relief was short-lived. No sooner did I arrive at my summer quarters, than I spotted a spray of bullet holes in the sliding glass door running the length of my bed. Answers for my queries came quickly. "That's the PLO camp just down the hill," the host's son pointed through the strafed door. "They get in gun battles pretty often with the Lebanese gendarmerie just up the hill. . . . Where are the bullets? They're lodged in your mattress. No problem."

A fresh case of nerves would temporarily prompt me to scout out the shortest route home. But the Word of God brought peace. "For it has been granted to you on behalf of Christ not only to believe on him, but also to suffer for Him" (Phil. 1:29). Occasional warnings from the embassy about a potential evacuation of American citizens would test the newfound calm, but nothing could ruin what God had begun.

Three Dangers

Just as I felt nervous in Beirut, so I feel nervous broaching this subject of counseling. Why? Because of three dangers. First, there is the danger of displeasing God (Heb. 10:31). If the fear of the Lord is the beginning of wise living (Prov. 1:7), then the fear of the Lord must certainly be the beginning of wise writing. Since God will one day judge every motive (1 Cor. 4:5), every word (James 4:11), and every deed (Jude 15), no reverent writer could engage this subject with a careless attitude.

Second, there is the danger of displeasing sincere counselors. Just as teachers merit a stricter judgment (James 3:1–2), so writers merit stricter judgment. And since Bible-believing clergy with mental-health credentials have urged counseling trainers to distinguish between pastoral counseling and psychotherapy,[3] a book of this nature owes respect to these colleagues. Taken to the extreme, some Bible-believers may feel that any integration from the counseling field is at risk of trying to combine two fields of study that, like oil and water, don't really mix. On the other end of the continuum, some counseling specialists may feel that any use of the Bible in counseling risks layering a veneer of quick-fix impatience over profoundly complex human problems.

Third, there is the danger of displeasing actual counselees. If this one book found its way into the hands of a thousand caring counselors, some lay, some pastoral, and some professional, this book over its shelf life could help or hinder many thousands of counselees. Counting the cost in such a human-capital project (Luke 14:28) raises the bar high for both risk and reward. The potential of helping or harming a host of vulnerable people is humbling indeed.

Three Virtues

But God has not given us the spirit of fear; rather, we are beneficiaries of His love, power, and discipline (2 Tim. 1:7). In that spirit let's describe why "biblical" is married to "counseling."

The same Timothy who had learned to trust deeply in the Word was guided by the apostle Paul to do more than preach and teach that Word (1 Tim. 4:13, 16). He was also instructed to guard his personal life (4:16). This same apprentice who was under orders to "fight the good fight" (1:18) was also trained to win that fight by holding on to his faith and a good conscience (1:19). In short, Timothy needed to treasure both his public ministries for God and his private walk with God. Like all Christians, Timothy was commissioned to love both Christ and neighbor, learning to live out his Christianity in the vertical *and* horizontal dimensions.

Whether or not we call Timothy's work "counseling," his commission included an intense focus on relationships. He was to be ready "in season and out of season" (2 Tim. 4:2), ready to preach when the offertory ended and ready to care when someone knocked on his door at night. Like his mentor, Timothy was obligated toward both public proclamation and private exhortation (Acts 20:20, 31).

The whole counsel of God, which Timothy was to preach and teach, would also be profitable, as we noted earlier, for "rebuking . . . correcting . . . and training" (2 Tim. 3:16). Thus besides preaching and teaching, Timothy was commanded to "correct, rebuke, and encourage—with great patience and careful instruction" (4:2). In an obedient Timothy, how would these other ministerial activities look?

First, Timothy would be doing the ministry of "rebuking" (3:16; 4:2). As our Lord taught (Matt. 18:15–20), Timothy was to arrange a private conversation with any brother or sister who had behaved sinfully against him. The goal of such a confrontation was to win the brother or sister back to a reconciled relationship with Timothy and God. Presumably Timothy was also to coach people in this process throughout the church, issuing public "rebukes" when the personal, plural, and prohibitive stages of rebuke had proved ineffective at gaining reconciliation. Perhaps then as now it would have been easier for Timothy to just rail at people during public sermons and lessons than to do the harder work of seeking repentance and reconciliation in the smallest spheres of life.

Second, Timothy would be doing the ministry of "correcting" (2 Tim. 3:16). Once the sin of a brother or sister had been adequately identified, Timothy's work was not done. He, and all like him, were to seek a way "to restore [the erring one] to an upright position."[4] The scene painted here by the Greek word for correcting (*epanorthōsis*) suggests that Christians who get snared by sin are sometimes left spiritually hunchbacked, limping, or wounded. To restore spiritually good posture, the Lord's people are not content merely to arrest the prodigal behavior; they seek to so rebuild backsliders that they regain a hatred for evil and a love for good (Rom. 12:9).

Third, Timothy would be doing the ministry of "training" (2 Tim. 3:16), best pictured as parents raising their children (Eph. 6:4; Heb. 12:11). Knowing that children will face increasing degrees of independence and adversity in life, proactive parents are diligent to encourage their offspring toward greater levels of steadfastness. Not content simply to move a failure back to neutral, Timothy was committed to using the Word of God to build positive moral strengths. Like a fine athlete rehabilitating from an injury, the goal is for the wayward one to be reconditioned to win when faced by the same temptation next time.

In personal terms the ministries of rebuking, correcting, and training are developmental:

- Rebuking means identifying moral delinquence.
- Correcting means restoring moral innocence.
- Training means building moral competence.

If a wayward person were heading 180 degrees in the wrong direction, a *rebuke* would seek to name the path he or she is on and, ideally, to stop that person in his or her tracks. *Correction* would seek to bring about a pivot, reorienting the prodigal back toward the right goal. And *training* would seek to get the wanderer to begin recovering the lost moral ground, traveling forward toward greater maturity in godliness.

When Peter proudly defied the Lord (Matt. 26:33, 35, 69–74), the Lord rebuked him (26:34, 75). When this backslider met the Lord again, the risen Christ corrected him, soliciting a complete confession and a return to a spiritually good posture (John 21:3, 15–17). As Peter repented, Jesus began training him for a future of renewed obedience (21:15–23).

At times all three elements of rebuking, correcting, and training are clearly in view in Jesus' ministry encounters. For example, He said to Peter, "Simon, Simon, Satan has asked to sift you as wheat [rebuke]. But I have prayed for you, Simon, that your faith may not fail [correction]. And when you have turned back, strengthen your brothers [training]" (Luke 22:31–32).

Timothy was to carry out all these ministries "with great patience and careful instruction" (2 Tim. 4:2). For the Bible-centered servant of God to identify moral delinquence, restore moral innocence, and build moral competence, he or she needs a generous portion of God's patience. Though the Lord saw Peter's failures as clearly as if they were under a microscope, He empathized with him, praying for him and speaking of a day when the prodigal would return (Luke 22:31–32). In patience Jesus waited until His third resurrection appearance to confront loudmouth Peter in private (John 21:14).

Twentieth-Century Timothys

Since the Bible is relevant for today and since God is faithful to finish the work He began (Phil. 1:6; 1 Thess. 5:24), modern Timothys are still to minister in a biblical way. At 11:00 P.M., the phone startled one such pastor. A distraught mother and a rebellious daughter were "on the way," the dad reported. As the pastor's children continued their sleep upstairs, the power of the Word would soon be tested downstairs.

"She's on LSD," the mom soon summarized, slumping exhaustedly into the high-backed chair in the opposite corner of the living room. "I keep thinking I want to kill myself," the teen related flatly. "Don't you hear that?" she would ask, her eyes darting off toward an empty part of the room. "A physical problem?" the pastor wondered. "This drug does give schizophrenia-type attacks." "An emotional feature? Suicidal thoughts are right at home there." But sensing evil in the atmosphere, he waded in spiritually. "That's the devil," the minister pointed out. "Jesus came to give life, and to give it abundantly, but the thief comes to steal, to kill, and to destroy. He wants to destroy you. He's the one who whispered in Jesus' ear to jump." With a deliberate pause, the pastor pulled his chair squarely in front of the girl's.

By 1:00 A.M. time had disappeared. The anguished mother across the room had reached up, blanketing the battle zone with earnest prayer. No doubt the dad at home had likewise been begging heaven's help.

Like two rock climbers on the sheer face of granite, the clergyman and his charge were soon drained of energy. The evening had begun with a confused adolescent staring downward, mesmerized by the seductive chasm below. At times she had seemed to rise onto the balls of her feet, balancing herself with arms outstretched, steeling herself for the foolish courage to jump. But before the night died, the daughter leaned hard into the mountain, securing some excellent handholds and footholds. Sometime before 2:15 A.M., she angled toward the veteran climber and began to ascend slowly with him back toward the top.

What had happened? A recent sermon series on 1 Samuel had snagged the attention of an otherwise-bored teen. The study on Saul and the medium of Endor (1 Sam. 28) had climaxed with two messages on the strategies of Satan, earning some credibility in the mind of the young rebel. But as her behavior continued to spiral downhill at home, the parents' strained grip slipped to the end of their rope. On the night of their call, they were "putting her out."

As the script unfolded, it had been like the Lord whispering in the ear of the pastor. As he rebuked the suicidal urge as "a hand grenade from hell," the Holy Spirit scored a direct hit on the conscience of the young person. Then the story began to come out piecemeal. The girl had been recruited to join a witch's coven several years before. The bait in that trap had been the promise of sex, drugs, grades, and popularity. But the bondage in the trap was the fear of death (Heb. 2:14–15), with members of the coven threatening to kill her if she ever quit or if she ever named anyone else in the coven.

The pastor declared that Satan "is a liar and the father of lies" (John 8:44). "Look at it," he said. "The very one who promised you life, the bait in his trap, is now threatening you with death: suicide or murder. Take your pick. He is speaking through these voices and these friends." The teen saw her moral crossroads.

A rash of excuses followed, but after each utterance, the pastor was able to declare, "That's the truth!" or "That's a lie!"

With such a prelude God brought the juvenile to the crux in her crisis. She was exhorted to speak the name of her recruiter, to renounce him and Satan. After a seeming eternity Christ won!

The pastor sent the girl home with her mother promising to be at their house in the morning. The Lord led him to give them a Bible-based book on spiritual warfare for them to study together. And he emphasized two verses to the teen: "Submit yourselves, then, to God. Resist the devil, and he will flee from you. Come near to God and he will come near to you. Wash your hands, you sinners, and purify your hearts, you double-minded" (James 4:7–8).

The pastor gave two brief applications about the hands and the heart. First, the repentant teen had objects she needed to destroy, things in her "hands." Second, she had thoughts she needed to withstand, thoughts in her "heart." After prayer, the meeting ended, but the obedience continued.

As the pastor drove away, the teen began collecting various possessions, including an antique nightstand. Piling these possessions in the backyard, the parents and daughter burned this pile of dark rubble. Some of the artifacts had been purchased at a hefty price from people bartering bondage. Their fiery destruction brought an end to oppression in the home.

Over the years leading up to this crucial juncture the pretty teen had walked deeply into an ugly forest. That night she did a spiritual about-face. By morning she was taking some giant steps back toward the light, though the journey would be long.

Although the apostle Paul wrote twenty centuries ago, his directions are timeless for modern Timothys—"teaching... rebuking... correcting ... and training." Whether in the sands of Samaria or on a sofa in the suburbs, biblical counseling can teach prodigals by rebuking devilish lies, correcting destructive loyalties, and training in new disciplines.

Contemporary Biblical Counseling

This book seeks to take a modest but straightforward approach to biblical counseling. In the first part, definitions are provided. In the second, skills are discussed. In the third, models are described.

In addition to being straightforward, the project seeks to be holistic, recognizing that God treasures each person, "spirit, soul, and body" (1 Thess. 5:23), and He wants each believer to contribute to the maturity of other believers (Eph. 4:11–16). Thus whether you are a busy pastor, a professional therapist, or a godly layperson, my prayer is that this book would help improve your ministry (John 13:14–15; Eph. 4:12).

CHAPTER TWO

Biblical Counseling: What It Isn't

WHAT DOES "BIBLICAL COUNSELING" MEAN? This question, no doubt, has occurred to every thoughtful person who has seen this primer advertised or thumbed through it. While no single book other than the Bible could hope to unify thousands of readers, we seek in these next two chapters to provide a tenfold summary, clarifying what biblical counseling is not (chapter 2) and what biblical counseling is (chapter 3).

While chapter 1 purchased some conceptual real estate on which to build our "goodly house," chapter 2 seeks to post ten "No Trespassing" signs on our property. As newcomers walk the perimeter of our site, they can read signs that say that biblical counseling is not . . .

- a recipe for quick or guaranteed success
- an exercise in value neutrality
- an excuse for hostility
- an attempt at mind reading
- a confusion of human emotion and spirituality
- a promise of absolute confidentiality
- a breeding ground for antigovernment sentiment
- an excuse for inappropriate disclosure
- a way to play doctor
- a ritual in the idolatry of self.

BIBLICAL COUNSELING IS NOT A RECIPE
FOR QUICK OR GUARANTEED SUCCESS

The phone rang loudly. When the TV preacher himself did not answer the 1-800 line, the caller seemed irritated.

"But I am his assistant," the calming voice tried to reassure. "How can our staff help you?"

The caller had fallen on bad times. He was a pastor, a college graduate. But his wife had become "disobedient," he lamented. "She hasn't gone to church for months! Says there are only two pastors in the world she trusts . . . and your preacher is one of them. Please just tell him that if he'll get on the phone for two sentences, I'll put the phone to her ear. If she just hears him say, 'Go to church; obey your husband,' things will change. We'll be able to go back to the way it used to be when she loved church."

Tragically, even clergy—shepherds who are educated and ordained to lead congregations—can get trapped in quick-fix, recipe-type thinking. Problems that may have been a long time brewing can be seen as mystically dismissible. If some kind of trouble could only be blessed by the right magic wand, the impasse might end. At least that's what some think.

But what factors had brought about the wife's so-called disobedience and lack of trust? What had fueled her church life in the past and what was different now? Had she become disappointed with God? Her husband? Or the congregation? Had she been sowing seeds of lukewarmness, leading herself steadily down the path to apathy? And if she had been deafening herself to God through months of bitterness or fear, why should anyone expect her to hear God's perfect pitch amid two sentences from a famous stranger?

If ever there existed a perfect biblical counselor, it was Jesus, thoroughly wise and fully scriptural. But what would Jesus have said to this pastor or to his wife? Would Jesus have advised a two-sentence 1-800 call, or something like it, to fix the problem? In fact, did Jesus Himself always "succeed" with people, resolving their every problem?

By surveying Jesus' ministry through a results-oriented lens, we conclude that our Lord was sometimes a slow success with people (for example, Thomas) and sometimes not a success at all (for example, Judas). If we try to control our Lord, demanding that He suddenly fix people regardless of their will, we will be tempted to perceive Him as a failure and we will be unable to explain the theodicy of an eternal hell. As biblical counselors, if we buy into the myth of quick or guaranteed success, or if we allow the pain of our counselees to ambush us with that noble expectation, we could find ourselves sliding down a slippery slope, falling prey to a devilish slander against the competence or compassion of Christ.

Although Jesus Christ ministered to thousands (Matt. 14:14–21), he handpicked seventy-two preachers (Luke 10:1) and a dozen apostles (Matt. 9:36–11:1), including Thomas (10:3) and Judas (10:4). The examples of the apostle Thomas and the apostate Judas are a helpful caution against the success syndrome in the ministry today.

When Jesus called the Twelve to follow Him, they believed they had forsaken all (19:27). Thomas even urged the inner corps to steel themselves for a martyr's death in their loyalty to Jesus (John 11:16). But ironically, Thomas staggered with doubt (14:4–5) and was the last to repent of his unbelief (20:24–29). All fell away (Matt. 26:31, 56), breaking their naive pledges. Worse, Judas, a hypocritical thief (John 12:3–8), fell in love with a satanic thought (13:2) and betrayed Jesus for the price of a field hand (Matt. 26:14–16). In Judas's blind folly he tried to fool the omniscient One (26:25), exploiting Jesus' privacy and kissing Him with the poison of false affection (26:46–50). In Judas's final hours he became wickedness incarnate, eventually jumping to his death at the end of a rope (27:3–10). So, if there was any success with Judas, it is found in the predictive power of the Old Testament (Acts 1:16–20; 2:23) and the eternal justice of well-earned damnation (1:25).

The biblical counselor is wise to remember that Jesus never went into a self-esteem tailspin over the apparent failure of a Judas or the slow success of a Thomas. Nonetheless caring souls can expect to undergo a transient period of mourning when their help seems barren (Matt. 23:37). Like parents who grieve the folly of their offspring (Prov. 17:25; Heb. 13:17), counselors are often moved with a sorrow when a couple quits a marriage or when conflict erupts into violence. Although biblical counselors can harvest wisdom from every interaction (Prov. 9:7–9; 17:10), they must remember that fools often refuse to change (26:11; Luke 10:10–11). As such, biblical counseling cannot be held out as a recipe for quick or guaranteed success.

BIBLICAL COUNSELING IS NOT AN EXERCISE IN VALUE NEUTRALITY

The room felt nervous. As the nineteen-year-old and his therapist dropped decisively into their chairs, the camp director knew she was in for some kind of complaint. As a trained lay counselor and as the supervisor of all the summertime youth counselors, the camp director was no stranger to controversy. She deliberately sat straighter behind her desk and looked the unfamiliar therapist in the eye.

"You had no right to tell the Richardsons about my past!" The young man spit his words toward the camp director, glaring.

"Really, there are only a few reasons for breaking trust," the therapist waded in. "An active risk of homicide, suicide, or child abuse. As a counselor, you are expected to be neutral, not taking sides in an interpersonal conflict."

"Time out." The camp director's hands formed a deliberate T. "You feel like I wronged you?" She slowed the pace and softened the volume, looking specifically at the lad. "By breaking your confidence?"

"Yes!" he replied bitterly. "She even knows what she did was wrong," the boy whined, looking dumbfounded toward his therapist.

Taking a slow, deep breath, the camp director began to navigate the rough waters. "When did you ever counsel with me? How could I break your trust, if you never took me into your trust?"

"No, but . . . Sammy . . . ," the nineteen-year-old fumbled. "I figured Sammy told you. . . ." Now all three seemed nervous.

The director asked, "Were you angry because you thought you had told Sammy something in private and that he then told me and I told the Richardsons?"

"You mean Sammy never talked to you about me?" the boy queried. "So how did you know? How could you have told the Richardsons about the, uh, stuff?"

"How did I learn that you claimed a background in drug trafficking and the juvenile jails?" The camp director was becoming very systematic.

"Yeah, if Sammy didn't tell you, how did you know?" The nineteen-year-old seemed truly curious.

The director responded, "I don't even know, for a fact, what the truth is about your background. But I heard you speak about your past twice, once in a very loud voice at the lunch table and once in your chapel testimony. As I recall, the story seemed to change quite a bit between the two tellings. But I wondered, even if some version of it were true, why you would be sharing it in such conspicuous ways."

"And the Richardsons?" the boy volleyed back, timidly.

"Did you know their three kids are adopted?" the director asked. "When Mr. Richardson came to pick up the kids on the last week of camp, he asked me whether adopted children are more prone to rebel or to seek their birth parents during their teen years. At the end, he asked me if I would recommend you for a baby-sitter in the off season."

"Yeah, I know, Mr. and Mrs. Richardson had a disagreement about whether I'd make a good nanny for them." He looked down.

The director continued, "And I told him that we don't sponsor child-care in the off season. So he wanted to know if I would have personally hired you as a baby-sitter, if my children were still the same age as his. And I said, 'No.' He wanted to know if there had been any 'incidents' at camp with you and I also said, 'No.' But I summarized your public disclosures about your 'past.' True or not, I felt that you might tell that kind of a story to the kids and it could frighten them. That's the last I knew of it."

"Well, two weeks ago they told me they weren't going to use me as a baby-sitter anymore." After a long pause the teen and his therapist tied some loose ends together and dismissed themselves.

In a culture that treasures democratic equality and individual rights, counselors are sometimes trained to be neutral, theoretically unbiased toward clients, their beliefs, and their behaviors. Some therapists-in-training, for instance, have been taught in their graduate programs that they must be neutral or even positive toward some behaviors that the Bible describes as wrong. For instance, if trainees felt any psychological discomfort while watching homosexual videos in class, they might be scolded as "homophobic." Even a former Sunday-school-teaching president has joined the tirade against such alleged bigotry.[1] But biblical counseling is not an exercise in value neutrality.

Biblical counseling recognizes Dietrich Bonhoeffer's distinction between cheap grace and true grace; while cheap grace justifies the sin, true grace seeks to justify the sinner.[2] On the strength of a biblical whetstone, true character is sharpened like the blade of a knife (Prov. 27:17). While Christian caregivers want to avoid the follies of false superiority, and of judging motives, many times the Word of God judges explicit behavior (2 Chron. 19:6; Isa. 1:23; Jer. 5:28; 1 Cor. 5:1–13). The camp director, though not a private counselor for the nineteen-year-old, was biblically "biased" against dishonest or nonedifying speech (Eph. 4:25, 29; 5:12). As a mother herself, she was unable to remain neutral (2 Tim. 3:7) if her neutrality might put someone at risk. Before the nineteen-year-old left her office that day, she gently admonished him from the Word (Col. 3:16).

In a parallel vignette the New Testament reminds us about Barnabas, a compassionate man who was nicknamed "the Son of Encouragement" (Acts 4:36). When the Jerusalem Christians were afraid of their new spiritual brother Saul, Barnabas built a bridge of trust between them (9:26–28). When persecution scattered Christians in every direction, Barnabas traveled to confirm the new gentile believers in the faith (11:19–24; 15:1–35). When needs arose, Barnabas paired up with Paul, providing teaching and famine relief work in A.D. 46 (11:25–30). Despite martyrdoms and arrests, Barnabas followed the Holy Spirit and led the first missionary team, consisting of himself, Paul, and John Mark (12:1–13:3). Even when young John Mark quit before the first journey was over (15:38), Barnabas used some of his furlough time to restore John to the ministry, triggering the anger of Paul (15:36–40). But in the end, even Paul would see John Mark as a recovered teammate (2 Tim. 4:11). Biblical counseling, in New Testament times or the present, is not an exercise in value neutrality.

BIBLICAL COUNSELING IS NOT AN EXCUSE FOR HOSTILITY

Out of the senior class only one student could be chosen "Most Likely to Succeed." Even though it was a Bible college, success still had its trademarks: integrity, not money; soul-winning, not corporate-ladder climbing; orthodoxy, not mental paganism. When he rose to his feet, the West Coast chapel thundered with applause. He was not only well liked; he was handsome, soon-to-be married, and moving on to that heartland seminary where many of his profs had gone.

But success did not follow as expected. Moving to the big city posed its special problems. Ten weeks at a night job were supposed to enable the honeymooners to start paying the rent and to set aside a nest egg for his fall classes. Instead, moving away from parents, a home church, and a supervised dorm situation opened up a Pandora's box of temptation.

Night work made it easy to sleep through the day, including Sunday. The graveyard shift put the newlyweds on opposite schedules. Worse, the job drew the seminarian-to-be through the hooker district at the beginning and end of work. Friendless, the wife could only dream about the encouragement that might come with fall classes. But that fall never arrived.

Somewhere there was a "fault line" in his character and no one would ever be sure how long it had been widening. Before any students stood in the registration line, he had stepped across a different threshold into a greenhouse of wickedness. He began to experiment, even cross-dressing at times for quick infusions of cash.

The new bride's frantic calls home to her parents, in-laws, and pastor were met with denials. "You must be imagining things . . . Not him! . . . How dare you?" No one intervened, and the husband disappeared.

Alone and alienated, the young wife eventually fell prey to another man. Though not a Christian, he did offer her a sense of some security. In her mind she couldn't marry him; she wasn't even divorced yet. When their child was born, the family back home had enough excuses to cut her off—the parents because the baby was biracial and the pastor because of her sin. Buried beneath a mountain of shame, she wished someone would remember the lines from Sunday school, "Love your enemies . . . do to others what you would have them do to you" (Matt. 5:44; 7:12).

As the estranged wife of the one "Most Likely to Succeed," she drifted for years. Churchless, she saw men come and go. Her babies had different dads. Her jobs were low-end, geared toward survival, and complicated by the need for childcare. This Christian daughter of proud middle-class parents barely survived on underpaying jobs, food stamps, and Medicaid. But God had not given up. The Holy Spirit would stir her, again and again, to try a church, to begin doing what she knew was right.

Her courage mustered, she eventually readied her children for church and went. The message and the service seemed so familiar, yet like an event from another century. At the rear door she asked if she could talk to the pastor, in private. Reluctantly he agreed. Gathering her preschool trio into his office, she began to tell her story with a street-smart, matter-of-fact face; she didn't know what he would think of her. She was looking for permission to start over again, there.

The pastor, no doubt tired, hungry, and a bit nervous about this stranger in his office, kept biting his tongue. He was just sure she was going to ask for money. When she came to the so-there-you-have-it pause, he fired his Bible bullet: "You know, if you had lived in Old Testament times, they'd have stoned you!" He was unhappy that she hadn't expressed sorrow or repentance in her story. She felt like he had punched her in the stomach, or worse, wished her dead. As she prepared to leave, he stuck a brochure in her hand. "A church down the street has a counseling center; I'd suggest you try them." Scanning the brochure as she stuffed it in her purse, she was relieved to see a photograph showing that a woman served as one of their counselors.

Within a month this weary mother had met an angel, a professional therapist with a Bible-college background, a woman with convictions similar to those of the referring pastor but with an abundance of empathy for real-world hurts. A modest sliding-scale fee was negotiated, and the counselor confidentially secured a generous benevolent gift from the deacons of her church. On the very day the surprise gift was handed to the counselee, a story about God's timing unfolded.

"Today, my boss propositioned me. If I would allow him to come to my apartment for sex whenever he wanted, he'd pay my rent. He pressured me for an answer by tomorrow. Now I can tell him that God loves me more than he does, that God has met my need, no strings attached."

Like Job, this sufferer had had more than her share of adversity. She was a sinner but she had encountered some destruction not of her own doing. And despite her sinfulness, she had met some of "Job's comforters," people who had focused on criticism when comfort was due. Her parents, in-laws, and two pastors had all but revictimized her when she needed them most.

Charles Swindoll describes people who are like "Job's comforters," people who misunderstand the grace of God: "There are those who seem to be waiting for the first opportunity to confront. Suspicious by nature and negative in style, they are determined to find any flaw, failure, or subtle weakness in your life, and to point it out. There may be twenty things they could affirm; instead they have one main goal, to make sure you never forget your weaknesses. Grace killers are big on the shoulds and oughts in their advice. Instead of praising, they pounce!"[3]

Despite the sinful choices this woman had made, biblical counseling was no excuse for personal rejection and hostility.

BIBLICAL COUNSELING IS NOT AN ATTEMPT AT MIND READING

Most security guards struggle with boredom, but this night would be different, fatally different. As John stared at the bank of closed-circuit television screens in the lobby of the office building, he hummed along to country music on the transistor radio; it would be the calm before the storm.

Since John moonlighted as a night watchman, he didn't even know about the events of that afternoon, how the sullen law clerk in the seventh-floor office had been fired. Who knows why? Somebody said the senior partner had e-mailed the office manager, "The clerk has to go!"

Anyway the office manager did the dirty work and told the clerk it was time to clear out his desk that day. Angrily the ex-employee strode back and forth, boxing his possessions and marching them to his car. Before long the hubbub around the water cooler had developed a consensus: "The jaw-clenched clerk should have seen it coming. Maybe he was even a little 'mental.'"

By the time the discharged employee had left, the other employees were back at their desks. No one noticed that he had come back up and stepped into the storage closet. No one noticed the pistol under his jacket or could have known the vengeful scheme under his breath: "Tomorrow when Marty gets off the elevator at 6:30 A.M., he'll have the surprise of his life! We'll see how courageous Mr. Courageous is, the coward who from his fancy laptop in Colorado e-mailed somebody else to fire me. He's so arrogant. He probably already told them to cancel my magnetic passcard. I won't need it; I'm not coming back in. I'm spending the night, just for the pleasure of the look on his face. One last look!"

As expected, the law offices emptied out by about 9:00 P.M. The blanket of quiet covered the suites, lit only by emergency lights. As the night wore on, John felt sure he could move around. "A bathroom break . . . a drink at the water fountain . . . no harm," he figured. But the camera spotted him. Almost immediately the guard was ringing the office manager's phone on an idle desk.

With the sound of the elevator, the ambush was put in motion. Crouching behind the trash can, the trembling gunman waited. Within seconds, the seventh-floor elevator doors were opening. Just as the guard stepped through the doors, he felt the hot puncture of two bullets pierce the left side of his rib cage. In the doctor's words, "He was dead before he hit the floor."

As news of the ambushed security guard hit the media, the whole city mourned for two days. And a seminarian pondered what he could say to the widow and children. As the adult Sunday school teacher, he knew the pastor was counting on him to help shepherd this grieving family. Muttering all the way to the funeral home, this young pastor-to-be tried to perfect the art of mind reading. "What would they be thinking? How do I explain why this happened?" He dreaded being speechless, or worse, crying.

Preoccupied, trying to get God off the hook, the aspiring pastor walked into the funeral home and met strangers, the dead man's brother and wife. Before he could get his first religious line out, the woman turned and pointed at the casket. "I hate this place! That's exactly where my baby boy was, and I feel so guilty!" The woman hung her head.

The seminarian's prearranged speech no longer fit. Stammering, he grasped for any material he could find. "It's a terrible thing when a child dies. You know, King David's son could not come back to him. But there is the age of accountability. It's not your fault; you shouldn't feel guilty, you know."

The conversation ended with an awkward silence, typical of the whole night. In the weeks that followed, the widow calmly explained why her brother- and sister-in-law were feeling so much guilt during the viewing. Two years earlier their four-year-old had died at Mercy Hospital. Though the death was not the doctor's fault, some mistakes were made. The parents had pushed hard for a big settlement. But throughout the long months of litigation, despite all the dramatic rhetoric about their precious son, they had never even visited the boy's grave site or bought a grave marker. The funeral director had recognized them, prompting them to mutter something about "not enough money for a tombstone." To anesthetize their pain, they had vacationed away the whole settlement on Caribbean islands and still had never bought a marker or visited the grave. True guilt!

Sadly, the seminarian was so busy trying to read minds and to prepare speeches that he missed the beauty of simple prayer (1 Sam. 12:23; 1 Thess. 5:17), reflective listening (Ps. 46:10; Isa. 30:15), and empathic sorrow (Rom. 12:15). Like judging motives (1 Cor. 4:5), attempts at mind reading risk infatuation with the covert and the subconscious (Eph. 5:12–13). At times, efforts at mind reading grow out of fear, pride, and a need to control.

When Agabus warned Paul about his impending arrest, some Christians couldn't believe the apostle insisted on going to Jerusalem anyway (Acts 21:10–12). Perhaps they feared he was disobeying the Holy Spirit or that he selfishly craved the limelight. Even when he was in jail, some preachers were caught up with judgmental attitudes (Phil. 1:15–16), perhaps indicting the methods that had supposedly landed Paul in jail or quibbling over reputation and results. But Paul refused to get caught up in their mind games; instead he focused on their overt behavior: "It is true that some preach Christ out of envy and rivalry, but others out of goodwill . . . . But what does it matter? The important thing is that in every way, whether from false motives or true, Christ is preached. And because of this I rejoice" (1:15, 18). For Paul and for us biblical counseling was never intended to be an attempt at mind reading.

BIBLICAL COUNSELING IS NOT A CONFUSION OF HUMAN EMOTION AND SPIRITUALITY

As the jail chaplain stepped up to the prison microphone, he felt clear-headed. "The gospel, nothing but the gospel today!" he reminded himself silently, as he scanned the crowd.

This chaplain was a tough man, a diesel mechanic before he had gone to seminary. Before that, he had spent time in prison. When he stood nose-to-nose in a cellblock, he had a single mission: to get the inmate saved. Once saved, there was another mission: to get the convert to grow.

Everything had gone according to plan with prisoner Lester. The chaplain had met him during his first week in prison. Back then, Lester wouldn't even talk to a white man. He just stared, as if he was in a police lineup. But when the chaplain sent volunteers to deliver Christmas presents to Lester's children, his stony face softened. After that, Lester became a person. In the chaplain's mind, Lester now had a story. Sometimes he smiled, and once he even cried.

During one of his softer times Lester trusted Christ for salvation. And for the next six months he came to about half of the Bible studies offered by the chaplain's office. It seems he was expecting God to make him a new man and to restore him someday to his wife and children.

Then it happened. On the morning circuit the inspector found Lester dead by hanging. The denim work shirt had become his noose, his escape hatch, his exclamation mark. Friends said news of his wife's boyfriend had sent him into a downward spiral for several weeks. He never pulled out.

As the chaplain cleared his throat, he began the funeral sermon. "Today we bury Lester's body but only God can describe the plight of his soul, that unholy place of torment, the sulfuric streets of the damned." The audience winced. "God is a God of hope and Christians are people of hope; but suicide is an act of utter hopelessness. Like his suicidal forbear, Judas, biblically known as the 'son of perdition' (John 17:12, NASB), Lester showed us last Tuesday that deep down he did not believe." The sermon went on, but its essence had been telegraphed in the first few sentences.

Several days later a prison-ministry volunteer asked to have lunch with the chaplain. He too had been puzzled by Lester's fatal choice, but he was even more puzzled by the chaplain's all-or-nothing logic. "Didn't Lester show us some of the fruit of salvation? Didn't you know his wife said she was dumping him?"

The chaplain barely paused. "Man, if I preached that funeral like he was a Christian, we'd have suicides here by the dozen. I can hear it now, 'Lester got saved, killed himself, and went to heaven. Anybody else want to get out of here?'"

The volunteer thought about it, trying to appreciate the leadership dilemma the chaplain had faced in his sermon. "But what about 1 Thessalonians 5:23, which says we are made up of spirit, soul, and body, like three concentric circles?" As he talked, the volunteer quickly diagrammed his thoughts on the chaplain's white board, labeling the circles from the inside out, "spiritual ... emotional ... physical." "Couldn't Lester have been saved on that innermost, spiritual level, but been sad or depressed on the emotional level?"

"Listen," the chaplain jabbed back, looking down at his watch. "You can't buy into that psychobabble, like they try and teach us at our chaplains' in-services. If a kid fell out of a tree and broke his arm, we'd take him to a doc. The doc would x-ray the break, reset his bone, and put him in a cast. But anything that isn't physical is spiritual." As the chaplain walked from his desk, he smudged out the smallest circle and the middle label, "emotional." "Spiritual and emotional, one and the same," he smiled, as if he had just won an argument.

Though the conversation was over, the controversies it touched on were not. Just as certainly as the chaplain had lumped the emotional and spiritual dimensions of life together under one religious umbrella, some best-selling social scientists have lumped the same elements together as if they are an indivisible whole.[4]

The chaplain's two-dimensional model, emphasizing the physical and nonphysical, could find wide support in Christendom and Scripture (Matt. 10:28). Even the hymn writer Charles Gabriel interpreted Jesus' tears in Gethsemane as an expression of spirituality, not emotionality (26:37–39).

> For me it was in the garden
> He prayed, "not my will, but Thine";
> He had no tears for His own griefs
> But sweat-drops of blood for mine.[5]

Though Jesus had tenderly grieved for Jerusalem (23:37) and Lazarus (John 11:35), was it beneath Him to weep for Himself? Are we sure Jesus' spirituality canceled out His emotions? "During the days of Jesus' life on earth, he offered up prayers and petitions with loud cries and tears to the one who could save him from death" (Heb. 5:7). "An angel from heaven appeared to him and strengthened him" (Luke 22:43). "He learned obedience from what he suffered" (Heb. 5:8). To argue that Jesus was too spiritual to cry for Himself would be like arguing that He was too spiritual to bleed for Himself. But God, in whose image we are all made (Gen. 1:26), designed the human body to bleed after certain physical injuries and the human soul to grieve after certain emotional injuries. Despite these injuries and these reactions, Jesus' spirituality led Him to pray, "Not as I will, but as You will" (Matt. 26:39). Similarly the apostle Paul reminded us (1 Thess. 4:13) that when our loved ones die (physically), even Christians grieve (emotionally), but not in a way that is hopeless (spiritually).

Perhaps the chaplain's true gift was evangelism. But even a burden for soul-winning, made rigid by a bipartite anthropology and a fear of copy-cat suicides, does not excuse an end-justifies-the-means rationalization. Biblical counseling is not a confusion of human emotion and spirituality.

BIBLICAL COUNSELING IS NOT A PROMISE OF ABSOLUTE CONFIDENTIALITY

"Can I tell you something? Promise you won't tell anyone else?" It was a hard question but he'd heard it before, and he paused before answering. He was an elder in the church and almost like everyone's uncle, a kind of Gentle Ben among the congregation's leaders. Many people found it easy to talk to him; he seemed to have a God-given knack for encouraging people. These qualities made him a very popular teacher at the Christian high school.

"Why do you need that promise?" he explored. "I've never listened to something in confidence and then gone and told anybody before."

"Well, I've never had a problem this big before," the fifteen-year-old girl said with a look of shame. "I have a decision to make and there are only two options, but I want your opinion, confidentially. I don't want you bringing anyone else into this. Promise?"

He felt she had thoroughly rehearsed this conversation in her mind, resolving not to speak further without the promise of permanent privacy. To this tender-hearted shepherd, the conversation had all the earmarks of a confession. The teen seemed repentant to him, so why would he need to tell anyone anyway? "Besides," he thought, "since she has put her trust in me, I can probably get her to do whatever I think is necessary, including telling somebody else if need be."

"Okay," he smiled hesitantly.

She sighed, as if hoping for that answer. "I'm pregnant and nobody knows!" Worry drew quick lines across her face, dreading his reaction. "Part of me wants to get an abortion; part of me wants to let the baby live. What should I do?" She got very still, studying his eyes for some clue.

He wanted more of the story, but she didn't budge. He tried to get the name of the boyfriend, but she was tight-lipped. The elder shifted uncomfortably in his chair; now it was his turn to sigh deeply.

"Do your parents know? Does your boyfriend know?"

Twice she nodded no. "I told you nobody knows!" she shot back with impatience.

"Well, we can't handle this alone," he replied quietly. "Your original question, to abort or not—you can't kill the baby." His sentence ended with an intentional staccato.

She seemed to appreciate his decisiveness about abortion. Maybe that's why she came to him in the first place. But she didn't appreciate what he did next. He pushed her a second time for more information, insisting that she go to her parents. He threatened that he might go to them anyway.

Nothing doing. She reminded him of his promise, pointing at him like a young lawyer.

For the next two months this elder tried to unlock the oath of silence. He prayed that she would confess to her parents; she didn't. He queried a couple of people about how she was doing, generally. To no avail. He even called the house once, trying to get another conversation with his pregnant counselee, but her mother answered. After answering his roll call about everybody in the family, the mother insisted on knowing why he had called. Grimacing in silence, he lied, "I wanted to set up an elder visit to your home."

The elder visit turned into a two-family meal. With both sets of parents and all the children present, the visit stayed tame. A couple of times the elder caught an angry glare from his young confidante. But the subject never came up and the evening ended.

Before the elder could ultimately choose between his personal promise and his public responsibility, he got nailed. Noticing her daughter's nausea and rounding figure, the mother eventually put two and two together. But when the parents learned that only two people in the world knew about the pregnancy—their daughter and this teacher—they hit the roof. With the help of a lawyer they launched a career-ending info-missile. Quoting an old state statute, they alleged that any adult male who has exclusive knowledge of a minor's pregnancy is presumed to be the father! Using this statute, the family's attorney insisted that the church leader pay all medical, legal, and adoption expenses for the upcoming birth. In exchange the family would not reveal what this elder had done. On a meager salary he paid. But when the birth finally took place, someone in the family failed to keep their promise and the story leaked out.

The elder was forced to resign his roles at the church and the Christian school. Though DNA tests were never done, even those who joined the girl and the elder in denying the paternity implications agreed that he had shown very poor judgment. In time he became a painter and began to sit in the back pew of another church, one large enough to keep him anonymous.

In our American culture, which treasures individual rights, the counseling tradition is firmly built on the medical ethics of patient autonomy, informed consent, and confidentiality. In the typical doctor-patient relationship modern medical values imply that patients should be able to make choices for themselves based on information provided them by the doctor. Furthermore this entire decision-making process is presumed to be entirely private. Hence people who describe themselves as "doing counseling" of any sort are at risk of being seen through the contractual eyes of the doctor-patient framework. However, the expectation of absolute confidentiality challenges many Christian notions about parents' rights (Josh. 24:15), the danger of secrets (Gen. 37), and the potential requirement to "tell it to the church" (Matt. 18:17). Judging from these notions, as well as legal requirements to report the suspicion of ongoing child abuse or impending homicide or suicide, biblical counselors should not offer absolute confidentiality.

BIBLICAL COUNSELING IS NOT A BREEDING GROUND FOR ANTIGOVERNMENT SENTIMENT

Delaware churches were abuzz with the news: A local pastor had been arrested! Before sunset on Sunday, volunteers had passed out leaflets at congregations throughout the southern part of the state, leaflets designed to raise legal fees for this "falsely accused" clergyman. After all, they reasoned, he had done so much for the pro-life movement. He had started the local crisis pregnancy center, placed pregnant teens in good homes, picketed and lobbied as needed. His closest friends said he swore that he had nothing to do with the string of abortion-clinic bombings in several bordering states.

But the FBI had a different story. His pro-life friend had a construction license to buy dynamite. Together they owned a storage shed where some bomb-making ingredients had been found. A fender bender and a gasoline credit card receipt showed they had been hundreds of miles from their homes at 2:00 A.M., just hours before an explosion in that vicinity. In fact, two blond hairs, found on the black electrical tape from the bombing debris, apparently matched the accused pastor's DNA.

While awaiting trial, he posted bond and lived at home. He was not to leave the state, nor go near any abortion clinics. But what surprised people was the publicity he seemed to seek during this intervening period. He regularly denied any involvement in the bombings, and he began to preach, teach, and debate about Rahab's "lie" (Josh. 2:1–24; Heb. 11:31). She lied, he argued, in order to fulfill a higher command, namely, to save lives. He said it would be parallel to French resistance forces in World War II breaking padlocks off Nazi railroad cars. Destroying property, technically a crime, was forgivable if hundreds of innocent people bound for the ovens were set free. In fact, it might actually be a moral duty to break those locks. The duty to protect lives outranked the duty to protect property. In the words of the apostle Peter, "We must obey God rather than men!" (Acts 5:29).

Eventually this man went to prison. And when his years were up, he returned to pastoring with the same perspective: Government was supposed to be a theocratic republic. When government falls short of its obvious responsibilities, he contended, its citizens have the option, if not the duty, to challenge the system. At times, challenge was framed like the colonists withstanding Lexington's Redcoats or like "Indians" dumping barrels of London tea into Boston harbor. Some Christians in his orbit also focused on the dangers of the "Philistine schools" (that is, public schools) or Big Brother's control via the Social Security number system.

Unfortunately this convicted pastor, often the spark plug to individual and group action, had frequently provided counseling with an antigovernment bias. Too often his counseling sessions had functioned as conspiratorial enclaves, fueled by the paranoia of doomsday thinking. Granted, government errs, such as when gynecological exams were forced on all the females at a public school without parental notification or child consent. Even some secular critics argued, in that instance, that the local health officials were guilty of invasions of privacy and of sexual battery.

But with a more pro-government approach, some biblical counselors entered a cooperative relationship with child-protection officials and the FBI. Blessing the partnership, God allowed this unusual tandem to accomplish what none of the subgroups could have done alone: discover and prosecute an interstate child-abuse network.

Christians know that God has not given us "a spirit of timidity, but a spirit of power, of love, and of self-discipline" (2 Tim. 1:7). Even in relation to our elected officials, Christians know that their higher citizenship calls them to pray for their human leaders (Phil. 3:20; 1 Tim. 2:1–8), trusting God to use government as a tool of justice (Rom. 13:1–7).

In drawing the parallel between clinic bombings and Peter's preaching, antigovernment advocates set themselves up for sharp scrutiny. For instance, Peter had been commanded to preach to all nations (Matt. 28: 19–20), so when the Sanhedrin forbade him to preach (Acts 5:17–18, 26–28), he obeyed God rather than his unbelieving persecutors (5:29). But Peter did not lie to the Sanhedrin; he did not insist that he hadn't preached. And when arrested and punished (5:17–18, 26–28), he didn't bemoan his ill-deserved fate; instead he rejoiced that he could suffer for righteousness' sake (5:41; see also Matt. 5:10–12; 1 Pet. 2:11–17). Furthermore, if the Christian church had been given an explicit commission to bomb abortion clinics, biblical counselors could rightly urge many more people to follow suit and would correctly expect the pastor, once out of prison, to resume his conscience-based civil disobedience. In actuality, he did not resume it.

Christians who despise the world (1 John 2:15–17; 5:19) still remember to love their enemies (Matt. 5:43–48), to be "salt" and "light" in society (5:13–16), to render Caesar his due (22:21), and, at times, to appeal to Caesar for help (Acts 25:11). So, when biblical counselors are faced with helping folks who are in the troubled spotlight of the hospital, the school, or the court, they must help their counselees strive to live like Joseph in Egypt. While Joseph had good reason to believe there had been conspirators working against him, still he sustained a spiritual optimism about his adversities. In fact, Joseph, a government official at the time, saw God's hand in the public-welfare program of Egyptian granaries. To his biological brothers, he painted an amazing contrast: "You intended to harm me, but God intended it for good to accomplish what is now being done" (Gen. 50:20). Although biblical counselors today hold to conservative or traditional values, true biblical counseling should not become a breeding ground for antigovernment cynicism.

BIBLICAL COUNSELING IS NOT AN EXCUSE FOR INAPPROPRIATE DISCLOSURE

Biblical counselors often have the opportunity and the social skills to get close to people; that's the positive side of the ministry coin. But with that reward comes risk. In gaining the trust of a counselee, biblical counselors can sometimes be tempted to step onto the slippery slope of inappropriate disclosure, asking for or telling information that is nobody's business. While this may seem to help the relationship grow by closing the distance between counselor and counselee, at the same time it can create inherent relational dangers.

Little did the Christian radio counselor know, but such a danger was just around the corner. Combining a seminary education and a university specialization, this radio minister had become a popular people-helper. His topics were practical (such as depression, communication, fear, and forgiveness), and he became a popular speaker at banquets, retreats, and seminars. So when the pastor for Grace Church called, requesting a ten-week seminar on "Improving Communication," the radio host gladly accepted. From it, he gained an honorarium, a wider listening audience, and the thrill of live interactions.

Saturday morning sessions at the church, kicked off by coffee and doughnuts, would allow about twenty members of the congregation to take the training without the cost of going away to another site. A small per-person tuition was much cheaper than ten sessions of professional therapy or a full weekend retreat. But for two of the participants, the cost would be far greater.

The counselor knew that in the first week people would be defensive, inclined to hide their problems and act as if they really didn't need to be there. Rather than engage in ten Saturdays of cognitive dumping, and wanting to avoid boredom, he did his usual thing: He hung out a little bit of dirty laundry. Taking some risks, he told the group about some of the more personal communication problems he had experienced with his wife, his kids, and his colleagues. By doing this, he intended to soften the crowd, to show his vulnerability, and to invite honesty among his seminar attendees. But to at least one seminar participant, he communicated a different message, a message that he had a very unhappy marriage. She understood that; she had been through an ugly divorce herself.

At the end of the first session she lingered to speak to him. "Thank you for being so honest today," she said softly as she left the room. Somehow the brief encounter gave him a flattering rush.

The next Saturday the same woman raised one question during the discussion period: "Do you do counseling?" He made it clear that his schedule didn't allow for long-term counseling, but that he often talked to callers by phone or seminar participants over lunch to evaluate their situation and to make referrals. "Whatever they need," he said.

By the end of the day the divorcée took him up on his offer. "How about next Saturday? Lunch?" Part of him tried to say, "Why?" But the other part of him smiled, "Sure!"

As a standard part of the communication seminar, session three focused on nonverbal communication. That segment, "The Royal Route to the Heart," emphasized the power of one's tone of voice and facial expression. "Based on surveys," he reported, " we know that people trust facial expression 55 percent of the time, tone of voice 38 percent of the time, but words only 7 percent of the time."[6] Spontaneous stories from attendees proved his point throughout the final hour of the morning. By lunchtime he was ready for a mental break.

After gathering up overheads and brochures, the teacher and learner made quick work of deciding where to chat; they would take their own cars to that little diner down the street. Once there the meeting had all the earmarks of caution: a public table, simple fare, separate checks.

By the time the food arrived, he had made his inquiries, all polite. "What do you do for work? How long have you been going to this church? Did you grow up here? Any kids? Are you in a relationship now?" He had a way of zeroing in and setting people at ease.

She was a nurse . . . worked nights . . . had found this church two years before . . . wasn't really too connected, since their singles ministry was geared to college students away from home . . . no kids of her own . . . had grown up in a sound church across town, but left when her marriage ended and her ex-husband stayed. . . . she wasn't currently involved with anyone, but was "hungry" for a relationship. The counselor realized he had to concentrate to hear her answers. With his energy drained during the morning, he found it easier to mirror her smiles, to study her eyes and complexion, and to enjoy her personality.

Her questions seemed innocent enough. "How'd you learn all this stuff you're teaching us? How can a person learn to trust again when she's been hurt? How do I know which criticisms from my ex-husband were valid, which ones might resurface in my next relationship?"

She then told the counselor some intimate details of problems in her married life. It became clear that she was longing to be loved.

While some counselors would disagree with the interactions the woman and her counselor already had, even more would reprimand the two for what followed. The fourth and fifth Saturday sessions ended with quick hugs. She would wait to be the last to speak with him as the crowd thinned out. He started to look forward to the hugs, but never discussed these feelings with anyone.

Somewhere along the line the weekly hug included a quick peck on the cheek. By the last session, she whispered, "Whenever you want me." He said nothing.

When the thank-you note arrived at the radio station, he had an address and phone number. Several months later, bored at work and irritated at home, he dialed her phone. In the end no one knew they had begun to meet until he left a note for his wife and children. Now, according to the good-bye note, he had supposedly "found the right one."

The radio counselor had been deceived by his own lusts (Eph. 4:22), indulging in "the passing pleasures of sin" (Heb. 11:25, NASB).

After months of spiritual havoc and years of sorrowful reaping (Gal. 6:7–8), God's kindness would lead the former radio counselor to repentance. With the help of several godly men the once-wayward husband faced his prodigal behavior. He saw the pride of prayerlessness (James 4:6–8), the folly of independence (Prov. 27:17; Rom. 12:3), and the risk of an unguarded heart (Prov. 4:23; Heb. 4:12, 15–16). Most of all, he discovered the incendiary nature of his sexual discourse and feelings toward his client. In restoration he came to love the power of prevention found in Scripture. "Do not let any unwholesome talk come out of your mouths, but only what is helpful for building others up according to their needs, that it may benefit those who listen. . . . For it is shameful even to mention what the disobedient do in secret" (Eph. 4:29; 5:12). In hindsight the wounded helper began to emphasize to his former counseling colleagues that counseling should not be an excuse for soliciting or providing inappropriate disclosure.

BIBLICAL COUNSELING IS NOT A WAY TO PLAY DOCTOR

The seminary movement has seen a kaleidoscope of trends, many related to modernity. "If theologians could get university degrees in philosophy or religion, perhaps the gospel could gain a respectful audience among its critics," some have reasoned. "If the art of communication could improve pulpit speech, perhaps the television generation would stay tuned in to God's word," others proposed. "If leadership techniques were honed in seminary, maybe clergy could model their not-for-profit churches on successful business practices," the pragmatists have offered.

Despite the many advantages to a broad education for seminary professors, at least one disadvantage seems obvious: the potential for unwanted cross-contamination. While some Christian scholars have brought Christianity into their fields of study, others have brought the nomenclature, methods, and presuppositions from their respective fields into Christian scholarship. To one observer, these latter have acted like "eager-to-please puppies underfoot an indifferent master."[7]

In some modern ministerial schools students have been delighted to be able to take courses from psychologists and psychiatrists they trust. For one bright student his seminary coursework gave him the first opportunity he had ever had to discuss his sister's chronic mental illness with a Christian medical doctor. Since the student was talkative and the professor ambitious, the sister became a case study for the class. By having students study the *Diagnostic and Statistical Manual of Mental Disorders*,[8] a reference volume known as "The Psychiatrist's Bible," students were shown how to diagnose their classmate's sister, as well as those they would one day serve in some assigned congregation. The students were assured, "When you get out, at least you won't be putting every problem into a John 3:16 bag and trying to dump out a solution!"

For some students the training was very valuable. They could debrief on any eccentricities in their families of origin, and they now had a way to classify what they had seen. The training also convinced a certain portion of the students to make referrals to mental-health providers when needed or to see to it that another staff person was available to do the bulk of the counseling. However, another group of students emerged from the course quite convinced that the average church leader could and should classify mental disorders according to the *Manual*. Unfortunately these naive optimists were never educated about the *Manual's* weaknesses,[9] nor were they told that the majority of clinicians do not use it for treatment purposes.[10]

In time, some of the naive optimists would play doctor in the church office. Clients would come for weekly fifty-minute sessions; each week the counselor would file progress notes using terms like "depression" or "chronic anxiety." At times some of these fledgling counselors would advise their counselees to quit medications, to discontinue outside therapy, or to ignore certain components in hospital discharge plans and court orders. This was appealing to the counselees because it seemed spiritually safer. There was just one problem: the law.

By describing themselves as "counselors," these clergy were unconsciously setting themselves up to be tested against state statutes that govern the doctor-patient relationship. By interfering with existing doctor-patient relationships, these religious people-helpers acted as if they knew as much as the mental-health provider whose treatment plans they were countermanding. For those counselors who advertised, there seemed to be a front end to the implied contractual relationship, while those who collected a fee seemed to complete the contractual loop. When subpoenas arrived, those with medically oriented progress notes were sitting ducks for malpractice actions.

While counselor education programs in Bible colleges and seminaries have readied many graduates for America's growing appetite for counseling, the lack of caution may have tempted some students to "love the world [system]" (1 John 2:15). By learning to speak the language of therapy, some ministerial trainees have unwittingly accepted the supposed power of "wise and persuasive words" (1 Cor. 2:4). And though such training has marginally demystified some of the priestcraft in the medical profession, it has also risked the snakebite of unforeseen consequences.

Who could have foreseen a sincere phone call resulting in a violent death? When the church member asked if the pastor would begin counseling her best friend, a nonchurchgoer, the pastor accepted. Though difficult, the problem seemed straightforward: the husband, a policeman, occasionally battered his wife at home. On inquiry, the pastor learned that the husband had often expressed an unwillingness to attend counseling with his wife, anywhere. So in their first-and-only counseling session, the pastor pulled out a well-worn strategy: "Tell him if he doesn't come in for counseling, you'll have him arrested for past battery or you'll leave him for incompatibility." Though she insisted that the paradoxical strategy was an empty threat, she delivered the message.

It provoked a reaction: The batterer killed himself.

Though the strategy had seemed doctor-tested, the pastor and counselee had engaged in deception and manipulation. Though the wife would forever pay emotionally, the counselor would forever pay professionally. In tragic proportions the pastor learned that biblical counseling is not a way to play doctor.

BIBLICAL COUNSELING IS NOT A RITUAL IN THE IDOLATRY OF SELF

When the imprisoned apostle Paul wrote Timothy, he predicted a spiritual future shock. "But mark this," Paul wrote. "There will be terrible times in the last days. People will be lovers of themselves, lovers of money, boastful, proud, abusive, disobedient to their parents, ungrateful, unholy, without love, unforgiving, slanderous, without self-control, brutal, not lovers of the good, treacherous, rash, conceited, lovers of pleasure rather than lovers of God—having a form of godliness but denying its power. Have nothing to do with them" (2 Tim. 3:1–5). And our Lord prophesied that evil would flourish and that true love would diminish (Matt. 24:12). Similarly Jude foresaw a callous cadre of "grumblers and faultfinders [who] follow their own evil desires and [who] boast about themselves" (Jude 16). As if writing a diary for twenty-first-century culture, these prophets zeroed in on an impending spiritual implosion, an end-times obsession with self.

Today many people focus on self-concept, self-esteem, self-determination, and self-expression. Some have even been coached toward personal rebellion masquerading as freedom. For example, G. Brock Chisholm, Canadian psychiatrist and cofounder of the World Federation for Mental Health, challenged traditional authority this way:

> We have swallowed all manner of poisonous certainties fed us by our parents, our Sunday and day school teachers, our politicians, our priests, our newspapers and others with a vested interest in controlling us. 'Thou shalt become as gods, knowing good and evil,' good and evil with which to keep children under control, with which to prevent free thinking, with which to impose local and familial and national loyalties, and with which to blind children to their glorious intellectual heritage. . . . The results, the inevitable results, are frustration, inferiority, neurosis, and inability to enjoy living, to reason clearly or to make a world fit to live in. If the [human] race is to be freed from its crippling burden of good and evil, it must be psychiatrists who take the original responsibility.[11]

Tragically, many have donned the mantle of counseling, mesmerized by an idolatry toward self. Counseling techniques, thus employed, invite counselees to vent their most basic thoughts and feelings, to be "true to themselves," to be free of the burden of externally imposed guilt. And depending on the counselor's theoretical orientation, clients may not be considered "healed" until they have recognized their childhood fantasy to murder one parent and have sex with the other.

Even Christian counselors can be attracted to the idea of making self the magnetic field for the counseling ritual. A young woman, whose parents were renowned missionaries, was coaxed by her Christian counselor into "telling all" and ventilating her "true feelings." In time she revealed that she felt caught in a battle between her two selves, one public and one private. Her public self was an overachieving actress, an aspirant to the mission field, and the compulsively polite child of highly revered parents. Her private self was manipulative, promiscuous, and bitter.

By milking the venom of her bitterness in their sessions, the counselor learned that the young actress had always felt anxious, worried that she was going to let her famous parents down. Perfectionistic and overbearing, her parents had rarely let her act like other children. If she had a conflict with neighbor children, she was severely disciplined, regardless of the circumstances. After all, anger was the unpardonable sin. And growing up in a home that was frequently shared with traveling missionaries, the daughter learned to perform and to put on an insincere show. The therapeutic goal seemed simple: Get the counselee to merge her two selves, learning to communicate her anger toward her parents more directly.

Anxious to play out the script for therapeutic change, the young actress immediately revealed her Dr.-Jekyll-and-Mr.-Hyde personality. She broke several of her personal commitments, pronounced her parents "hypocrites," and moved in with the boyfriend she had so diligently kept secret.

The parents, now heartbroken and embarrassed, learned about the counselor and placed a phone call. Concerned about privacy, the counselor simply summarized her perspective: "Your daughter's self-esteem is probably healthier now than it's ever been." With the mystery of that summary etched in their memory, the parents were invited to "just be good parents." In a rapid succession of events the daughter was excommunicated from her local church, the family was emotionally fractured, and the once-secret self became her public persona.

Using the analogy of a boiler, some therapists feel that conflicted feelings, like steam pressure, must be ventilated. "After all, if we don't ventilate these inner impulses, we'll explode," they imply. Unfortunately people-helpers who share this view do not always anticipate the lifelong scars their counselees may inflict when they scald someone in the name of self-expression. Indeed, some boilers are trained during counseling to explode, but few are warned that exploding can leave irreparable damage and become a progressively reinforcing habit.

Enriched by the wisdom of Scripture, biblical counselors understand that we all live in a honeycomb of relationships and that God must be the measure of our lives. "For none of us lives to himself alone and none of us dies to himself alone. If we live, we live to the Lord; and if we die, we die to the Lord. So, whether we live or die, we belong to the Lord" (Rom. 14: 7–8). Where self stands prominent, the Bible warns about fleshly selfishness (Gal. 5:16–26), about the perversity of the Luciferian "I will" (Isa. 14: 12–14), and the tragedy of disobedient willfulness (Matt. 23:37–38). Instead of spewing evil from a putrid heart (Jer. 17:9; Matt. 12:34–37), we are challenged to cultivate virtue in a charitable heart (22:36–40; Phil. 4:8). In essence, biblical counseling is not a ritual in the idolatry of self.

CHAPTER THREE

Biblical Counseling: What It Is

WHEN CUSTOM-BUILDING A HOME, an owner buys a piece of ground and marks off the boundaries; this we sought to do in chapters 1 and 2. To prepare for the construction phase, chapter 3 seeks to drive in some stakes, indicating the exact shape of the foundation. On our site each of the construction stakes flies a bright plastic ribbon describing what biblical counseling is. As the excavation foreman walks through the foundation area, he reads ribbons that successively announce biblical counseling is . . .

- a call to respect scriptural process
- a call for principled intervention
- a call for compassion with integrity
- a summons to excellent communication
- a commitment to regard each person as an interdependent whole
- a call to privacy with permeable boundaries
- a coaching session for resilient coping
- a private version of public speech
- a way to shepherd souls
- a practice in relational accountability.

Each of these descriptions stands in contrast to the series of disclaimers in chapter 2 that clarify what biblical counseling is *not*.

BIBLICAL COUNSELING IS A CALL
TO RESPECT SCRIPTURAL PROCESS

As evidenced by Jesus' ministry to Thomas and Judas, biblical counseling is not a recipe for quick or guaranteed success. Instead biblical counseling is a call to engage interpersonal relationships in a way that respects scriptural process. While every biblical counselor, ancient or modern, seeks to be clear on product, each biblical counselor must also grapple with process. For instance, our Lord was crystal clear in His goal for Nicodemus: "You must be born again" (John 3:7). Yet Jesus' one-on-one nighttime conversation with Nicodemus revealed His respect for divine timing and change.

Nicodemus, a respected lawyer, had been a religious unbeliever. After watching Jesus for some time, Nicodemus then sought out the Lord in private (3:2). But before the conversation was over, Jesus had engaged Nicodemus's curiosity, compelling him as a master teacher in Israel to search the Old Testament for analogues to the "born-again" imperative (3:3, 7). Nicodemus became a genuine seeker (7:45–53).

After two years, perhaps through the arrest, trial, and crucifixion of the suffering Servant, Nicodemus became a secret disciple (19:38–42). Then, sometime after the Resurrection, Nicodemus and Joseph must have gone public with their faith, resulting in their story now being included in the Gospel of John. While Jesus had longed to see this particular product in Nicodemus's life, He pursued the relationship with great respect for spiritual due process, sowing and watering with patience and hope (Ps. 126:5–6; 1 Cor. 3:6–9).

In our results-oriented culture, some might deem Jesus' ministry with Nicodemus or with Thomas (John 11:16; 14:4–5; 20:24–29) as taking too long. Others might critique the Lord's work with Judas as a failure. But even secular researchers acknowledge that there is no such thing as a 100-percent cure rate, regardless of whether the rate is reported by type of problem, type of counselor, or type of cure.

First, success rates often vary, depending on the type of problem encountered. People-helpers often find it easiest to produce information change (the cognitive domain), less simple to achieve behavior change (the psychomotor domain), and most difficult to obtain attitude change (the affective domain). For instance, a high-school guidance counselor would be progressively less likely to succeed in the following scenarios. (1) A junior comes for an appointment and asks, "How long do you have to go to college to become a lawyer?" (2) The same junior comes for a second appointment and asks, "I have a C- minus average so far in high school, but I have found out that pre-law programs are looking for people with at least a B+ average. What can you do to help me get my GPA up to B+ before I graduate?" (3) By the third appointment, the eleventh-grader becomes more candid. "My folks say they'll pay for my college education only if I train to become a lawyer. But I hate going to school; I hate reading and I hate writing. They are hoping that you can talk some sense into me." The guidance counselor who simply answered information questions (the cognitive domain) would typically have a higher success rate than one that sought to change a student's study habits (the psychomotor domain). But the biggest challenge for any guidance counselor would be to produce a lasting shift in the counselee's attitude toward schooling (the affective domain).

In a similar way a Sunday school superintendent could experience varying degrees of success, depending on the type of success he sought. For instance, on the first Sunday of a missions conference, the superintendent could ask the classes who are gathered for opening exercises, "What is the gospel?" In quick order he could answer his own informational question: "The gospel is the 'good news' that Christ died for our sins . . . was buried . . . and was raised on the third day" (1 Cor. 15:1–8). That's why we witness; it's good news!" With due pride the superintendent could feel glad to hear his Bible students grasp the informational truth of the gospel.

But what if the superintendent took the intervention a step farther? What if on the following Sunday he explored the same subject in more depth? "This was missions conference week. How many of you remember what the gospel is?" A good number of hands would probably go up. Continuing, he could ask, "How many of you shared your faith verbally this week with an unbeliever?" The superintendent might be disappointed to see fewer hands going up, silent testimony to the greater difficulty of securing behavior change. And then if he took his own class into their room and led them in singing the gospel song, "I Love to Tell the Story," he could invite an honest discussion about how people feel toward witnessing. Unfortunately he might find that even some percentage of those who did witness during the previous week did so out of a sense of obligation or fear, not for the sheer love of witnessing. Creating information change would be one thing, but motivating behavior change or attitude change would probably be progressively more difficult. He could judge himself, therefore, to be progressively less successful, depending on the type of solution he was targeting.

Second, success rates may also vary depending on the type of counselor involved. Some master's-level counselors, for instance, have a better success rate than doctoral-level counselors, especially psychiatrists. However, this trend should not be interpreted as showing a paradoxical relationship between the counselor's education and the counselor's expertise. Rather, the trend may show that problem complexity goes up by specialty. For example, when a person needs help, he or she usually seeks it from family and friends. If that works, that's where the help seeking stops. However, if the problem persists or becomes more acute, the individual may seek out a pastor or a guidance counselor at a school. If that works, that's where the help seeking stops. But if things continue to go downhill, the needy person may feel obliged to seek out a physician or a mental-health provider; sometimes the court or the employer requires it. To illustrate this inverse relationship between problem complexity and success rates, one might expect the survival rate for neurosurgery patients to be lower than the survival rate for oral surgery patients.

Third, success rates can also vary depending on the type of "cure" defined. For instance, approximately 50 percent of the people who get on a counselor's waiting list say they "got well" while they were waiting for their first appointment. Among those who enter counseling, 60 percent end up "cured," as mutually defined by the counselor and the counselee. But if cases are included where only one of the parties, counselor or counselee, says the problem was resolved, there is a 90 percent success rate. Rather than becoming cynical about the small margin of difference between wait-list success (50 percent) and mutually defined success (60 percent), there seem to be five positive outcomes for counseling: (1) some problems just go away; (2) some counselees on a wait-list begin to take responsibility for their problems, receiving help from God or others; (3) some counselees and counselors develop a mutually beneficial collaboration; (4) some counselees get just enough help to return to mental health, falling short of the counselor's complete treatment plan; or (5) some counselees get better with treatment without completely understanding why.

Biblical counsel, whether offered by a professional therapist, a pastoral counselor, or a layperson's loving admonition, is not automatically destined for quick or guaranteed success. Rather, biblical counseling is a call to engage interpersonal relationships in a way that thoroughly respects the often-complex processes of change.

BIBLICAL COUNSELING IS A CALL
FOR PRINCIPLED INTERVENTION

Biblical counselors do not enter into helping relationships as if the moral Governor of the universe were asleep or indifferent. Instead of practicing value neutrality, biblical counselors follow two God-given principles for intervention: truth and love. By striving for the elegant balance of "speaking the truth in love" (Eph. 4:15), mature counselors avoid unspiritual extremes. After all, truth without love would be brutality, while love without truth would be mere sentimentality. By avoiding these extremes, biblical counselors seek to model genuine spirituality and to respect tolerable differences in spiritual intervention.

First, biblical counselors recognize that therapy tends to function with a higher ratio of love, while counseling typically functions with a higher ratio of truth. Though the distinctions may seem merely semantic, the chart below distinguishes some of the characteristics of therapy and counseling.

	Therapy	*Counseling*
An exchange:	Between near-equals	Between non-equals
Seeking to:	Heal perceptions	Solve problems
By:	Guiding communication	Giving communication
Over:	Many sessions	Fewer sessions

For example, if a rape victim were suffering from depression born of sleep-onset flashbacks, a therapist might seek to travel back with the survivor to the site of the trauma through reassuring conversations. Over time the survivor might gain greater skills to control the power of the posttraumatic stress and to talk herself through the flashback episodes with a loved one. However, a different woman might find herself raising a nine-year-old granddaughter who is chronically underachieving at school. This custodial grandmother could hire an educational psychologist to conduct a series of assessments and write a psychoeducational plan for the girl. Based on these recommendations, the family might retain legal counsel to petition the public school to provide appropriate accommodations for their granddaughter's special needs.

Of the two foregoing scenarios the former tends to picture therapy, while the latter pictures counseling. Though therapy leans toward the "love" part of the helping equation, counseling leans toward the "truth" side. In balancing truth and love, biblical counselors can never lower themselves into using mere therapeutic techniques in a morally flat universe; similarly biblical counselors can never justify using religion as an attack weapon in a morally rigid universe. Hence, whether one is seeking to provide a core service of biblical counseling in the context of professional therapy or in the context of expert counsel, each must seek God's grace to balance the two virtues of truth *and* love.

Second, biblical counselors recognize that some counselees voluntarily seek help (Prov. 11:14; 15:22; 24:6) while others are sought out for help by their would-be counselors (Gal. 6:1–2). While counselee-initiated helping relationships begin more like therapy, counselor-initiated helping relationships start more like expert counsel. Helpers in the former scenario need to be willing to speak up with the truth, even though it may feel flattering to be sought out voluntarily for help. Helpers, in the latter context, need to be willing to speak as gently as possible, although it may feel like a moral duty to propose help to someone not seeking it at the time. While the former model is typically the focus in counselor education and therapeutic training, the latter model is very common in life.

The Bible illustrates both counselee-initiated and counselor-initiated helping relationships. For instance, when the pharaoh of Egypt was haunted by two bizarre dreams (Gen. 41:1–7), he asked Joseph for help. "His mind was troubled, so he sent for all the magicians and wise men of Egypt . . . but no one could interpret them for him. . . . So Pharaoh sent for

Joseph . . . [saying to Joseph], 'I had a dream and no one can interpret it. But I have heard it said of you that when you hear a dream you can interpret it'" (41:8, 14–15). "I cannot do it," Joseph replied to Pharaoh, "but God will give Pharaoh the answer" (41:16).

Similarly, when Nebuchadnezzar's advisers proved fruitless, the king turned to Daniel for help (Dan. 2:1–49). As with Joseph, Daniel resisted the flattering notion that he was the source of help and truthfully turned the needy person's gaze toward God (2:27–28).

From a different starting point the apostle Paul initiated a counseling exchange with the apostle Peter, even though Peter had not yet recognized he had a problem: "When Peter came to Antioch, I opposed him to his face, because he was clearly in the wrong" (Gal. 2:11). Guilty of hypocrisy sourced in fear, Peter had waffled between eating nonkosher foods with the Gentiles and endorsing the legalistic, kosher cookbook (2:11–21). By lovingly speaking the truth, Paul initiated a helping relationship with a brother who had caused others to stumble (2:13). As illustrated by the positive examples of Joseph, Daniel, and Paul, biblical counseling is not an exercise in value neutrality; rather, it is a call to intervene by "speaking the truth in love" (Eph. 4:15).

BIBLICAL COUNSELING IS A CALL
FOR COMPASSION WITH INTEGRITY

Biblical counseling is not an excuse for hostility; biblical counseling is a call for compassion with integrity. By "speaking the truth" we minister with integrity; by speaking it "in love" we minister with compassion.

On a sunny morning in the temple court our Lord showed the beauty of balanced ministry, a ministry of compassion with integrity. The self-righteous religious leaders of Jesus' day had made a citizens' arrest of an adulteress (John 8:1–4). Exploding with religious pride, the legalistic posse pushed Jesus toward an indictment. To their minds her adultery had violated the seventh commandment (Exod. 20:14), making her a candidate for capital punishment (Lev. 20:10).

But even before the adulteress had been hustled into the courtroom of public opinion, our Lord had detected her failure on the radar screen of

His omniscience. Yet Jesus' integrity was bigger than any selective application of rules, even divine rules. Christ not only recognized that she deserved to be put to death (John 8:5). He also knew that adultery required at least two people. He discerned that the Pharisaic bureaucrats had somehow let the man go, even though the Mosaic Law would have called for the man to be executed too (Lev. 20:10). To appear biblical, the prosecution could at least have dragged the man into the same circle of stigma.

The Pharisees placed the adulterous woman in front of the crowd and painted her, as it were, with a scarlet letter. With compassion for her, Jesus perceived their trap (John 8:6). Since the Roman government had revoked the Sanhedrin's right to try capital offenses (18:31), Jesus' adversaries were trying to put Him in a no-win situation: "Opt for stoning her and you'll be in trouble with the Romans; opt for anything less and you'll be in trouble with God, or worse, us!"

In a brilliant and balanced maneuver Jesus did not get caught in the whirlpool of their conniving energy. He remained quiet, broke eye contact, and doodled in the dust as if He were deaf (8:6).

But the legalists kept questioning Jesus. As they pushed and pushed Him, He patiently stood up. Looking them in the eye, He gave instructions on how to start the stoning: "If any one of you is without sin, let him be the first to throw a stone at her" (8:7). If only those who were morally perfect could reach for a rock, her execution would be stayed. More than that, if Jesus could indict the prosecution team for its sins of favoritism and hypocrisy, perhaps more than she would learn a lesson.

When Jesus returned to his legal pad on the ground, something mysterious happened. As he wrote (8:8), the plaintiffs excused themselves one by one, from the oldest to the youngest. In a short while, only Jesus, the accused woman, and some original bystanders remained (8:9). Though the Bible does not record what He wrote, one wonders if He may have listed the name of each accuser from the oldest down, scribbling some secret sin beside each name.

When the King of righteousness stood up, His opponents were gone; the prosecution had vanished (8:10). According to the Mosaic Law a minimum of two firsthand witnesses were needed to testify (Deut. 17:6; 19:15; John 8:17). Without these witnesses, the arraignment ended (8:11). Nonetheless in a moving sidebar the Judge of inner justice told her, "Go now and leave your life of sin" (8:11). In the beauty of spiritual balance, Jesus delivered the iron fist of conviction toward the woman and her accusers, but He wrapped it in the velvet glove of compassion and meekness.

In modern times biblical counselors still strive for the same balance of compassion with integrity. Rather than falling prey to a dichotomous victim/victimizer notion, caring Christians seek to see the truth clearly in order to speak about it lovingly.

While it is tempting for counselors to align with counselees, as if counselees were pure victims in life, the truth may be found in some hybrid of responsibility. For instance, a newly arrested young woman may need considerable support just to prevent her from taking her own life or from becoming the newest prodigal fleeing church. Patient listening may reveal that she has been "the black sheep" of her pagan family for years. But integrity also requires the biblical counselor to indict her behavior, the molestation of a neighbor boy a half-dozen years previous, long before the perpetrator was ever converted. Compassion, on the other hand, says that this regretful woman should name the teacher at the high school who first abused her; in that part of the story, the young woman was truly a victim. Integrity says that the abusing teacher should at least be fired, possibly halting a habit that has harmed many students for many years. And compassion says that any other children whom the defendant has touched should also be named, so that they can get the help they need to stop the cycle of destruction. Integrity says the church needs to remove the woman from any program with minors and to assist in her recovery and accountability. Despite the ugly nature of many sins, biblical counseling is no excuse for hostility; it is an invitation for the counselor's compassion and integrity.

BIBLICAL COUNSELING IS A SUMMONS TO EXCELLENT COMMUNICATION

Biblical counseling is not an attempt at mind-reading; rather, it is a summons to excellent communication. God warns us not to judge other people's motives (1 Cor. 4:5). And though we are commended for identifying with other people's feelings (Rom. 12:15), we are cautioned about jumping to conclusions (Prov. 18:13) and about assuming that we are the measure of another person (2 Cor. 10:12). In all of life, and especially when human passions are stirred, God calls His people to communicate in an excellent manner (Prov. 15:1).

When the call went out over the prayer chain, most of the people in the Bible-study group immediately recognized that this might be the end for their friend's dad. The father had been sick for months, but now the doctors were calling the family in. "Kidney failure . . . pericardial edema . . . coma," they said.

The coleader of the group, a middle-aged woman, whom we'll call June, was like a big sister to most of the people in the group. The miniflock had been together for three years and some of them had known each other for twenty. In some ways June felt like her own father was dying. Heading straight for the ICU, she hoped to bring comfort to her friend, remembering what it was like to lose a parent.

After a little searching at the hospital June spotted the family huddled in the corner of a dimly lit waiting room. Her friend, the church member, noticed her and came over to give her a long hug. Then, leading her by the hand, he stood in the middle of the family circle, introducing her to each relative: brothers and sisters, nieces and nephews.

After gathering some details, June and her friend went to the bedside and prayed with the dying dad. Then they reentered the family huddle, drawing two chairs into the circle, side by side. A lively discussion was being monopolized by one brother. Plunging into his oversize Bible, the brother systematically "disproved" prayers to Mary, Mormon polygamy, and food stamps. With every new topic, he gave June a chance to agree with him and to add more proof. June declined politely but she was puzzled: Why the need to throw Bible daggers at every variant idea by the bedside of a dying father?

Before excusing herself June offered to pray. Grateful, the family members quickly rose to their feet and joined hands in a circle for the prayer. The visit had lasted about an hour and had seemed positive to June as an outsider. As she raised her hand in a little farewell gesture, her fellow church member again gave her a hug.

Walking briskly to the car, June soon realized she was being shadowed by the know-it-all brother. Smiling to acknowledge him, she slackened her pace. Amid small talk, they walked side by side to the parking garage. Assuming that the brother was heading to his car too, June wished him God's blessings as she stepped off the curb toward her van.

"Just a minute! I was offended back there and I need to confront you on it," he blurted.

"Oh?" June was surprised.

"Yeah. If you were a man, I woulda knocked your head off . . . the way you were caressing my brother! He's a married man, you know! I don't know what kind of a thing you two have going, but it's not right!"

"I'm sorry," she mumbled, frantically remembering that she had rubbed her right palm back and forth across her friend's shoulder blades as they sat in the circle. "Yes, I know your brother's married; we've known each other for almost twenty years, since we met as couples in the young married's class. Our kids are like cousins."

"Well, if your husband had touched my wife that way, I woulda knocked his head off too! We didn't know who you were . . . the way my brother hugged you when you showed up. Just wasn't right!"

"I hope you'll forgive me; I didn't mean to offend you or your family. Let me assure you, we've never touched inappropriately," she offered softly.

"What you did in there was inappropriate. You show me from the Bible where what you did was right. I go on visitation every Tuesday night with Brother Phil and we use that verse about 'the right hand of fellowship.' The only thing God permits between a man and a woman who are not married is a handshake. We know about that 'holy kiss' verse but that's not what it means. They kissed on the cheek back then; so, the only thing that's right is a handshake, unless you can prove it from the Bible."

The story of this family was all coming back to her: alcoholic parents, zero warmth, sibling relationships fractured for years at a time.

"I apologize . . . but I don't want to argue," she said with a very deliberate staccato. "I assure you that I'm very happily married. When we meet, it's at church or as couples." Pausing, she looked him right in the eye, "I'm very concerned that you're going to march back in there and make some big issue over this in the waiting room while your father is dying. Maybe my family is more expressive, more physically affectionate than you are comfortable with. I promise you I'll be very careful around your brother from now on." After a slow exhale, she continued, "I'm concerned that I've apologized three times to you and you've ignored it. Twice, you've said I should have had my block knocked off."

"And every law in the land would've said I had the right to do it," he interrupted. They stood there, uncomfortably staring at each other.

"Well, do you forgive me?" June persisted.

"Yes, since you can't prove it from the Bible." He stuck out his hand like a punch toward the gut. They shook hands and walked off in opposite directions.

As illustrated by the painful strain in this real-life interaction, God does not want His children trying to read people's minds (Prov. 18:13) or to judge people's motives (1 Cor. 4:5). With empathy for one another's feelings (Rom. 12:15), Christ's followers are called to respect the uniqueness of each individual (14:5; 1 Cor. 3:12–15), practicing the art of wise and loving conversation (Eph. 4:29). Though biblical counselors may be as scripturally literate as the know-it-all brother, the ministry of biblical counseling seeks to model conversational meekness (Matt. 5:5; James 1:19–20), not indictment by cross-examination (Gal. 5:14–15; Phil. 2:14–16).

BIBLICAL COUNSELING IS A COMMITMENT TO REGARD EACH PERSON AS AN INTERDEPENDENT WHOLE

Biblical counseling is not a confusion of human emotion and spirituality; instead, biblical counseling is a commitment to regard each person as an interdependent whole. Though concentric circles may oversimplify the trilogy of personhood, biblical counselors perceive the "spirit, soul and body" (1 Thess. 5:23) more like interconnected clover leaves or orbits of spinning electrons.

In the events leading up to the suicide of Lester, the prison convert discussed in chapter 2, each dimension of his life seems to have played a part.

Physical: Lester strangled himself, using the combined effect from his shirt-noose and gravity. Self-strangulation brought on acute anoxia, cardiac arrest, and, within minutes, brain death.

Emotional: Lester was very attached to his wife and children, or at least to the idea that they were on the outside waiting for him, inspiring him to change for the better. He became angry at his wife's reported infidelity, jealous of the boyfriend's opportunism, and fearful that life was no longer worth living.

Spiritual: Lester chose not to humble himself, nor to grieve his loss in a cleansing way, nor to seek help from those who could coach him. He chose not to forgive his wife and her suitor, failed to recommit justice to God, and did not draw sufficient hope from the presence and promises of God to survive another day. He grieved the Holy Spirit.

Although biblical counseling prioritizes spiritual intervention, it does not deny or dishonor the physical and emotional aspects of sincere care or human need. When the prophet Elijah was challenged by the darkest forces of his day (1 Kings 18), he knew he was engaged in Israel's spiritual battle of the century. But after riding the roller coaster of success and failure, Elijah also wanted to die (19:1–14). However, God did not look at him in a one-dimensional way. God ministered to this "man just like us" (James 5:17), granting him sleep, shade, an angel, touch, food, water, empathy, shelter, and a divine word (1 Kings 19:5–9). Even afterward, when Elijah sent out invitations to his pity party (19:10), God showed up with an object lesson (19:11–13). And when Elijah continued to feel sorry for himself, God patiently gave him companions (19:14–21). Though the priority for care may have been on the spiritual level, God regarded Elijah as an interdependent whole: body, soul, and spirit.

Rather than diagramming human beings as concentric circles of spiritual, emotional, and physical life, the image of a spinning gyroscope may better capture the dynamic interdependence of these dimensions. Bump the gyroscope and it will wobble, at least momentarily, out of sync. Give it a serious knock on any level and the impact will be distributed to some degree onto every level.

Imagine visiting someone in the hospital two days after she has had major surgery. It's quite likely that this patient is physically devitalized, in a "postsurgical depression," the physicians call it. During the visit you may sense that she is in pain, emotional and physical. She may even be doubting certain spiritual realities.

If you were some kind of universal caregiver for this patient, you might want to respond from the joint expertise of biology, psychology, and theology. You might wish you could prescribe a diet with antidepressant qualities, talk her through the stages of change and loss, and offer a prayer while holding her hand. Or if you were the hospital chaplain, attending a case-management meeting for this patient, you might help the whole team see her wider range of needs, personally providing the spiritual dimension in the plan. And if someone joined the team who was new to the interdisciplinary approach, you might point out that our words "whole, holy, and health" all derive from the same old English word "halus," suggesting that one is not truly whole or healthy until he or she is right with God.[1] Yet the average biblical counselor operating outside of such a team would seek to provide a spiritually rich support system, while trusting God to meet the larger array of needs through other means.

Although holistic thinking became unpopular during Western society's infatuation with microbes, interdisciplinary theories have now regained support among many health professionals. This renaissance in holism can be seen in many forms.[2]

Luke, the physician who wrote the Gospel of Luke and the Book of Acts, included fewer references to physical healing than either Matthew or Mark. Perhaps this suggests a message for the current healthcare system: The needs of the physical body do not supersede the needs of the whole person.

Similarly, when the Lord commended the ministry of visiting the sick (Matt. 25:36), He used the word *episkeptomai*, which means "to look at, examine, inspect, go to see, be concerned about."[3] According to James Epperly, "The gist of the word implies a vision of the person which involves an overarching panorama of the needs of the whole person."[4]

Just as physicians are being encouraged to honor the spiritual dimension of health,[5] religious caregivers are urged not to underestimate their role in good medical care. As Judith Shelly wrote, "Spiritual care is more than a nice 'extra'; it is a vital ingredient in health care. Each person is a biologically, psychosocially, and spiritually integrated being, created to live in relationship with other people and with God. Illness disrupts the harmony of that integration . . . . Respecting and encouraging a person's spiritual and religious interests and concerns enhances the healing process. Spiritual support includes communicating love, forgiveness, meaning, purpose, and hope in a time of discouragement and anxiety. It is not a frill. It is basic to good health care."[6]

By recognizing the interplay between the physical, emotional, and spiritual realms, a biblical counselor can better explain how spiritual traumas can ripple over into psychological and biological consequences (see, for example, 1 Sam. 3:10–21) and how excellent treatment includes attending to the whole person (James 5:13–20). Biblical counseling does not confuse human emotion and spirituality; rather, biblical counseling regards each person as an interdependent whole: body, soul, and spirit.

BIBLICAL COUNSELING IS A CALL TO PRIVACY WITH PERMEABLE BOUNDARIES

Biblical counseling is not a promise of absolute confidentiality; instead, it is a call to privacy with permeable boundaries. Everyone needs boundaries. Without them, we wouldn't know where our property ends and our neighbor's begins. Without such definition, drivers couldn't keep their cars in their own lane. Without spiritual boundaries, there would be no way to separate between the true God and false gods (Exod. 20:3), between the Lord's Day and other days, and between appropriate and inappropriate forms of ownership or intimacy. "You shall not commit adultery. You shall not steal. . . . You shall not covet your neighbor's house. You shall not covet your neighbor's wife, or his manservant or maidservant, his ox or donkey, or anything that belongs to your neighbor" (20:14–15, 17). Sin is transgressing a God-given law, overstepping a spiritual boundary (1 John 3:4).

In clinical circles confidentiality is nearly absolute, unless the counselor foresees a homicide or suicide, suspects child abuse, or receives a written release from the counselee that authorizes the sharing of specific information to a specific party. While this stance has its defenders in the therapeutic context, biblical counselors wrestle with its applicability to the ministry milieu.

When our Lord analyzed the path to spiritual maturity, He pointed to childlike humility (Matt. 18:2–6) and interpersonal simplicity (18:7–35). With omniscient realism, our Lord predicted that even in the best of relationships, people would sometimes hurt themselves or one another (18:5–10). But always, in the will of God, true disciples would be challenged to pursue forgiveness, restoration, and a return to relational innocence (18:11–14, 18–35).

How can Christ's children pursue family-like simplicity in their lives together? How can they incorporate the Lord's noble ideals of forgiveness, restoration, and innocence in the real world that is scarred by deep interpersonal wounds? By purposing to follow Jesus' guidelines for innocence lost and found (18:15–17).

Like the English poet John Milton, Christians understand that there was an Edenic paradise where all was "good" and none were "ashamed" (Gen. 1–2). Tragically, that paradise was lost (3:1–24). But Christ has revealed history's last chapter, aiming the world back toward a new dawn of innocence (Rev. 21:1–7, 9–24; 22:1–17).

From the beginning God has sought to have people live in voluntary fellowship with the Creator and His creatures. But the abuse of freedom (Gen. 3:1–6) resulted in the loss of virtue (3:7–10). And once paradise was lost, relationships began to deteriorate (3:11–13). But God, the ever-persistent Restorer, began to build toward a new creation (3:14–24; 12:1–3; Rom. 16:20; Rev. 21–22).

Christ has revealed the way of restoration for His followers. Indeed, He taught us how to try to regain the innocence and trust that is lost every time someone feels hurt by another person. In this difficult work of reconciliation, our Lord described four steps.

Personal rebuke: "If your brother sins against you, go and show him his fault, just between the two of you. If he listens to you, you have won your brother over" (Matt. 18:15).

Plural rebuke: "But if he will not listen, take one or two others along, so that 'every matter may be established by the testimony of two or three witnesses'" (18:16).

Public rebuke: "If he refuses to listen to them, tell it to the church" (18:17a).

Prohibitive rebuke: "And if he refuses to listen even to the church, treat him as you would a pagan or a tax collector" (18:17b).

Lest one misread these steps as limited to the Gospels, Paul paralleled these efforts in seeking to resolve interpersonal conflicts with church leaders: personal rebuke (1 Tim. 5:1), plural rebuke (5:19), public rebuke (5:20a), and prohibitive rebuke (5:20b).

Although there are a number of interpretive variables in this would-be conflict-resolution procedure, at least two things are clear. First, our Lord endorsed privacy by teaching His followers that the Christian way requires an offended individual to go speak privately with the perceived offender (Matt. 18:15; 1 Tim. 5:1). This principle, combined with a willingness to forgive (Eph. 4:32), would enable Christ's followers to live above the sins of gossip (1 Pet. 4:15), slander (Prov. 10:18), backbiting (Gal. 5:15), divisiveness (Prov. 6:16–19), and bitterness (Eph. 4:31). Such simplicity would model a unique love to the world (John 13:35; 17:15, 21–23). Second, our Lord did not endorse absolute confidentiality; instead, He taught His followers that there are occasions when it is appropriate to include one or two credible witnesses (Matt. 18:16; 1 Tim. 5:19) or even the church leaders and members (Matt. 18:17; 1 Tim. 5:20) in what had begun as a private matter.

Borrowing metaphors from the field of cell biology, family therapists have begun to study boundaries.[7] Cells with rigid membranes are seen as pathological, unable to jettison waste or receive nutrition. Cells with diffuse membranes are viewed as equally sick, unable to maintain sufficient boundary strength to rebuff toxins or to retain useful nutrition. In a social sense relationships characterized by rigid boundaries are prone to being secretive, hierarchical, authoritarian, and disengaged. In contrast, relationships with diffuse boundaries seem symbiotic, enmeshed, and incestuous. The ideal is the permeable boundary, sufficiently strong, yet appropriately flexible. In the beautiful balance of Christ's teaching in Matthew 18:15–17, individual responsibility works toward private reconciliation, yet community support expands the efforts at reconciliation when the ideal fails. By following these principles, Christ's disciples can avoid hiding pockets of bitterness in secret enclaves, yet they can also avoid hanging out dirty laundry in an inappropriate sense.

By following Jesus' model of privacy with permeable boundaries, a men's-ministry leader was able to face a difficult challenge. A college student had asked him for counseling. Though the leader made it clear that he was not a mental-health professional, he agreed to meet weekly with the college senior for prayer and accountability. Because of the leader's gifts and the younger man's "father hunger," their rapport grew quickly and his story unfolded over several weeks. The younger man was unmarried and an active homosexual. He had experimented heavily with drugs and the gay lifestyle since he was fourteen. Having taken nearly three years of his college education at a renowned school a thousand miles away, he had transferred to the local Christian college after his secret life became known to three people: a dorm friend, the dean of women, and a psychology professor. Now in a new setting, the wandering senior was still in bondage to the flesh. In fact, he was dancing on gay bartops each night, ostensibly "to pay his college bills." But he also served as an assistant pastor at a church thirty minutes away from school, and fully expected to be ordained and sent to the mission field after graduation, an event that lay only two months away.

The men's-ministry leader spent hours with the disobedient student, praying, hoping, and admonishing. Eventually the leader was convinced that there were no Christians in their metropolitan area who knew his story. How could he utilize formal witnesses, if there were none? The leader also ran into a brick wall, urging the student to confess his sin voluntarily to his own senior pastor or to his college adviser. The leader's offer to accompany the young man at the time of his confession was rejected.

In their meetings it soon became clear that the college student took a sinister delight in the layman's inability to fix him. Sexual binges preceded their meetings; disgusting stories were soon being told with a smirk. So after much prayer the layman met privately with the college adviser, someone previously unknown to him. Without detail the men's-ministry leader summarized his relationship to the young man and said, "Sir, I believe this fellow is very far from God. I would advise you to pray with me toward his repentance and that you or someone confront him as an unknowing Nathan."

As strange as the intervention seemed, the adviser sensed God's will and met with the prodigal. After expressing deep concern for his welfare, the adviser queried, "I'm worried about you. How is your relationship with God?" With the force of a dam breaking, the young man confessed everything. His college studies and church leadership came to an abrupt halt. His care was put into the hands of his church, and the layman breathed a sigh of relief. In a chilling example the men's-ministry leader confirmed that biblical counseling is not a promise of absolute confidentiality; it is, however, a call to privacy with permeable boundaries.

BIBLICAL COUNSELING IS A COACHING SESSION TOWARD SPIRITUAL RESILIENCY

Although people of faith often feel like political outsiders, no one could have felt more disillusioned about earthly governments than Daniel. Judah, Daniel's own government, had wandered away from God, inviting a hostile takeover by a super-wicked Babylon.

As an adolescent, Daniel had seen his nation living in rebellion against God. Instead of humbly obeying the Lord, Judah had concocted feeble alliances with Egypt and Assyria, behaving like an unfaithful wife. Even the priests and prophets failed to clarify God's will for the people. "The visions of your prophets were false and worthless; they did not expose your sin to ward off your captivity. The oracles they gave you were false and misleading" (Lam. 2:14).

Judah's worldly hopes were dashed by its infidelity; neither a Jewish king nor a foreign ally would be able to rescue that erring generation from God's wrath (4:17, 19–20). Accordingly Jerusalem became a morgue: "Young and old lie together in the dust of the streets; my young men and maidens have fallen by the sword" (2:21). In the end the Neo-Babylonian bulldozer barricaded famished citizens into one final siege. The leaders of the nation dressed for death; malnourished mourners shed their last earthly tears (2:10–11). Starving mothers failed to live up to even the standards of the animal kingdom; they cannibalized their own children (4:10).

How cynical Daniel could have become! How great a burden it might have seemed to bear the name of Daniel, meaning "God is my judge." How fair could Daniel's God be, allowing Daniel's family, friends, and neighbors to be decimated or deported by blaspheming pagans?

As one of the "lucky ones," Daniel survived the Babylonian onslaught, only to be taken in chains to a gentile metropolis seemingly light-years away from home. Even there things were not much better. Refusing to eat the king's gourmet meals, he suffered a veiled death threat (Dan. 1:10). Yet he maintained his integrity, offered a creative alternative, and gained the respect of the royal court (1:8–9, 11–21).

Later an impetuous monarch put Daniel in danger of execution (2:12–13), but God rescued him. Daniel, filled with heavenly insight, showed the folly of trusting in earthly kings or kingdoms, whether Babylonian, Medo-Persian, Greek, or Roman (2:14–49; 7:1–12:13). Trusting only in God, Daniel received a promotion in Nebuchadnezzar's administration.

Surrounded by a culture of idolatry, Daniel suffered the indignity of working for a boss who was filled with himself. Nebuchadnezzar, erecting a ninety-foot statue to his ego, demanded that all loyal citizens worship him on cue or be burned alive (3:1–7). Daniel's best friends, willing to serve God with life or death, refused to compromise their conscience (3:8–18). Refusing to espouse a "name it, claim it" sassiness, they rested their fate in the hands of God. God caused the very flames, which cooked the death squad, to cool the trio. With ropes burned away, the three heroes were blest by a Christophany and a kingly confession (3:19–30).

In the course of Daniel's seven decades of public service, he witnessed a king go mad with pride (4:1–37) and watched a Tinkertoy throne slip through puny hands (5:1–31). Though Daniel had consistently sown the seeds of wisdom and prayer while in office, there were times when he faced jealous colleagues and hungry lions (6:1–28).

In contemporary biblical counseling the problems of life are rarely so severe as in Daniel's day. And yet for counselors and counselees who hold a high view of Scripture, it is tempting to develop a "Woe-is-me!" attitude. Modern culture has sometimes caricatured Bible-believers as ultraconservative, like vestigial organs from a bygone era. At times media images and editorial discourse have implied that religious conservatives are intrinsically hostile: Islamic and Irish fundamentalists in city streets . . . "pro-life" killings at abortion clinics . . . militaristic enclaves at Waco, Ruby Ridge, and Oklahoma City. For some critics it is a small leap to equate people of faith with medieval Crusaders, Nazis, and Klansmen. Yet if Christian people allow themselves to be put on this cultural defensive, they can devolve their counseling sessions into sophisticated pity parties: "The government is not doing what it ought to do . . . Hollywood is doing what it ought not do . . . and the public schools are not doing what they used to do!"

Instead of developing a victim mentality, Daniel, Shadrach, Meshach, and Abednego were spiritually resilient. Rather than getting caught up in the blame game, these godly souls stubbornly refused to get bitter at Judah, at Babylon, at God, or even themselves. They took responsibility for their own attitudes and actions, practicing integrity, creativity, and wisdom. Without stooping to pessimism or cynicism in life, these government officials were realistic about the world but optimistic about God (3:17–18). When facing what appeared to be dead ends, these separatists generated wise alternatives (1:12–13). In scriptural prayer they looked ahead to the crucifixion of Christ (9:1–27), the source of true justice and peace. From a New Testament perspective these men learned how to maintain their higher citizenship, becoming mega-conquerors despite their earthly sufferings (Rom. 8:28, 37). In terms of folk wisdom our elder brothers did not write another "somebody-done-somebody-wrong song"; instead they received the serenity to accept the things they could not change, the courage to change the things they could, and the wisdom to know the difference. As biblical counselors, we use our influence not to breed antigovernment skepticism, but to coach spiritual resilience.

BIBLICAL COUNSELING IS A PRIVATE VERSION OF PUBLIC SPEECH

Biblical counselors are wise to guard against a downward drift in conversation, that natural gravitational pull toward seeking or providing inappropriate disclosures. Indeed, biblical counselors are wise to remember that all of their private caregiving dialogue needs to be consistent with their public discourse and that whatever is said in private could easily become public.

In a virtual zoo Jesus projected four animal images in rapid fire, teaching His disciples about the nature of their coming ministry: "I am sending you out like sheep among wolves. Therefore be as shrewd as snakes and as innocent as doves" (Matt. 10:16).

Sheep	Christ's followers will be vulnerable . . .
Wolves	. . . to savage forces that could kill them.
Snakes	They need to learn how to withdraw into quiet, hidden spaces . . .
Doves	. . . seeking to do no harm.

One biblical counselor, seeking to do no harm, was surprised to hear the name of a church elder on the lips of a stranger. The young woman had walked into the church office on a weekday, asking to talk to a pastor. She explained that she had been mentored years ago at another church by the elder she named, now retired in Florida. "He was the greatest man," she reminisced. "Without him, I'd be dead."

Within the hour her story had been told. She had been a child of abuse, drug addicted, and in bondage to invisible forces. With sincerity painted all over her face, she reported, "He saved me while he was my Sunday school teacher." Parts of the story made sense and seemed believable. But other parts were weird. Was she really drug addicted as an elementary-age Sunday-school child? If she had enjoyed such a powerful relationship with the retired elder, why had she been out of touch with him and any church for so many years? Praising the elder, she said, "Whenever he was in the county, crime would drop; whenever he would leave the county, crime would soar. It was as obvious as night and day. You knew that, didn't you?" Every additional exploration revealed her extreme dependence on him, her magical thoughts about the relationship between his presence and her security. More questions filled in more gaps. She was a long-term psychiatric patient, diagnosed with manic depression with psychotic features. As far as she was concerned, she needed either of two things from the pastor: the address and phone number of the former mentor or someone to pray with her like he used to do.

With Christ's animal metaphors in mind (Matt. 10:16), the pastor knew that there were several vulnerable sheep in this story: the young woman, the former mentor, and himself. Wolf-like forces could tear at the sheep. Her disorders could drive her to stalk the elder psychologically, potentially invading his privacy or worse. Impulsive speech on the part of the counselor could revictimize the young woman, caricaturing her as crazy. Or the counselor's need-to-please could push him to give out the Florida phone number that hundreds of people in his congregation already knew, since it had been published in the church bulletin when the retired couple relocated. Worse yet, the pastor could volunteer to become the new "magician" for this troubled soul.

Withdrawing into quiet prayer, the pastor sought to coil up in the shade of caution. "Well, you have obviously been through a lot, and you love this elder as a lot of people do. I don't have his number at my fingertips, but if you'll write out your name, address, and phone number, I'll make sure he gets it. He can communicate with you, if that's how God leads him. Whoever your doctor is, stay in touch with him or her; that's important. And just like you did years ago, find a church again. With the encouragement of a whole congregation, not just one person, you'll be able to keep on reading your Bible and praying. I'm not sure any one person dictates the crime rate, but if we all work together, we can be salt and light in our community." The meeting ended without the pastor leading in prayer.

As soon as the woman drove away from the church parking lot, the pastor telephoned the retired elder, summarized the interaction that had just taken place, and conveyed her information. Somewhat surprised, the elder confirmed parts of her story and agreed that he and his wife would pray for her, without communicating with her directly. At least in this way the retired couple knew what was happening back in New Jersey, if the young woman did contact them somehow. Then the biblical counselor met with the church secretary and the other pastor on staff and summarized the woman's two requests and what he had done about them. "I didn't pray with her at the end of our session, as I normally would have, because I felt she was begging me to become her new lightning rod for God. And I didn't give out the elder's information because I didn't have his permission to do that—I don't want you to give it out either."

In the weeks that followed, the wisdom of respecting the yellow caution lights became a little clearer. The young woman, unable to find the elder, cornered the other church pastor and tried to get him to become her personal security blanket. Then a church member called the office to get the retired elder's address and telephone number so she could give them to the distraught woman. And though the woman never attended a worship service, several church people became snared in a slander which originated with the woman. "Did you know that the pastor doesn't even pray with his counselees? What kind of a Christian is he?" With a spiritual innocence that sought to do no harm, the dove-like church staff handled these delicate challenges with meekness and prayer.

Biblical counselors are becoming wiser about the wiles of the devil (Eph. 6:11). By engaging in the art of biblical conversation, these caregivers are seeking to do God's will; yet this work is not without opposition. Therefore biblical counselors have become sensitive to the two-way dangers of gossip (sharing information that no one has the right to know), slander (sharing information that harms the reputation of another person), and unprofitable speech (sharing information that does not edify). In theological terms biblical counselors know that they will one day give an account for their motives, their words, and their actions (1 Cor. 3:13; 4:1–5). In political terms biblical counselors understand that whatever they say to a counselee in the here-and-now can and will be used against them, at times, in the court of public opinion. Hence wise counselors never share something with a counselee that he or she is unwilling to have shared with that individual's spouse, parent, lawyer, physician, congregation, or local newspaper. Resting in the preventive power of Scripture, biblical counselors seek to obey the apostolic maxim, "Do not let any unwholesome talk come out of your mouths, but only what is helpful for building others up according to their needs, that it may benefit those who listen" (Eph. 4:29).

BIBLICAL COUNSELING IS A WAY
TO SHEPHERD SOULS

Biblical counseling is a not an opportunity to play doctor; it is a way to shepherd souls. In his farewell speech to the Ephesians the apostle Paul spoke about the noble work of shepherding souls (Acts 20:17–38). Organizing his parting thoughts around the past (20:17–21), the present

(20:22–27), and the future (20:28–38), Paul asked and answered key questions about the ministry: Who should be leading? What should the leaders do? How should leaders lead? Why should leaders lead?

Within his chronological framework Paul intertwined his answers to key questions. First, Paul taught about the ideal qualities of "elders . . . overseers [who] shepherd the church of God" (20:17, 28). With descriptions like these, we infer that those who care for souls should be above average in their maturity (as elders), looking out for the good of the group (as overseers), and spiritually nurturing (as shepherds). With Paul as their example these individuals strive to be accountable (20:18), other-oriented (20:24), above reproach (20:26), nonpossessive (20:28), nonmaterialistic (20:33), and hardworking (20:35).

Second, Paul profiled two things the spiritual leaders should seek to do: evangelize (20:21) and edify (20:27). Because he steadfastly sought to win unbelievers to faith, Paul suffered persecution (20:19). Earnestly working to strengthen believers in their faith, the tentmaking apostle frequently engaged in large-group and small-group teaching sessions (20:20) during his time in Ephesus.

Third, Paul, the veteran church planter, modeled how the care of souls is done: with a deep commitment to relationships. In caring for the Ephesians Paul had cultivated friendships known for their generosity, prayer, and affection (20:35–37).

Fourth, the soon-to-be imprisoned missionary revealed why spiritual leaders lead: to protect Christ's flock from danger. Potential dangers could arise from within or without, from unbelievers or believers (20:29–30). Based on this kind of personal concern, Paul had consistently delivered specific admonitions to his Christian kin. He said, "Remember that for three years I never stopped warning each of you night and day with tears" (20:31).

Instead of completely patterning one's ministry on the paradigms of psychology or psychiatry, men and women in the care of souls can offer a lifestyle of shepherdly influence. Ever in pursuit of richer character, biblical counselors often enjoy the privilege of seeing God enlighten the unbeliever and fortify the believer, manifesting the twofold work of the Great Commission (Matt. 28:19–20). In essence this kind of spiritual care is "the communication of God's love to persons in need . . . an art more than a science, a living relationship more than a theoretical discipline, a perspective more than a category of work, a way of being more than a way of doing."[8]

In church ministry biblical counseling may have become increasingly common in our day because the practice of pastoral visitation has become more and more uncommon. According to pastoral mentor Howard Hendricks, "You can influence people at a distance, but you can only impact people up close. You can't minister across a chasm. I think when we left the field of pastoral calling and went to an emphasis on professional counseling, we lost something. We were no longer in the homes and in the businesses, the places where we had exposure to people on a deeply personal basis."[9]

Aware of these kinds of changes in cultural routines and rhythms, some churches have begun to offer a generous variety of small-group ministries, some oriented to study, some to service, and others to support. Through meaningful Sunday-school classes, miniflocks, or support-oriented small groups, much biblical counseling is done. Some congregations have even discovered the strategic benefit of having a female counselor on staff, trained in theology and therapeutics.

At first a church in the Midwest was hesitant, but the proposal made sense. For several years the church had enjoyed a paid staff of four full-time clergymen, two full-time secretaries, and a variety of part-time leaders in music, education, and ministry to senior adults. However, there was a noticeable limitation: All the pastors were males. On those occasions when a female parishioner requested a female counselor, the church was awkward. In some informal ways laywomen in the congregation could fill the need, but none of them could bring professional skills to the task. Another problem: Sometimes the male pastors also wanted a way to refer one of their female counselees to a female counselor, based on the nature of the presenting problem. But their staffing resources did not allow room for an internal referral.

The proposal identified a woman who held degrees in biblical studies and counseling. With experience in church and parachurch people-helping, the candidate seemed ideal. But how could the church pay her salary?

Their solution was to hire the counselor full-time, print brochures, provide an office, share the receptionist, grant health insurance, and ask her to accept financial donations when offered.

After nine months it was obvious that this woman's ministry had blossomed. Her counselees' love gifts for the church had exceeded her salary needs. Once the anxiety over money and gender had passed, the board relaxed its financial monitoring and began to treat the new staff person "as one of our own." This Christian counselor soon came to be recognized as a major strength of the church. The board now recognized that most people who seek counseling are female and therefore it is wise to provide female counselors. Adding this woman to the professional staff also allowed the pastors to provide joint pastoral and marital counseling sessions of high quality. Over time she became famous for her insight, courage, and shepherdly admonitions. Lives were saved through her ministry. Though she was a beneficiary to some of the psychotherapeutic tradition, she did not view biblical counseling as a way to play doctor. Rather biblical counseling for her was a way to evangelize and to shepherd souls in the context of a congregation.

BIBLICAL COUNSELING IS A PRACTICE
IN RELATIONAL ACCOUNTABILITY

Biblical counseling is not a ritual designed to raise the self-esteem of counselors or counselees. Instead, biblical counseling seeks to engage Christians in the practice of spiritual accountability.

Though a church on the West Coast had been founded by Christians who believed that a disciple should live a life of discipline, the practice of interpersonal accountability in this congregation had seen a variety of different outcomes. Over the years the leaders had taught that church discipline was not something the pastors do *to the people*. To the contrary, church discipline was something *Christians do for one another* (Gal. 6:1–5). "In the Lord's teaching about accountability," the elders periodically rehearsed, "there is a priority on graduating the efforts at relational reconciliation: personal, plural, public, and prohibitive (Matt. 18:15–20)." But despite the solid teaching and sincere modeling about accountability, there were no easy solutions to real-life spiritual conflict. Sometimes people sought to skirt or sabotage accountability, while other times the practice seemed blessed by heaven itself.

Stanley, a university student, reared in the church, had joined David, a local Bible-college student, to provide nursing-home chapel services each Wednesday afternoon. But only when spiritual push came to shove did David show his true disdain for accountability. The duo had been doing chapel services for almost six months when a controversy arose in the retirement facility. The local priest, unhappy that Catholic residents were being brought to the Protestant services, asked the administrator to segregate worshipers by denomination. Irritated at the risk of losing attendees, David offered to lead or read prayers to Mary in each service. "Hey, if it keeps the people coming, what's the harm?" he rationalized. But Stanley challenged him, saying, "I feel praying to Mary would be hypocritical; you and I don't believe in the intercession of Mary and neither does our church."

When his personal rebuke went unheeded, Stanley asked two elders to attend their next chapel service. The elders were shocked to hear one of their own congregants asking "the Blessed Virgin" to heal the sick who sat around in wheelchairs. After the meeting Stanley reiterated his conviction to David that these prayers manifested the sin of hypocrisy or heresy; in a plural rebuke the elders agreed. But it was to no avail.

After committing the matter to prayerful review in the subsequent meeting of all the elders, the board unanimously agreed to ask David to stop praying to Mary. Although Stanley and the two involved elders offered to do weekly Bible study on the subject with David, he refused. Unwilling to attend such training or to meet with the convened board, David fired back. "I'm not coming to any meeting with you hypocrites. You board members don't come to my chapel services, so don't pretend to care about me or my senior citizens. Besides, I'm not an official member of your church anyway, and I won't be caught dead in there again. Go ahead and tell the Bible college; they are parachurch, not church. Throw me out of your little cult; I don't care." Unable to win David, the board committed the matter to ongoing prayer and withdrew their official endorsement of the Wednesday chapel services.

Several years earlier the church had grieved over another unrepentant brother. Despite the board's best efforts to practice biblical accountability, one of the church leaders himself sabotaged the very accountability system about which he had so often taught.

Anxious to succeed the outgoing principal in the church-run Christian school, the vice principal (an elder) tried to win the vacant position by volunteering to serve as the interim principal, teaching extra classes, tutoring, and coaching. While the search committee welcomed the vice principal to apply for the job, after six months he wasn't chosen.

Jealous of the new successor appointed from Arizona, the vice principal made a series of attempts to overturn the decision. Stirring up his miniflock, the angry elder convinced some of his followers that there had been an abuse of process. Convinced that God wanted him to become the new principal, he used a pretense to send faxes to the new appointee. Running down the school in the faxed messages, he hoped the appointee would withdraw. As the sabotage continued, various elders rebuked the brother for lying, for slander, and for creating divisions in the church. Personal and plural efforts at reconciliation proved fruitless. The vice principal even thumbed his nose at the public session of the elders when they spoke with one voice about his behaviors.

The church board felt they had to revoke the brother's membership in the church, which meant he would no longer be an elder or a school staff member. Though they hoped that a grass-roots commitment to prayer and admonition might win their brother back, the congregation saw one of their own leaders spiritually self-destruct before their eyes. This beloved brother, personally and plurally rebuked, was eventually rebuked publicly and excommunicated.

Although the congregation maintained a clear conscience about their practice of relational accountability, they wrestled with the feeling that it was un-American. Nonetheless over the years they enjoyed a deep sense that God had blessed their exercise of tough love. Even though some brothers and sisters skirted or sabotaged the process of accountability, many more were rescued from ongoing waywardness.

One single mom had been the concern of several families. Chronically "out of money," this young mother of three had often been helped with her unpaid bills. The confusing element was the contradiction in appearances; despite frequent unpaid bills and creditor threats, she was always dressed in the most current styles and drove a late-model car.

Because of their love for this woman, two couples in her discipleship group admonished her about the dangers of coveting. The confrontation brought tears to her eyes. "You seem resentful that you have helped me out in the past—and now you want to blame me for it?" Her friends stayed the course. They said, "No, we just feel that you've been overtaken in a fault. We've been praying about this for some time, but we have no regret for past times when we've helped you or your kids; they're like our kids and we'd do it again, as often as the Lord leads. We just want you and your children to learn how to live without going from panic to panic."

Within a few days the single mom accepted the offer of her two best friends and their husbands. She agreed to be instructed by one of the couples on personal finance and to make her personal checkbook and credit cards accountable to the other couple. Within six months she had stopped buying on credit, had developed a debt-repayment schedule, and had almost completely overcome her chronic episodes of spastic colon. In time she downsized her car, learned to ask for brotherly help with small repairs, and became an expert at saying no to her children and to advertisements. In a true biblical sense these couples at church had "won their sister." As illustrated, biblical counseling was not a ritual in the idolatry of self; it was a practice in relational accountability.

In the first section of this book we have sought to paint a verbal portrait of a "house" called biblical counseling. So far, we have purchased some theoretical ground (chapter 1), posted "No Trespassing" signs (chapter 2), and hammered in ten construction stakes (chapter 3) that describe what biblical counseling is intended to be.

PART TWO

Skills for Biblical Counselors

CHAPTER FOUR

Helping People Tell Their Stories

Every counselor needs to cultivate three fundamental skills:
- helping counselees tell their story
- helping counselees choose their goal
- helping counselees practice change.

In three successive chapters we will explore these skills, drawing on the interactions of Christ (chapter 4), the commands of Scripture (chapter 5), and the actions of the apostles and prophets (chapter 6).

HE WILL BE CALLED "WONDERFUL COUNSELOR"

Born into an influential Israelite family, Isaiah had grown up rubbing shoulders with royalty. Unimpressed with earthly monarchs, Isaiah envisioned a coming king: "The virgin will be with child and will give birth to a son, and will call him Immanuel. . . . For unto us a child is born, to us a son is given, and the government will be on his shoulders. And he will be called Wonderful Counselor, Mighty God, Everlasting Father, Prince of Peace. Of the increase of his government and peace there will be no end. . . . A shoot will come up from the stump of Jesse; from his roots a Branch will bear fruit. The Spirit of the Lord will rest on him—the Spirit of wisdom and of understanding, the Spirit of counsel and of power, the Spirit of knowledge and of the fear of the Lord—and he will delight in the fear of the LORD. He will not judge by what he sees with his eyes, or decide by what He hears with his ears; but with righteousness he will judge" (Isa. 7:14; 9:6–7; 11:1–4).

Imagine. Eight centuries before Bethlehem, Isaiah offered up brilliant foreign policy advice: National security begins with God. Just as Judah's northern neighbors had been scourged by the Assyrians, so their southern counterparts were headed toward defeat at the hands of Babylon. Unless they repented, the people of Judah were staring down the barrel of trouble (Isa. 1–39).

In the end, blessed comfort would come (Isa. 40–66), but it would come only through a right relationship with the Davidic offshoot, a virgin-born King, rich with exquisite qualities and an unending reign. Among His attributes, the predicted Savior would be a Wonderful Counselor (9:6). Imbued with the very wisdom of God, Jesus Christ would not be fooled by appearances or mere words; to the contrary, He would always make the correct appraisal in His dealings with people (11:2–4).

Although mere mortals can never expect to have Christ's x-ray vision for the soul (1 Sam. 16:7; John 2:24), we who are growing in Christ's likeness (Rom. 8:28–30; Phil. 1:6) can count on the help of the Lord, the One who will one day permit us to know as we are known. In the meantime even those with gifts in counseling only "see through a glass, darkly" (1 Cor. 13:12, KJV).

Polar Bears on Icebergs

This chapter explores the first skill in biblical counseling: helping counselees tell their story. Drawing on the earthly interactions of the wonderful Counselor, we will examine how biblical counselors can help counselees reveal their burdens and clarify their problems. By analyzing several of Jesus' interpersonal exchanges, we will illustrate some problem-exploration principles involving the power of nonverbal behavior and the use of interview questions.

To overview the first skill—helping counselees tell their story—readers are asked to visualize polar bears on icebergs. With apologies to our elementary-school spelling teachers, we will use the P-O-L-E-R bear acronym to remember our nonverbal behaviors.

P   Physical presence
O   Open posture
L   Leaning in and out
E   Eye contact
R   Relaxed style

And picturing icebergs, we will train ourselves to recognize that there may be more to the counselee's story, as if we've only seen the tip of the iceberg.

Although some skeptics may see professional therapy as nothing more than a $2.5 billion annual fraud,[1] critics should remember how easy it is to slip into tunnel vision. Even some of the world's experts have jumped to regrettable conclusions.[2] "The abdomen, the chest, and the brain will forever be shut from the intrusion of the wise and humane surgeon" (Sir John Ericksen, Surgeon-Extraordinary to Queen Victoria, 1873). "Everything that can be invented has been invented" (Charles H. Duell, commissioner of the U.S. Office of Patents, 1899). "Who . . . wants to hear actors talk?" (H. M. Warner of Warner Brothers, 1927). "Stocks have reached what looks like a permanently high plateau" (Irving Fisher, Yale University professor of economics, 1929). "I think there is a world market for maybe five computers" (Thomas Watson, chairman of IBM, 1943).

Yet without swinging to an opposite and naive extreme, readers are encouraged to admit that *some* counselors have had significant success in helping *particular* counselees with *certain* kinds of problems.[3] The issue, of course, is to discover which counselors are more likely to experience success and why. One thing is crystal clear: Effective counselors are good at helping counselees tell their story.

The Danger of Foolish Listening

In the Bible would-be counselors and friends are warned about poor listening: "He who answers before listening—that is his folly and his shame" (Prov. 18:13). By halting the potential flow of a story and by mentally jumping to conclusions, counselors have sometimes wasted time, lost credibility, or even inflicted harm. Think about it. Physicians diagnose their patients before they treat. Lawyers depose their witnesses before they litigate. Orators study their audiences before they speak. Builders study their blueprints before they break ground. By parallel, biblical counselors help counselees tell their story before moving them toward goals and action.

A phone call triggered a series of counseling sessions, illustrating the need for counselors to help counselees tell their story. The caller told the receptionist she needed "to talk to the counselor himself as soon as possible!"

"I've called you because you come highly recommended by two different people," she hurriedly relayed to the counselor. "Can you tell me how a person gets over anger?"

What an open door! Any counselor seasoned by experience or saturated by professional literature could have had a field day. A mental toss-of-the-coin could birth a variety of realistic scenarios. "This woman is angry," the counselor could scribble onto his imaginary notepad. "Angry at someone important to her. Why else would she inconvenience herself, calling on a stranger for help? But angry at whom? Her husband? Her father? Her boss? God? Angry over what? Abuse? Adversity? What could it be?"

But reining in his imagination, this counselor slowed down the process. "What's the chance we could get together and talk about it?" Resisting the pressure he felt to make it a quick question-and-answer telephone call, the counselor negotiated for a face-to-face meeting during office hours. Pleased that he had redirected the initial mood of vague panic, he penciled in the counselee's name on his appointment calendar. Beside her name, he jotted down the single word: "Anger."

Over the next two days the counselor's mind drifted to the upcoming appointment twice. The first time, he found himself mulling over the names of the two people who had referred the woman to him; they mattered and he wanted to do a good job for them. The second time, he found himself like a race car, revving its engine at the starting line. "If she has an anger-management problem, I should give her this book to read. Maybe during the first session we can try to size up the type of anger problem she has: exploding? underhanding? somatizing?"

When the woman arrived, the counselor resisted his compulsion to confess the woman's sin for her, and he resisted his inclination to embark on a multiple-choice expedition to fix her. Instead, he remembered the advice of Solomon: "He who answers before listening—that is his folly and his shame" (Prov. 18:13). He remembered that he really didn't know very much about this woman or her situation. So following the principles in P-O-L-E-R bears and icebergs, he helped the woman tell her story.

After several sessions and a disciplined use of nonverbal behavior and interviewing strategies, the counselee's story was told. Anger was an issue, but not her own anger. The woman had called in hope that the counselor could tell her how she could stop somebody else's anger from flowing toward her.

Besides unwisely trying to get the counselor to fix someone who was not present in the counseling relationship, the woman had made other mistakes. A married mother of six, she had recently abandoned her family, and she had ignored the rebukes of her pastor-husband and their congregation—all because she had "fallen in love with another man."

Although the woman admitted to the facts of her affair, she refused to repent. She reasoned, "The first time we slept together, it was sin; but after that, it wasn't sin because we had confessed it."

This prodigal pastor's wife wanted the counselor to prescribe an over-the-counter antidote to her husband's anger, a man still in pursuit of marital reconciliation. She claimed by now to have "found another life." In fact, she and her suitor had supposedly "found another church" where they wouldn't be "judged for getting a divorce."

Imagine how ridiculous the counselor would have looked if he had nibbled on her first bait. What if he had kept her original question out of context, as if he had seen her whole iceberg at first glance? He would have given her advice about anger that was totally irrelevant. Based on first impressions the counselor could have trained the counselee on the danger of unresolved anger, easily fueling the wife's self-righteous dialogue toward her "too angry" husband. Without realizing it, the biblical counselor might have been perceived as agreeing with her adultery, desertion, and rationalization. It would have been a small step for her to report to those who cared enough to inquire, "I'm counseling with Dr. So-and-So and he thinks my husband just has to get over his anger." Though Jesus Christ, the wonderful Counselor, would never have been fooled by her mere words or sincere appearance, a presumptuous earthly counselor could have missed a significant part of her story as if it were an iceberg floating largely beneath the surface.

The Hierarchy of Two-Way Communication

To avoid the folly of presumptive listening, it's important to recognize the power and the two-way nature of nonverbal behavior. This off-the-record behavior typically creates a hierarchy in communication, ranging from our actions, to our face, our voice, and our words.

Those who know us judge us by the way we treat people. But for brand-new relationships, the kind often sparked by a counseling need, there is typically very little past history on which the counselee can draw. Therefore counselees tend to judge the quality of the counselor-counselee relationship by interpreting the counselor's words (7 percent), voice (38 percent), and face (55 percent).[4] Therefore, if we model behaviors that suggest that we are offering a warm, open, safe relationship, it is more likely that the counselee will trust us and allow more of the iceberg to rise above the surface of the water. And as they tell more of their story, we have a greater likelihood of communicating God's will in the matter.

Imagine the difference in two hypothetical situations. A young man is shopping for professional premarital counseling, hoping to begin as soon as his fiancée arrives home from college in mid-May. The groom-to-be finds two identical ads in the *Christian Yellow Pages* and decides to give both operations a dry-run visit. He's planning, after comparing the two providers, to debrief with his lucky lady and to choose a starting date for joint counseling with one of the centers.

Judging from the ads, the phone contact, and the waiting-room brochures, the two counseling operations are mirror-images. Without telling the centers that he's comparison shopping, the groom-to-be schedules one premarital counselor for Monday at 7:00 P.M. and the other for Tuesday at 8:00 P.M.

Now pretend you're the counselee and it's Monday night. The receptionist indicates that it's your turn and so you step to the counselor's door and knock. A businesslike "Come in" resonates, with the higher pitch landing on "Come." As you step into the room, you see the office is split in half by a large government-style desk, surrounded by walls dripping with credentials. Inside the fortress, the counselor remains seated in a high-backed, swivel chair, dressed in a suit and tie. As the counselor brushes crumbs from his mouth, your nose tells you he's just eaten a fast-food dinner, perhaps explaining why the door was shut. Plain-faced, the therapist chops the air once with his hand, indicating that you are to be seated in the rickety chair opposite the throne. Having looked you straight in the eye since you stepped into the throne room, the counselor seems like an old-world king for whom the rules of court jesters still apply (for example, "Don't speak unless spoken to"). Moving like he's about to speak, the counselor drops his mouth open and freezes his index finger in mid-thought. Everything suggests he's just remembered something important. Flattening his right palm toward you, he implies, "Halt!" Swiveling on his throne, he madly jots himself a note on a scrap of paper and then turns back to you, ready for you to begin again. Assuming his working pose, the counselor crosses his legs and folds his arms. With furled brow and pursed lips, the counselor lowers the conversational drawbridge toward you, the intruder, and asks an opening question, "What can I do for you?" Although these are the first words voiced in the thirty seconds since "Come in," you feel like you've been drinking water from a nonverbal fire hydrant, gathering in gallons of communication easily missed by someone reading only the transcript.

On Tuesday night a different receptionist in a different center indicates that it's your turn. As you rise to your feet, she opens the door for you before you get to it. Almost simultaneously the counselor pulls the door open from the inside with a smile. He intones, "Come in" with the higher pitch on the second word. Identical in age, fitness, and education to his Monday-night counterpart, the second counselor seems more relaxed; his open-collar shirt looks more comfortable. This office, with the same dimensions as the previous one, feels more like a living room with a modest desk facing into the side corner. With a soft flex of his hand, the Tuesday counselor points toward a small grouping of three identical chairs. His chair, located beside the desk, is faced by two more that complete a kind of semicircle. A quick glance at the desk and walls reveals several family photographs, a bowl of candy, and a couple of framed posters—one humorous and one tranquil. Standing until you're seated, the counselor sits down, letting his hands come to a comfortable rest on his lap. In no apparent hurry he smiles and says, "So what can I do for you?"

Even if the engaged couple knew that both counselors would be saying exactly the same things throughout the same number of upcoming premarital sessions, it's likely that they would choose the second provider. It's also likely the second counselor might do a better job helping them tell their story before they choose goals and act on them.

JESUS' NONVERBAL BEHAVIORS

Of course, Jesus of Nazareth never had an office, never scheduled weekly fifty-minute appointments through a receptionist, and certainly never wrestled with finding the best DSM-IV[5] label for third-party billing purposes. Yet despite the obvious—that Jesus never functioned as a professional therapist in the modern sense—He did understand and practice the power of nonverbal communication. By a straightforward reading of the Gospels, we detect that Jesus often communicated with more than words. He also used body language: (P) physical presence, (O) open posture, (L) leaning in and out, (E) eye contact, (R) in a typically relaxed style.

Jesus' Physical Presence

Isaiah had underscored the coming physical presence of Jesus; the Messiah would be "Immanuel . . . God with us" (Isa. 7:14; Matt. 1:23). He who would serve the world as the Wonderful Counselor (Isa. 9:6) would interact with the world in a concrete, physical sense. No longer would God be seen as the unseen, the invisible presence on Sinai known only through His astounding words to Moses and His miraculous effects on the earth: "A mountain . . . burning with fire . . . darkness . . . gloom and storm . . . a trumpet blast . . . a voice speaking words that those who heard it begged that no further word be spoken . . . trembling with fear. . . . I will put you in a cleft in the rock and cover you with my hand. . . . I will remove my hand and you will see my back; but my face must not be seen.... No one has ever seen God."

According to Isaiah, this awesome God would become a "child ... a son ... a shoot from the stump of Jesse ... a Branch" (9:6–7; 11:1). The Son of David would become the suffering Servant. In His six-hour agony on the cross, He uttered a mere seven lines. And, according to Isaiah, "Many ... were appalled at him: ... disfigured ... marred.... They will see ... a tender shoot ... a root ... no beauty ... despised and rejected ... stricken ... smitten ... pierced ... crushed ... wounds ... oppressed and afflicted, yet he did not open his mouth. He was led like a lamb to the slaughter, and as a sheep before her shearers is silent, so he did not open his mouth ... taken away ... cut off ... stricken ... assigned a grave ... to crush him and cause him to suffer" (52:14–15; 53:2–5, 7–10).

Biblical Christianity affirms the fact of the Incarnation, in which Jesus Christ was virgin-born and took on Himself a human nature. In the words of Charles Wesley:

> *Christ, by highest heaven adored;*
> *Christ, the everlasting Lord!*
> *Late in time behold Him come,*
> *Offspring of the Virgin's womb.*
> *Veiled in flesh the Godhead see;*
> *Hail the incarnate Deity,*
> *Pleased as man with men to dwell,*
> *Jesus, our Emmanuel.*[6]

He who was first wrapped in swaddling bands would be finally wrapped in Palestinian death garb. Not a mirage (1 John 1:1–4) or an apparition (Luke 24:36–37), Jesus would rise bodily (24:38–43), ascend physically (Acts 1:9–11), and promise to return gloriously (Matt. 24:30–31; John 14:1–3).

God, who had whispered in Joseph's dreams and Daniel's visions, now thundered through Jesus' incarnation. Through the Incarnation, the immutable One become hungry (Matt. 4:2), thirsty (John 19:28), tired (John 4:6), and sad (11:35)—He was even tempted to sin (Heb. 4:15). But this volunteer for vulnerability, by His ministry of physical presence on the earth, could say, "Come and see Me, come and follow Me, come and be with Me."

Because Jesus was not locked inside the fortress of heaven, the world could literally hear Him say, "Come to me, all you who are weary and burdened, and I will give you rest. Take my yoke upon you and learn from me, for I am gentle and humble in heart, and you will find rest for your souls" (Matt. 11:28–29). And because Jesus could be seen and handled (1 John 1:1), He is our example, offering credible sensitivity to our shortcomings and modeling God's way for us.

In reviewing the ministry of our Lord and comparing it to modern analogues, we realize that Jesus never phoned a client, faxed a colleague, taped a sermon, broadcast an appeal, gave away a paperback, scored a questionnaire, or e-mailed a friend. His ministry was always a ministry with intense physical presence. Even when healing from a distance, He did so in the presence of distraught relatives or friends (Matt. 8:5–13; 15:22–28; 17:14–21).

Jesus' example challenges us as biblical counselors to examine our own people quotient. How often do we seek to be in the physical presence of people? How often do we skirt face-to-face contact because we say we don't have the time? How often do we make excuses for the fact that face-to-face contact is more intense, more draining, more risky? Don't we see that it is also potentially more rewarding?

As counselors, do we pay attention to the people quotient of our counselees? Does it register with us when our counselees refuse to meet with us face to face? Do we pick up on the downward power spiral when counselees miss appointments, come late, or choose to communicate by impersonal means like answering machines and letters? As counselors, does it send off an alarm to our nonverbal radar when we ask a counselee to confront someone personally, but instead the counselee wrote a note, placed calls, or gossiped to some third party? For biblical counselors and counselees alike, Jesus presents the ideal of total honesty. Two-way communication blossoms in the garden of physical presence.

Jesus' Open Posture

Jesus also practiced the skill of maintaining an open posture. We infer this by reading about the children who wanted to climb onto His lap and about sinners who wanted to invite Him to their parties. Imagine if Jesus had been physically present with people, but typically maintained a cold, rigid, closed posture—fists somewhat clenched, stomach muscles tight, lips pursed. The quality of His interpersonal relationships would have been profoundly weaker.

Normally when a king speaks, subjects listen—or so they should. So it seems remarkable that when Matthew introduced the King (Matt. 1–4) and invited Him to speak (Matt. 5–7)—to lay out His credentials (Matt. 8–9) and program (10:1–16:12)—that the King continued to welcome peasants into His chambers. Although this King of kings was nearing a head-on collision with the corrupt governors of the nation and although He was still unwavering in His declaration of authority to rule the world (Matt. 24–28), He continued to listen to common people (16:13–20:28).

Interacting with His subjects, the beloved King asked His disciples for the people's pulse, blessing the one who came up with the best answer (16:13–20). And when the toughest subject came up—His death—one of Jesus' followers felt that he had enough rapport with Him to object strenuously to His words (16:21–23).

Now if Jesus had been merely human, wearied by the busyness of His campaign for kingship, He would have welcomed some time with His family. But instead, this King of caregiving invited three of His campaign staff to a mountaintop audience with the Father, Moses, and Elijah (17:1–13). And when the three interns were frightened, Jesus touched them and comforted them (17:7).

So humble is this King, that He praised the simplicity of children (18:1–6), encouraging His followers to resolve their differences in a way that was likewise simple and direct (18:7–35). Concerned about people's needs (19:1–20:28), whether physical, marital, parental, financial, or spiritual, Jesus reminded His followers about true greatness. Welcoming a child into His inner circle (18:2), He warned the adults who were thronging around not to despise little boys and girls (18:10). Open to the many families who wanted Him to hold their children, He gladly agreed to pray for them (19:13–15; Mark 10:13–16), suggesting that spiritual greatness is not measured by who notices us, but by whom we notice (Matt. 18:1–20:28).

The element of children in Matthew's pedagogical narrative (16:13–20:28) is intriguing. Though we have no videotape of Jesus' nonverbal style, we infer that children wanted to be around Him. If they were afraid of Him, none of them would have come when bidden (18:2). If boys and girls were intimidated by "that scary man," the disciples would not have tried to keep them away (19:14). Instead, the parents would have protected their sons and daughters from Jesus, and the reluctant little ones would have thrown tantrums if forced in His direction. Very likely, Jesus' smile and His welcoming wave were social "green lights" to new relationships.

Indeed, children are often more attentive to tone of voice and body language than adults, since adult vocabulary and reasoning often exclude them from the complexities of higher discourse. Judging from the behavior of these kids, Jesus' nonverbal manner must have communicated warmth and openness.

Another group of people spotted the Lord's sense of humor and pleasure in companionship. Why else would Jesus be criticized for partying with the wrong crowd (Luke 5:27–39)? Jesus' reputation differed considerably from the reputation of His cousin: "For John came neither eating nor drinking and they say, 'He has a demon.' The Son of Man came eating and drinking and they say, 'Here is a glutton and a drunkard, a friend of tax collectors and sinners' " (Matt. 11:18–19).

Jesus also enjoyed being with the social lepers of his day. Otherwise why would these social outcasts share mealtimes with Jesus? My guess is that He did not seem self-righteous or uptight around them. They sensed that His love for them was genuine and open. If Jesus' body language had broadcast that He was easily angered by their shortcomings or worried about whether He would have the right answer for them, they would read that dissonance in a minute and would have kept their distance from Him.

Instead Jesus' critics sensed that He was a "friend of tax collectors and sinners" (11:19). Why? Because He didn't shy from them or look down on them. By the way Jesus stood around these folks, by the way He chatted and dined, He showed Himself to be their friend. His body language communicated that He was open toward them as people, though not open toward their sins.

While many people look on the outward appearance, God always looks on the heart (1 Sam. 16:7). While legalists and materialists consistently value how we look, what we own, and what we do or don't do, God has always valued who we are and who we can become.

Biblical counselors attend to the whole person, noting their own posture and the posture of their counselees. When we as counselors find ourselves tightening up, we do a self-check. If our face, our torso, our limbs are tensing up, we ask the Lord for help. In those moments we seek a divine peace that goes beyond our understanding. If we are feeling revulsion, fear, anger, or fatigue, we pray a silent prayer for personal wisdom. And if we spot our counselee closing down physically, we consider it possibly significant, possibly a barometer of spiritual conviction or personal offense or a historical tenderness. While physical posture isn't everything, it is worth noting.

Though Jesus had the courage and prerogative to cleanse the temple, His body language and His words were congruent throughout that event. Loving the good—His Father's house of prayer—made Him hate the evil, exploitive hypocrisy of the temple merchandisers (Mark 11:17; see also Rom. 12:9). Though counselors and counselees experience the full range of emotions and spiritual reactions, the most effective counselors pay attention to feelings and reactions that show up physically as well as those that show up verbally. When words and actions are out of sync, biblical counselors study both carefully.

Jesus Leaning In and Out

When Jesus wanted to express interest in a person or group, He no doubt leaned toward them, tilting his head, or bending a little at the waist, or even taking a half-step toward the object of His concern. This nonverbal phenomenon, nearly invisible to us through the Scriptures, is suggested by various Gospel narratives such as the Last Supper in the Upper Room (Matt. 26:17–30).

On Thursday night of Passion week, Jesus celebrated the Passover meal with His disciples. But one person was definitely not there: Domenico Ghirlandajo. In 1480 Ghirlandajo beautified the Church of Ognissanti in Florence with a fresco of the Last Supper, and in so doing he distorted our idea of what took place.[7] One inaccuracy stands out: the misplacement of

Jesus and the Twelve around the table. While Ghirlandajo placed the men at what seems to be the head banquet table, we now understand that this sacred event took place around something more like a low coffee table. While the artist has the men sitting upright in straight-backed chairs as if facing a camera, the New Testament seems to have them reclining on an elbow, with their heads positioned toward the low dinner table and their feet pointing away like spokes from a wheel. Though the Exodus generation had eaten the original meal standing and ready to flee (Exod. 12:11), Jesus' generation lounged as they ate (Mark 14:18), reveling in their freedom from slavery.

As the disciples entered their night of destiny (Matt. 26:17–19), a drama unfolded. "When evening came, Jesus was reclining at the table with the Twelve. And while they were eating, he said, 'I tell you the truth, one of you will betray me'" (26:20–21). Catching Peter's eye across the table, John easily read the fisherman's lips as Peter nodded and mouthed, "Ask him, 'which one he means?'" (John 13:24).

With each disciple angled toward the shoulder blades of the one next to him, John easily leaned back on Jesus' chest, expressing a nonverbal interest in private conversation. Reciprocating John's concern for privacy, Jesus probably tilted his head, answering barely above a whisper, "It is the one to whom I will give this piece of bread" (13:22–26).

Met with a dozen puzzled denials (Matt. 26:22), Jesus identified and indicted His would-be saboteur (26:23–24). His so-called friend (Luke 22:21) was in the sour business of filling his own pockets with thirty silver coins, the price of a common slave. As if his own spiritual darkness could shroud the Light (John 9:5), the greedy treasurer tried to deflect the truth by asking, "Surely not I, Rabbi?" (Matt. 26:25). Recoiling from the revelation, Judas departed into the darkness (John 13:30).

But in the thunder clouds of Judas's evil, God painted a silver lining; though Jesus was soon to be snatched by evil hands, He rested in everlasting arms (Deut. 33:27; Acts 2:23). With perfect peace, He broke the bread and blessed the wine, pointing toward the New Covenant that is filled with forgiveness and was purchased by His death (Matt. 26:26–29). That invisible horizon filled the Savior with spiritual eagerness (Luke 22:15).

Acting more like Judas than Jesus, the Eleven began arguing about their own spiritual pecking order (22:24–30), denying their own vulnerability (22:31–37) and imagining themselves to be self-sufficient (22:38–39). Acting out His sermon, Jesus got up and bent over the outstretched feet of His eleven disciples (John 13:4–17). Washing their feet as if He were their servant, Jesus rinsed the dust from that day's wanderings. Insisting that they had already been spiritually bathed, Jesus modeled their need for daily cleansing from broken fellowship. He touched them, drying their feet with His towel. With thanksgiving for what God had already done and what God would soon do, the remaining men lifted up their voices in the customary Hallel ("praise") psalms (Pss. 115–118; Matt. 26:30).

Like Jesus, biblical counselors seek to help counselees tell their stories, to communicate clearly. In doing so, the counselor who invests the time to hold face-to-face conversations often reaps better understanding. For counselors who practice an open posture and who note its absence, hints are available about welcome and unwelcome explorations. And when anchoring interest in a particular person or a topic, a skillful counselor avoids boredom and sharpens storytelling by a nod of the head, a lean from the waist, sliding forward in a chair, and stepping toward a person's gaze. Bending over the disciples' dirty feet and leaning toward John with His private concern, Jesus placed a listener's exclamation mark behind elements in the teller's story.

Jesus' Eye Contact

Without idolizing technique, biblical counselors recognize that the eyes can play a powerful role in communication. Blending both attitude and affect, one eyewitness wrote, "Jesus looked at him and loved him" (Mark 10:21). According to biblical wisdom, "A cheerful look brings joy to the heart" (Prov. 15:30). Although eye movements can be deceptively quick and subtle, one's full gaze can signal focused attention. Like a window to the soul, the eyes sometime reveal deep attitudes like sadness (Job 16:20; 17:7; Ps. 6:7) or pride (Prov. 6:16–17; 30:12–13, 17). The eyes might even convey hints about behaviors such as alcoholism (23:29–35).

As counselors, we ask God for spiritual insight when we read the Word (Pss. 19:8; 119:18) and for grace not to focus on the less important attributes of our counselees (such as affluence or physical beauty; 119:37; Prov. 4:25). In humility, we ask God to grant us eyes of compassion (Ps. 119:136) in the ministry of "the hearing ear, and the seeing eye" (Prov. 20:12, KJV).

Jesus' ministry certainly included the use of the eyes. In the heart of the Passion narrative Luke recorded, "The Lord turned and looked straight at Peter. *Then* Peter remembered the word the Lord had spoken to him . . . and he went outside and wept bitterly" (Luke 22:61–62, italics added).

This deep interpersonal gaze is highly dramatic, given the Lord's clear predictions and Peter's rigorous denials. When Jesus alerted Peter to his coming failure (22:31–32, 34), Peter rationalized away any sense of vulnerability to this temptation (22:33, 38). Even when Jesus rejected Peter's stab at the temple officer (22:49–54; John 18:10), Peter refused to get the point that the Good Shepherd has a kingdom not of this world (18:36), a kingdom that would be secured by the Shepherd voluntarily laying down His life for the sheep (10:15, 17–18). Earthly bluster, pride, and violence could never obtain God's blessings.

Even when Peter was confronted three times by witnesses who confirmed that he was Jesus' disciple (Luke 22:54–60), he branched from rationalization to rationalization. In trying to deceive others, Peter actually deceived himself. And in bouncing from excuse to excuse, he used his mind *not* to seek what he ought to do *but* to justify what he wanted to do. Jesus' intense eye contact, combined with His prophetic irony, caused Peter to burst into tears (22:61–62).

On another occasion Jesus commanded His disciples to open their eyes and look directly at the Samaritans. While the disciples were preoccupied with why their Master would talk to a woman (John 4:27) and how He had gotten food while they were at the grocery store (4:31–35), He challenged them to see people: "Lift up your eyes, and look on the fields . . . they are white for harvest" (4:35, NASB). Overflowing with the joy of her first love, the woman was in the process of leading the village and their white-robed priests to test the credentials of this Messiah (4:28–30, 39–42). In essence, our Lord may have been saying to His followers, "Stop staring at your lunchboxes; look up and look those people in the eye, especially the Samaritan priests—what a redemptive feast!" (4:35).

Even in our Lord's final hours He probably spoke with the help of His eyes. With hands and feet nailed to the Roman execution post, Jesus was left to communicate with His words, His tone of voice, His eyes, the expression on His face, and the nod of His head. His final seven words may well have been enunciated with nonverbal accents (Matt. 27:35–54; Mark 15:24–41; Luke 23:33–49; John 19:18–30). (1) Grimacing from the penetration of the nails, Jesus' eyes may have darted from His executioners toward the sky when He said, "Father, forgive them, for they do not know what they are doing." (2) Rotating His head to the side, Jesus may have looked deeply into the eyes of the repentant thief when He told him, "Today you will be with me in paradise." (3) Looking down, as if He were two feet taller than Mary and John, Jesus' eyes may have traveled back and forth several times between His beloved mother and His best earthly friend. "Dear woman, here is your son. [John], here is your mother." (4) Screaming skyward, Jesus' head may then have drooped when He exclaimed, "My God, my God, why have you forsaken me?" (5) In the throes of a raging fever, with His throat as dry as sand, Jesus may have looked to someone in the four-man execution squad, when in raspy voice, He uttered, "I am thirsty." (6–7) In prayerful simplicity Jesus may have bowed His head and closed His eyes with His two final sayings: "It is finished. . . . Father, into your hands I commit my spirit."

Just as Jesus utilized visual communication, skilled counselors pay attention to various forms of eye contact. When talking to a family, for instance, a biblical counselor can sometimes spot a parent giving the child a split-second "Don't-you-dare!" glare, a powerful effort to shut down communication during the session. That glare, in fact, is a part of that family's dialect, a kind of lexicon to their collective soul.

Similarly a marriage therapist might study the eyes of a couple as she helps them tell their relational story. With respect for their words, the therapist would also listen to the story being told by their eyes, their face, and their tone of voice.

Imagine a thirty-something couple arriving at the office of an unknown marriage counselor, ready for their first session. In the early minutes of their initial session, everything seems courteous, neutral, and behaviorally nondistinct. Then the therapist ventures her first probe. She observes, "I see from the notes my receptionist gave me that you two have come 'because you want your relationship to be better'?" Her intonation places a higher pitch on "better," as she slows her rate to signal her specific curiosity about that word. The therapist's body swings into a total reception mode, as if she has locked her story-seeking radar on the couple. Her eyes sweep up from her notes and begin to alternate between the two pair of eyes staring at her. Her body is relaxed and her feet are resting comfortably on the floor. Everything about the therapist says, "It's your turn; I'm all eyes and ears." Nothing about the therapist suggests that she has trivialized their reported reason for coming; nothing implies that she has a cookie-cutter solution to a preconceived problem. Nothing promises that it's going to be "twenty minutes and you're on your way." She anchors her question with another query. "If you could wave a magic wand over your marriage and change anything, what would it be?" As her question unfolds, she swings an invisible wand over the couple, concluding with both of her palms flexed upwards, ending as if she has just lightly tossed two nerf balls in the air.

The man's eyes climb the wall behind the therapist and he begins to select items that could be improved. "Well, I think we have a pretty good marriage, that we don't really need a therapist. But, hey, I'm here." Pausing, he brings his eyes back to a quick check-off with the therapist, and then looks to his wife as he asks, "Magic wand?" With his eyes again secured on the ceiling, he methodically begins: "We shouldn't have as much credit-card debt. I wish we had sex more than twice a month. I'd like her to stop nagging me about things; why does she have to say it twenty times?" Hearing his own question, his eyes come back to the therapist. With a slight smirk, his face implies, "That's not too bad, is it? So what's the answer, big shot?"

The wife, who acts as if she knew he'd go first, slowly exhales the breath she had been holding. Having studied his eyes from the side, she realizes he's done for now. Checking off with the therapist, she queries, "My turn?" With a sympathetic nod, the counselor gives her the green light.

Looking down, as if studying a crystal ball of emotion and experience, the wife speaks quietly, almost apologetically. "I'm sure I'm not a perfect wife. I'm sure we disagree about some things, sometimes. But what I'd really like . . ." She pauses as she looks cautiously his way. Showing signs of hurt, she sees him staring at his boots, drumming his fingers on the armrest. "I want to feel that he loves me and that he really loves the children." After twenty seconds elapse, the silence is deafening. The wife has studied her man up and down, waiting for a response. Still he stares at his boots. She glances at the therapist with a "Don't you see it too?" look.

Without going further, the case study suggests the valuable interplay of words and non-words. For counselors who are sensitive to body language, there is value in using their own eyes wisely and value in studying the eyes of their counselees—a potential window to the soul.

Jesus' Relaxed Style

Jesus' personal style was relaxed in spirit; after all, He is the Prince of Peace (John 14:27; Eph. 2:14). At our best we taste that peace from time to time (Phil. 4:7); but Jesus lived that peace, rooted in His perfect understanding (John 16:33; Rev. 21:6). Even when Jesus was angry, His omniscience and meekness granted Him the grace to be angry only at the right people for the right reasons, angry for the right length of time with the right expressions. His total spiritual calm allowed His voice and face to exude feelings of humor and sadness, affection and gravity, without confusion or selfish preoccupation with how others perceived Him.

In short, Jesus was touchable. Crowds sought to touch Him for help with their physical and psychic disorders (Mark 3:10–11; 6:56). Individuals sought to touch Him, such as the woman who had wasted her life's savings on inept healers (Matt. 9:20–21).

Jesus touched infants and children when the Pharisees wouldn't lift a finger to help the neediest of their day (Luke 11:46; 18:15). Jesus touched people on the hand (Mark 8:22–26), the eyes (Matt. 20:34), the ears and the tongue (Mark 7:32–35), praying with them and chasing away their leprosy (Matt. 8:2–3), their infections (8:14–15), and their blindness (9:27–28).

While I do not believe that Jesus was teaching us a healing technique, I do believe He was illustrating an interpersonal style: touchability. Jesus touched people to comfort their fears (17:7) and to heal their grief (Luke 7:11–17) as well as their diseases. And lest someone suggest that Jesus' patients healed themselves through positive thinking, remember the posse that arrested Him. A skeptic with an arrest warrant felt his amputated ear grafted onto his head in a healing instant (22:51). Wouldn't you love to hear how he explained those bloodstains on his shoulder when he got home from the night shift?

Among all of Jesus' ministry encounters, one stands out as a case study in touchability, as an example of the Lord's relaxed interpersonal style (7:36–50). The story unfolds as a religious dignitary, Simon the Pharisee, invites Jesus to an evening of fine dining. In the back of Simon's mind, apparently, Jesus is going to be checked out. Simon had been asking himself, "Is Jesus of Nazareth really a prophet?"

At some point in the evening, Simon and his guests are eating at the low living-room table when a neighbor shows up. With each man reclining on an elbow, their unsandaled feet are pointing away from the food; this is the perfect opportunity for the two men to chat and for the household servant, if there is one, to wash their dusty feet—just as Jesus did later in the Upper Room (John 13:1–20).

The surprise occurs when the neighbor quietly steps up to Jesus' feet. This "sinner" (Luke 7:37, KJV), as she is known in the town, begins to behave like the household servant—but with a brand-new level of affection and intimacy. Carried lightly in her hands is a fragile bottle of perfume, a thin-necked, alabaster flask shimmering with glass-like translucence. The visitor doesn't intrude on the conversation of the two men. In fact, she stands behind Jesus' feet, out of His direct line of sight. But He can hear her; she's weeping.

Without drawing water from a physical well, the penitent woman empties a fountain of tears from the reservoir of her painful memories. Remembering the faces, the places, and the rationalizations of her sin, she recognizes how far she has wandered from God. She measures the shame she's caused her family and other families. She admits how alone she is—except for the potential redemptive relationship with One who knows her completely and loves her without reservation. Her tears rinse His feet; her hair dries His skin. She leans slowly down and kisses the Carpenter's feet, showering on them an extravagance of sweetness.

As if there were a microphone inside Simon's head, Jesus hears him think: "Humph! There's my answer: He's no prophet. If He were, He'd know who she was. He'd know her by name; He'd know her by occupation—a woman of the night. He'd know she's a sinner, and He wouldn't let her touch Him!"

Enjoying his feeling of jealous superiority, Simon considered his evening mission done; the book was closed on Jesus, the prophetic impostor. But Jesus' mission was just beginning.

He told Simon a story about two debtors, one worse off than the other but both unable to pay a cent. Sidestepping Simon's rationalizations, Jesus touched his feelings by bringing the story to a surprising end, having the gracious creditor zero out both accounts. Then He asked a simple question: "Which of the debtors would probably love the gracious creditor the most?"

"I guess the one with the bigger debt," Simon ventured.

"Right," Jesus smiled. "That's why she loves me more than you do. That's why she washed my feet and you didn't, with her tears and hair no less. That's why she kept kissing me and you didn't kiss me even once. You didn't cologne my head, but she perfumed my feet. She has sinned against God many times, running up a big debt, but those sins are now lovingly forgiven and she's grateful for it. Anyone who has sinned very little—or believes he has—seeks God's forgiveness very seldom and takes God's grace for granted every day."

Setting off a quiet firestorm of debate among the guests, Jesus looked into the tear-filled eyes of the woman and said, "Your sins are forgiven. Your faith has saved you. Go in peace!"

And so this woman became one of the many whom Jesus led to repentance and comfort.

JESUS' USE OF QUESTIONS

A straightforward reading of a red-letter New Testament shows that Jesus asked more than three hundred questions in the Gospels. Although some of His questions are repeated in parallel accounts, the numbers still suggest that He averaged three to four inquiries per chapter. We therefore have no doubt that Jesus' work as the wonderful Counselor included a strategic use of questions.[8]

Whether heralding a crowd through the Sermon on the Mount or engaging Simon the Pharisee over dinner, Jesus often did the work of biblical counseling. In addition to noting elements of body language, facial expression, and tone of voice, Jesus helped His counselees tell their story by His queries. He didn't want just the "tip of the iceberg"; He wanted His counselees to float more of their thoughts, experiences, and behaviors above the dark surface of silence.

At first glance it seems mysterious that Jesus would ask so many questions. After all, He was omniscient! He didn't need His disciples to tell Him who had touched the hem of His garment, for instance, but He asked anyway (Mark 5:30). He didn't need Mary or Martha to guide Him to Lazarus's grave, but He inquired about its location anyway (John 11:34). Clearly, Jesus asked questions for the sake of His hearers, not for His own sake. In doing so He often leveled the playing field, showing a preference for dialogue over monologue.

Remember the encounter on the Emmaus Road? When the risen Christ caught up with the disciples, He acted more like an equal than Lord of the universe.

"What are you discussing?" He asked.

"Things," they responded sadly, referring to things that had recently happened in Jerusalem.

"What things?" Jesus followed up. When they explained that it had to do with His crucifixion, He pursued their sense of disappointment. "Did not the Christ have to suffer these things and then enter His glory?" (Luke 24:26). Rather than lecturing them, He invited them to walk with Him theologically.

Data Collection

In Jesus' ministry He used questions in many different ways. First, Jesus used questions to express interest by gathering data. "What is your name?" (Mark 5:9). "How long has he been like this?" (9:21). "What do you want me to do for you?" (10:36). "How many loaves do you have?" (6:38).

Biblical counselors who follow Jesus' example will develop a basic repertoire of interview questions. Where there are question marks, they'll usually get some fill-in-the-blank answers during a first meeting: name, address, phone number, age, occupation, marital/parental status, and a possible variety of other biographical markers.

Personal Exploration

Jesus also used open-ended questions to get people to think about themselves analytically. For instance, Jesus asked, "Why are you so afraid?" (Mark 4:40). "Do you want to get well?" (John 5:6). "Don't you know me, Philip, even after I have been among you such a long time?" (14:9). "Why don't you believe me?" (8:46). "Who do you say I am?" (Matt. 16:15). "Why did you doubt?" (14:31). "Can you drink the cup I am going to drink?" (20:22). "How will you escape being condemned to hell?" (23:33). "Where is your faith?" (Luke 8:25). "Dear woman, why do you involve me?" (John 2:4). "You are Israel's teacher and do you not understand these things?" (3:10). "Does this offend you?" (6:61). "You do not want to leave too, do you?" (6:67).

Using open-ended questions, biblical counselors can often get a deeper view of their counselee's perspective. The perceptive counselor might ask, "If you could change your life, what would you change? In trying to resolve this problem, who have you talked to and what have you tried? Why do you think these solutions didn't work? How did you decide to seek help from me?"

Spiritual Exploration

In Jesus' ministry He regularly inventoried people about where they stood in their relationship with God. He asked hard questions: "Do you believe this?" (John 11:26). "Why do you ask me about what is good?" (Matt. 19:17). "Do you believe that I am able to do this?" (9:28). "Who is my mother, and who are my brothers?" (12:48). "Why does this generation ask for a miraculous sign?" (Mark 8:12). "Why are you trying to trap me?" (12:15). "Could you not keep watch for one hour?" (14:37).

Biblical counselors express concern about their counselees' spiritual life. To get a handle on their spiritual state of affairs, a counselor might ask, "Have you come to the place in your spiritual life where you can say you know for certain that if you were to die tonight that you'd go to heaven? If you were to die tonight and God were to ask you why He should let you into His heaven, what would you say?" "Do you believe that God exists?" "Do you believe that Jesus is the only way to God?" "Do you believe the Bible is true?"

Biblical Exploration

Jesus often probed His listeners about their level of Bible knowledge and understanding. His questions often profiled certain texts as a part of the topical dialogue. "Haven't you read this Scripture: 'The stone the builders rejected . . .'?" (Mark 12:10). "Is it not written in your Law, 'I have said you are gods'?" (John 10:34). "Haven't you read what David did when. . . . ? Or haven't you read in the law that . . . ?" (Matt. 12:3–5). "But about the resurrection of the dead—have you not read what God said . . . ?" (22:31–32).

For a biblical counselor who seeks to imitate Jesus' approach, it would be wise to have a Bible with a concordance available. Some counselees may initiate specific questions focusing on particular texts, or the counselor may choose to direct the dialogue to a certain passage. Whether the counselor reads chapter and verse or simply engages in conversational paraphrase, the Scriptures should play an important role in the biblical counseling session. Soft, respectful introductions could begin as follows: "When you brought up that subject, it made me think about a line [or story, or person] in the Bible. It goes like this. [Cite the line or story.] Have you ever heard of that before? Let me tell you [or show you] what I'm thinking."

Logical Exploration

Jesus also seemed to ask questions to whet His listeners' appetite for more information, challenging them to think about the next logical step in the journey from the known toward the unknown. The master Mentor asked, "Are not two sparrows sold for a penny? . . . You are worth more than sparrows" (Matt. 10:29, 31). "What did you go out into the desert to see? A reed swayed by the wind? . . . A man dressed in fine clothes? . . . A prophet? Yes, . . . and more than a prophet. . . . Among those born of women there has not risen anyone greater than John the Baptist" (11:7–9, 11). "Do you think that these Galileans were worse sinners than all the other Galileans because they suffered this way? I tell you, no! But unless you repent, you too will all perish" (Luke 13:2–3).

Besides prompting His learners toward truth, Jesus also asked questions to reveal the logical fallacies that hindered His hearers from admitting the truth. These are some examples: "Doesn't each of you on the Sabbath untie his ox or donkey from the stall and lead it out to give it water? Then should not this woman . . . whom Satan has kept bound . . . be set free on the Sabbath day?" (13:15–16). "If Satan drives out Satan, he is divided against himself. How then can his kingdom stand?" (Matt. 12:26). "Do you bring in a lamp to put it under a bowl or a bed?" (Mark 4:21). "Am I leading a rebellion . . . that you have come out with swords and clubs to capture me? Every day I was with you, teaching in the temple courts, and you did not arrest me" (14:48–49). "If I spoke the truth, why did you strike me?" (John 18:23).

Biblical counselors who follow Jesus' way of extending good logic and confronting poor logic will help clarify the issues as counselees tell their story. For instance, a counselor might question the abortion decision of a young woman who is rationalizing her way out of a coercive marriage. The inquiry might focus on the spiritual soundness of her logic: "Tell me if I understand this correctly. Since your husband verbally harasses you, you feel you are the most vulnerable member of this marriage? So it's right for you to leave him and to abort the child? I'm wondering, isn't the unborn child the most vulnerable person in this conflict?"

Existential Exploration

In a profound way Jesus sometimes punctuated His dialogues with questions that had no obvious answer, questions that stunned and stopped His listeners. He inquired, "If you love those who love you, what reward will you get?" (Matt. 5:46). "What can a man give in exchange for his soul?" (16:26). "I have spoken to you of earthly things and you do not believe; how then will you believe if I speak of heavenly things?" (John 3:12). "When the Son of Man comes, will he find faith on the earth?" (Luke 18:8). "My God, my God, why have you forsaken me?" (Matt. 27:46).

At times Jesus asked questions that showed He could see through people, virtually reading their minds. "Why are you thinking these things?" (Mark 2:8). "How is it you don't understand that I was not talking to you about bread?" (Matt. 16:11). "Do you truly love me more than these? . . . Do you truly love me? . . . Do you love me?" (John 21:15–17).

Although no biblical counselor will ever be a match for Jesus, Christian helpers needn't avoid profound thoughts. Just because people-helpers are usually trained in basic empathy—the skill of accurately reflecting what the counselee has just said—there is no reason that the biblical counselor should not remain open to the possibility of advanced accurate empathy—the skill of tentatively jumping to a reasonable but intuitive conclusion. For instance, after a women's Bible study leader hears one of her members share her story of lifelong relational adversity, the leader might venture, "So you just want somebody to love you, right? To love you for who you are? Too often, the world loves you for how you look, what you own, and what you do. But God loves you for who you are and who you can become by His grace."

Power Exploration

When Jesus' questions had a punch to them, they were usually confronting an insincere person or trying to interrupt a behavioral cycle. To clarify the power issues with some insincere people, Jesus asked, "Why are you bothering this woman?" (Matt. 26:10). "I will also ask you one question. . . . John's baptism—where did it come from? Was it from heaven, or from men?" (21:24–25). "You hypocrites, why are you trying to trap me? . . . Whose portrait is this? And whose inscription?" (22:18, 20). "Do you think I cannot call on my Father and he will at once put at my disposal more than twelve legions of angels?" (26:53). "Is that your own idea?" (John 18:34).

To interrupt a self-perpetuating cycle and to change directions, Jesus often asked strategic questions. "Why all this commotion and wailing? The child is not dead but asleep" (Mark 5:39). "What are you arguing with them about? . . . How long shall I stay with you? How long shall I put up with you? Bring the boy to me" (9:16, 19). "Will you really lay down your life for me? I tell you the truth, before the rooster crows, you will disown me three times!" (John 13:38). "Are you still sleeping and resting? Enough! The hour has come. Look, the Son of Man is betrayed" (Mark 14:41).

Unfortunately biblical counselors will sometimes find themselves face to face with insincere, power-brokering "counselees." If the counselor doesn't discern the nature of the terrain, a lot of time and energy can be wasted; worse yet, the good intentions of biblical counselors could be used against them. At times a counselor may need to respond boldly. "Wait a minute. Let me get this straight. You are threatening to sue me, but you are demanding that I tell you everything that I said to so-and-so because your lawyer asked? Why don't you just load the gun and ask me to shoot myself?" Although Christians want to believe the best about people (1 Cor. 13:7), they are under command to "answer a fool according to his folly . . . without answering a fool according to his folly" (Prov. 26:5, 4). Such a principle requires discerning counselors to name the dirty trick without likewise threatening their own dirty tricks.

Jesus, the wonderful Counselor, utilized a rich array of nonverbal communication and interviewing skills. Since any counselee's story may be like the Petterman iceberg, showing only a few yards above the surface but measuring twenty-five miles wide under the surface,[9] skillful counselors try to help counselees tell the untold parts of their story. To aid them, biblical counselors behave like the seemingly clumsy polar bear. With an incredible sense of smell and the trademark fur on the soles of its feet, the polar bear—like the biblical counselor—is usually not fooled.[10] By meeting counselees face to face (physical presence) and by communicating with words *and* non-words (open posture, leaning in and out, eye contact, and relaxed stance), biblical counselors seek to avoid the folly of presumptive listening (Prov. 18:13). Instead biblical counselors strive to communicate as Jesus did, offering a varied assortment of gentle questions to help counselees tell their story.

CHAPTER FIVE

Helping People Choose Their Goals

THERE HE LAY: unconscious, silent, in a pool of his own blood, a baker's son on a mission for a grateful nation. The grenade had touched off a blistering village fight as the Blue Devils strained to push the Nazis out of the boot of Italy.

Missing in action and presumed dead, Watson lay crumpled on the dark cellar floor until the Brits discovered him. Far from a hospital, the two English infantry stitched his bleeding scalp together with a sewing needle and fiber from a rope. Hauling him to their camp, they wondered if their ally would live or die.

Days later the GI awoke from his coma. Wincing, he cautioned his hand along his swollen scalp.

"You're a lucky bloke. Thought you were dead when we found you. Your unit's moved off to the north."

As the boys from both sides of the ocean shared rations, one told the story of the fight, the others about the mopping-up operation. Like many who come for counseling, this twenty-three-year-old from the U.S. Fifth Army had a story to tell: He had nearly given his last full measure of devotion for a democratic ideal. Like many who offer counseling, the British soldiers who found him had no magic formula to specify what they or the American should do next.

Should the wounded private make a career of wearing the purple heart, lauding or lamenting his past? Should his newfound friends send him to the rear to look for a real doctor? Should he sit still, hoping some officers would find him and tell him what to do next?

As a matter of record, the GI stood up in his boots. Trying to blink away the dizzying migraine, the homesick combat soldier began his long trek toward the ever-rolling front lines. His mission? Do what the commander in chief would want. Act in concert with President Roosevelt's goals. Point northward, one boot in front of the other as if General Mark Clark were literally at his side.

Like undisciplined soldiers with no chain of command, many counselees approach counseling today as if it were an Aladdin's lamp for wishful thinking. Like generals with no battle strategy, many counselors today fail to lead their counselees out of the emotional fog of storytelling into the spiritual sunshine of biblical goal-setting.

CHOOSING JESUS' GOALS

Even Christians can come to counselors with dreams that scatter in more directions than a bucket of marbles dumped on a tile floor. "To lose twenty pounds; to increase my IQ; to know which model of car I should buy; to see if you'll agree with me that so-and-so has wronged me," and others. When confronted by such far-flung hopes, biblical counselors could paraphrase Paul's words and moan, "We don't know how to counsel as we ought" (Rom. 8:26). We are not to pray for things outside of God's will, nor are we to lead people confidently toward things not revealed as God's will.

Jesus made it clear that He wanted His followers to love God immensely (Matt. 22:36–40). Such love would blossom into an obedient lifestyle (John 14:15), energizing the disciples to win unbelievers to faith and to strengthen believers in faith (Matt. 28:19–20).

By counseling unbelievers toward the new life, these early Christians made God's will their will, "not wanting anyone to perish" (2 Pet. 3:9). By counseling their fellow believers to obey the ultimate Expert on life (John 14:6; Heb. 12:2), the first wave of Christian soldiers stood on sure spiritual footing (John 14:15; 15:10).

While God may have called some individuals to ministries of physical fitness, academic tutoring, consumer counseling, or abuse recovery, the church knows God's universal will only through God's universal Word. While it is noble to want to "do good to all people" (Gal. 6:10), the church must not lower herself to an "anything goes" kind of pragmatism. The church must not demean herself by becoming the doting parent who can think of nothing else than to please her spoiled child at all costs.

Jesus told His followers to disciple the world, converting the lost and maturing the found, teaching them to obey everything He had commanded. In eager pursuit of these commands one disciple-making pastor researched all of Jesus' imperatives in the Greek New Testament. By synthesizing Jesus' core requirements into thirty-one clusters of optimal behavior, Rick Leineweber Jr., has developed an authoritative primer for biblical goal-setting.[1]

THE COMMANDS OF CHRIST

Though a directionless counselor may groan, "We do not know how to counsel as we ought," spiritually directed counselors search the mind of God (through the Scriptures), interceding with goals provided by the wonderful Counselor. Sifting through the Lord's more than four hundred commands, biblical counselors understand that about half of the imperatives are historical or dispensational. For instance, Jesus' command for His disciples to "Come and have breakfast" (John 21:12) does not indict those who fast or otherwise skip the first meal of the day. His command is a piece of history, an instruction to *those* men on *that* day. Similarly Jesus' requirement for His disciples not to "go among the Gentiles" (Matt. 10:5) should not be read as a condemnation to missionaries who target a non-Jewish culture. Jesus' evangelistic boundary was a temporary rule, a kind of minidispensation to allow Israel sufficient exposure to accept or reject the Messiah. Their rejection, of course, led to His crucifixion, the good news of which is being heralded to all the nations of the world, including those of Hebrew descent.

Jesus' remaining two hundred commands in the Gospels cluster into thirty-one Christian duties, an excellent list from which counselors and counselees can select their goal(s) during biblical counseling. Because the remaining imperatives are not historical or dispensational, they easily correlate to timeless teachings throughout the remaining books of the New Testament.

Thirty-one Clusters of Jesus' Commands to His Disciples

1. Believing the gospel
2. Rejoicing in persecution
3. Listening to the Word
4. Pursuing the goal
5. Loving neighbors
6. Loving fellow believers
7. Serving with humility
8. Paying civil taxes
9. Not retaliating when wronged
10. Forgiving those who wrong us
11. Reconciling broken relationships
12. Keeping promises
13. Maintaining moral purity
14. Accepting God-given singleness
15. Avoiding greed
16. Serving as stewards of our possessions
17. Not worrying
18. Abiding in Christ
19. Following Christ
20. Bearing the cross
21. Reaching out to children
22. Honoring parents
23. Fearing only God
24. Praying
25. Avoiding hypocrisy
26. Not judging motives
27. Not opposing fellow believers
28. Confronting specific behaviors
29. Remembering the Lord's death
30. Being ready for the Lord's return
31. Obeying the Great Commission

Believing the Gospel

Throughout His public ministry Jesus preached, "The time has come. . . . The kingdom of God is near. Repent and believe the good news!" (Mark 1:15). Later in a Roman courtroom Paul confirmed that he did indeed believe. "I admit that I worship the God of our fathers as a follower of the Way, which they call a sect. I believe everything that agrees with the Law and that is written in the Prophets, and I have the same hope in God as these men, that there will be a resurrection of both the righteous and the wicked" (Acts 24:14–15). Even later from a prison cell, this apostle assured fellow believers of their eternal salvation. "And you also were included in Christ when you heard the word of truth, the gospel of your salvation. Having believed, you were marked in him with a seal, the promised Holy Spirit, who is a deposit guaranteeing our inheritance until the redemption of those who are God's possession—to the praise of his glory" (Eph. 1:13–14).

Biblical counselors, anchored in the evangelical imperative, will look for opportunities to sow and water the seed of the gospel, and at times they will share heaven's joy in the harvest of new fruit.

Rejoicing in Persecution

Knowing that the gospel would be profoundly controversial, Jesus prepared His disciples to face persecution. "Blessed are you when people insult you, persecute you and falsely say all kinds of evil against you because of me. Rejoice and be glad, because great is your reward in heaven, for in the same way they persecuted the prophets who were before you" (Matt. 5:11–12). Besides alerting His disciples to danger, Jesus taught them that their present suffering was small compared to their future reward; thus he challenged them to reframe their suffering. "Rejoice in that day and leap for joy, because great is your reward in heaven" (Luke 6:23). Because of the disciples' kinship to Jesus, preaching and persecution often went hand in hand (John 15:20; Acts 13:49–52). Nonetheless the apostle Peter counseled novices that self-inflicted punishment (for wrongdoing, for example) was not true persecution (1 Pet. 2:19–25).

Then as now, biblically oriented counselors help counselees distinguish between true persecution and a persecution complex.

Listening to the Word

Because the teachings of Jesus often sparked conflict, His followers needed supernatural help and character to discern the truth. Based on a farming analogy, Jesus said listeners were like different types of soil; the seed (the truth) remained the same but the yield (the listeners' response) varied dramatically. So He encouraged His audience to hear the truth of what He said (Matt. 13:9). As predicted, His disciples later encountered listeners who wanted to kill them (Acts 22:22) and others who begged for spiritual deliverance (16:25, 29–30). Thus the apostle James wrote guidelines on how to listen: "Humbly accept the word planted in you. . . . Do not merely listen to the word, and so deceive yourselves. Do what it says. Anyone who listens to the word but does not do what it says is like a man who looks at his face in a mirror and, after looking at himself, goes away and immediately forgets what he looks like. But the man who looks intently into the perfect law . . . and continues to do this, not forgetting what he has heard, but doing it— he will be blessed in what he does" (James 1:21–25).

Biblical counselors who yearn for their counselees to experience that blessedness will help them in their journey into the Word.

Pursuing the Good

Despite the potential adversities facing Christ and His followers, our Lord declared that Christians should be people of virtuous character and exemplary deeds: "Let your light shine before men, that they may see your good deeds and praise your Father in heaven" (Matt. 5:16). Though some early Christians, like Dorcas, were known for "always doing good and helping the poor" (Acts 9:36), Jesus warned that this kind of influence was not automatic. He asked, "Salt is good, but if it loses its saltiness, how can you make it salty again? Have salt in yourselves, and be at peace with each other" (Mark 9:50). According to Paul this kind of Christian credibility is anchored in excellent relationships, attitudes, and speech. "Do everything without complaining or arguing, so that you may become blameless and pure, children of God without fault in a crooked and depraved generation, in which you shine like stars in the universe as you hold out the word of life" (Phil. 2:14–16).

Though counselees may frequently come lamenting some circumstance, biblical counselors will wisely seek to reorient their perspective to what matters: character and lifestyle.

Loving Neighbors

When a scribe asked Jesus to select the single, most important command from the 613 in the Old Testament, Jesus answered, "The most important one . . . is this: 'Hear, O Israel, the Lord our God, the Lord is one. Love the Lord your God with all your heart and with all your soul and with all your mind and with all your strength.' The second is this: 'Love your neighbor as yourself.' There is no commandment greater than these" (Mark 12:29–31). In one breath Jesus summarized thousands of years of revealed truth, encompassing hundreds of particular commands and prohibitions. By loving God and neighbor perfectly, all spiritual duties would be met (Gal. 5:14). Such a love prevents Christians from harming their neighbors, even down to the small matters of owing debts (Rom. 13:8–10) or showing favoritism (James 2:8–9).

With this priority in mind, biblical counselors may imply, "Tell not what your neighbors can do for you; ask what you can do for your neighbors."

Loving Fellow Believers

Jesus taught that true love—the kind He modeled for us—would be the Christian "logo" (John 13:35; 15:12, 17). "As I have loved you, so you must love one another" (13:34). Jesus' followers were not allowed to playact for potential converts. Their love was to be an everyday affair between their most familiar brothers and sisters. For them, familiarity was not allowed to breed contempt. Drinking daily from the fountain of God's love, the early Christians overflowed with a spirit of generosity (Acts 2:44) and interpersonal concern (1 John 2:10). Perfect love, sourced in the Holy Spirit, demonstrated their salvation. And that kind of divine passion moved them toward noble deeds, harnessing them away from hatred and murder (3:10–23; 4:7–5:2).

Biblical counselors, in touch with such affection, are not easily cornered into simple alliances designed to orchestrate pity; instead, Spirit-filled counselors challenge counselees to rise above injustice with transcending love.

Serving with Humility

Although it is human nature to want to be top dog, Zebedee's wife and sons needed a lesson about humility and servanthood. When the three came asking for a place of special privilege in Jesus' coming kingdom

(Matt. 20:20–23), the other ten disciples became angry. So Jesus scolded the whole lot for their pride (20:24–25). "Instead," Jesus reminded them, "Whoever wants to become great among you must be your servant, and whoever wants to be first must be your slave—just as the Son of Man did not come to be served, but to serve, and to give his life as a ransom for many" (20:26–28). Indeed Jesus characterized the best leader as the one who takes the position as "the very last" (Mark 9:35). Such servanthood would beautify the early church as Spirit-filled deacons provided "meals-on-wheels" to Jerusalem's widows (Acts 6:1–7) and others modeled the gift of serving (Rom. 12:7; 16:1–2). Such servanthood beautifies any church today.

Paying Civil Taxes

Imagine Jesus in colonial Williamsburg nose-to-nose with Patrick Henry in the public square. Listen to the crowd chanting the revolutionary phrase, "No taxation without representation." Henry exclaims, "Give me liberty or give me death!" And then a preplanned question surfaces: "Jesus, should we pay taxes to Great Britain?" A smirk betrays the conspirators' pride; they have put Jesus in a no-win situation, or so they think. To answer no would put Jesus in a revolutionary posture; informants could see to it that Redcoats ride Him down before sunset. To answer yes would put Jesus at odds with the conservatives who detest the idolatrous image of an earthly ruler on English coins. But Jesus turns their logic upside down. He reasons, "If the denarius has Caesar's image on it, it must belong to Caesar! And if you have God's image on you, you must belong to God!" (see Matt. 22:15–22). Such civil simplicity prevented Christians from becoming just another political party, the perpetual antagonists of government (Rom. 13:6–7).

Even today biblical counselors redirect their counselees' attention from the misdeeds of government to the divine deeds of a higher citizenship (Phil. 3:20–21).

Not Retaliating When Wronged

In an age when Roman sentries stood on almost every street corner in Israel, Jesus' words must have stunned His audience. "You have heard that it was said, 'Eye for eye and tooth for tooth.' But I tell you, Do not resist an evil person. If someone strikes you on the right cheek, turn to him the other also. And if someone wants to sue you and take your tunic, let him have your cloak as well. If someone forces you to go one mile, go with him two miles. Give to the one who asks you, and do not turn away from the one who wants to borrow from you" (Matt. 5:38–42). When wronged by Roman soldiers or Jewish neighbors, Jesus forbade revenge. Even as Stephen was being gang-murdered on false charges, the first Christian martyr prayed for the forgiveness of his assailants (Acts 7:57–60). Far from the spirit of retaliation, Paul taught the Christian ideal: "If it is possible, as far as it depends on you, live at peace with everyone" (Rom. 12:18).

In this spirit and with this ideal, biblical counselors guide Christians who are in conflict today.

Forgiving Those Who Wrong Us

Besides requiring His disciples to pursue broken relationships, Christ challenged them to offer forgiveness in a generous way. "If your brother sins, rebuke him, and if he repents, forgive him. If he sins against you seven times in a day, and seven times comes back to you and says, 'I repent,' forgive him" (Luke 17:3–4). Even when a Christian has become a willing victim in a sin as ugly as incest, true repentance invites true forgiveness: "The punishment inflicted on him by the majority is sufficient for him. Now instead, you ought to forgive and comfort him, so that he will not be overwhelmed by excessive sorrow. I urge you, therefore, to reaffirm your love for him" (2 Cor. 2:6–8). Just as the Christian life is inaugurated through God forgiving us, our Christian lives are to be marked by our forgiving one another (Eph. 4:32).

Biblical counselors often find themselves serving as traffic cops, steering people through the crowded intersections of life where forgiveness is often needed but seldom granted.

Reconciling Broken Relationships

Although broken relationships have littered the human landscape since Eden, Jesus predicted an end-times escalation of cold-heartedness (Matt.

24:12). Similarly Paul prophesied a mushrooming movement toward sinful relationships, including the lack of forgiveness (2 Tim. 3:2–4). Jesus instructed His disciples to pursue reconciliation actively: "If you are offering your gift at the altar and there remember that your brother has something against you, leave your gift there in front of the altar. First go and be reconciled to your brother; then come and offer your gift" (Matt. 5:23–24). Even in relationships as private as marriage, Paul emphasized the principle of reconciliation: "To the married I give this command .... A wife must not separate from her husband. But if she does, she must remain unmarried or else be reconciled to her husband. And a husband must not divorce his wife" (1 Cor. 7:10–11). Counselors often face the challenge of seeking to repair broken relationships.

Keeping Promises

Some religions, cultures, and families justify lying to "outsiders," but Christian integrity demands truthfulness at all times. Some who are practiced in the art of lying have pushed everyone to the realm of "outsider," at times even lying to themselves. Yet in the face of trumped-up oath-taking (Matt. 5:33–36)—like "I swear on my mother's grave!" and "May God strike me dead!"—Jesus' instructions were crystal clear. He said, "Simply let your 'Yes' be 'Yes,' and your 'No,' 'No'; anything beyond this comes from the evil one" (5:37). Grounded in truth-telling, Paul kept his Nazirite vow, even in Gentile territory (Acts 18:18). Indeed, when Paul published his missionary itinerary, he considered it a matter of Christian duty to exercise all diligence to keep his word. "I planned to visit you.... When I planned this, did I do it lightly? Or do I make my plans in a worldly manner so that in the same breath I say, 'Yes, yes' and 'No, no'? But as surely as God is faithful, our message to you is not 'Yes' and 'No.' For the Son of God ... was not 'Yes' and 'No,' ... no matter how many promises God has made, they are 'Yes' in Christ. And so through him the 'Amen' is spoken by us to the glory of God" (2 Cor. 1:15–20).

Biblical counselors, convinced about verbal integrity, will guide counselees to keep their promises and to own up when promises are broken.

Maintaining Moral Purity

Based on a strange interpretation of Genesis 49:22, some famous rabbis taught that certain men had power "over the evil eye" (that is, that they could not be visually tempted).[2] Not surprisingly, some men reveled in this alleged immunity, parking themselves outside the public bath and engaging in girl-watching and flirtatious talk. Jesus was not on the fence about their behavior. He stated that physical adultery and fantasized adultery are both dead wrong. The solution? Deal with the source! Repent at the core! Regarding that lustful eye, that wandering hand or foot, Jesus was unequivocal. "Gouge it out . . . throw it away . . . cut it off " (Matt. 5:29–30; Mark 9:43–47).

In a sincere but mechanical effort to obey this dictate, Origen castrated himself. Although he survived the surgery, this church father failed to solve the problem of personal lust. This courageous pioneer for sexual purity discovered that the most powerful sexual organ in the body is the mind. If he were alive now, he would know that the second most powerful organ is the skin.

In biblical counseling, there should be zero tolerance for sexual impurity and a commitment to manage the mind and the skin. Even the Jerusalem Council made it clear that sexual purity was not "just a Jewish thing" (see Acts 15:20, 29; 21:25); it was and is God's will for all believers (1 Thess. 4:3–7).

Accepting God-Given Singleness

In Jesus' day, as in ours, most adults marry. However, some have a different calling, a calling to God-given singleness. Jesus taught, "Not everyone can accept this word, but only those to whom it has been given. For some are eunuchs because they were born that way; others were made that way by men; and others have renounced marriage because of the kingdom of heaven. The one who can accept this should accept it" (Matt. 19:11–12). While some people are born incapable of procreation, and others, like Origen, are rendered incapable by surgery, a third class also exists: those with a divine calling to practice singleness with contentment. While singleness has tremendous ministerial advantages, sexual purity for the Christian is not optional. Thus if some Christians have God's grace to maintain sexual purity and ministry intensity as unmarrieds, they should accept that grace (1 Cor. 7:7–9, 25–40).

So whether we are guiding children in their life choices or ministering to the divorced after a marriage breaks up, we must resist the cultural pressure to label singleness and celibacy as "abnormal" or "gay." Instead we can advise a prolonged and prayerful review of the possibility that God might have a particular individual remain single and celibate for a higher purpose.

Avoiding Greed

Jesus' followers were not only challenged to avoid sexual selfishness; they were also urged to avoid material selfishness. "Do not store up for yourselves treasures on earth, where moth and rust destroy, and where thieves break in and steal. But store up for yourselves treasures in heaven . . . For where your treasure is, there your heart will be also" (Matt. 6:19–21). So convinced was Jesus about the danger of material greed that He stung a young man who was whining that his older brother should split the family inheritance. "Watch out!" Jesus warned. "Be on your guard against all kinds of greed; a man's life does not consist in the abundance of his possessions" (Luke 12:15). True to this ethic, Paul testified to the Ephesian elders, "I have not coveted anyone's silver or gold or clothing" (Acts 20:33). Instead of playing the role of religious peddler or meandering philosopher, Paul worked as a tentmaker to provide for himself and the needy. After all, another apostle argued, a major source of conflict in our lives comes from believing the lie that things can make us happy (James 4:2). Amazingly, median family income and house size in twentieth-century America have steadily increased. Yet many American families, though smaller, have bigger debts.

Discerning biblical counselors will recognize that many of the stress-related problems that occur with individuals and families ultimately bubble up from the toxic fountain of greed.

Serving as Stewards of Our Possessions

Although Jesus is vitally interested in our attitude toward material things, He did not declare that financial status, by itself, is a matter of spirituality.

He did not announce that the rich are evil and the poor noble. Nor did He applaud the wealthy as heaven-blessed and excoriate the poor as lazy or ignorant. Instead, our Lord challenged His disciples to "use worldly wealth" (Luke 16:9) so long as it is honestly gained (Titus 1:7). Each Christian is to "use whatever gift he has received to serve others, faithfully administering God's grace in its various forms" (1 Pet. 4:10). In discharging our various stewardships—whether our time, treasure, or talent—there is only one standard: "It is required that those who have been given a trust must prove faithful" (1 Cor. 4:2).

Since money is merely a tool, a means to a nobler end, some Christians have begun ministries of financial counseling. An example is Larry Burkett, president of Christian Financial Concepts, Gainesville, Georgia. These teachers do not seek to exaggerate or gratify our greed; they seek to prepare us to answer to God for our stewardships in life. In concert with this goal biblical counselors will seek to prepare counselees to answer to God for their stewardships in life.

Not Worrying

Francis Schaeffer identified two primary values in modern Western culture: personal peace and affluence. He suggested that most of us are seeking both a high standard of living and freedom from personal stress. Unfortunately these two values are usually at war. Jesus warned, "Do not be afraid [that is, don't worry], little flock, for your Father has been pleased to give you the kingdom. Sell your possessions and give to the poor. Provide purses for yourselves that will not wear out, a treasure in heaven that will not be exhausted, where no thief comes near and no moth destroys" (Luke 12:32–33). The imprisoned apostle concurred, urging his readers toward the true contentment that comes from resting in the Lord's presence, living by a spirit of prayer, and engaging in constant "mind" baths. "Rejoice in the Lord always. . . . The Lord is near. Do not be anxious about anything, but in everything, by prayer and petition, with thanksgiving, present your requests to God. And the peace of God, which transcends all understanding, will guard your hearts and your minds in Christ Jesus. . . . Whatever is true . . . noble . . . right . . . pure . . . lovely . . . admirable . . . excellent or praiseworthy—think about such things. . . . And the God of

119

peace will be with you. . . . I have learned to be content whatever the circumstances. . . . I have learned the secret of being content. . . . I can do everything through him" (Phil. 4:4–9, 11–13).

To help counselees achieve victory over worry, biblical counselors need to mentor counselees in these principles of life.

Abiding in Christ

Since Eden, Jesus has sought a voluntary, permanent relationship with members of the human race, descendants of Adam and Eve. On His solemn stroll to a darkened Gethsemane the Savior spoke about that relationship. The Lord exhorted His eleven disciples to abide in Him. "Remain in me and I will remain in you. No branch can bear fruit by itself; it must remain in the vine. Neither can you bear fruit unless you remain in me. . . . Now remain in my love. If you obey my commands, you will remain in my love, just as I have obeyed my Father's commands and remain in his love" (John 15:4, 9–10). For them, abiding meant holding on to Jesus' core teachings (8:31). Such a relationship, solid and reciprocal, would last forever (2 John 2, 9).

The command "Remain in me" (John 15:4) calls the biblical counselor to minister to doubters and to backsliders, teaching them how to cultivate a garden of enduring fruit in their relationship with Christ.

Following Christ

Although many people were intrigued with Jesus and the temporary benefits they thought He could provide, He sought followers who would be marked by loyalty and perseverance. One day, having healed a series of very sick people, Jesus led His disciples to cross the lake and break company with the clamoring crowd (Matt. 8:1–18). Once Jesus was across, a scribe, volunteering to join His corps, promised, "Teacher, I will follow you wherever you go" (8:19). Apparently unimpressed, Jesus raised the bar higher. "Foxes have holes and birds of the air have nests, but the Son of Man has no place to lay his head" (8:20). So another disciple volunteered, "Lord, first let me go and bury my father" (8:21). Jesus was curt: "Follow me, and let the dead bury their own dead" (8:22). Although our

Lord never taught us to ignore the needy or to dishonor our parents, He pointed toward a higher camaraderie that could surpass what He might do in the here and now and what our parents had done in the there and then. In the will of God our long-distance sights are always to be set on Christ, not our favorite mentors (1 Cor. 1:12; 11:1).

And in the work of biblical counseling we will often find ourselves helping people who have been hurt by their favorite someone. We can help them heal, reminding them that only Jesus never fails.

Bearing the Cross

The loyalty Jesus sought was ultimately the same loyalty He offered, the willingness to give up everything, even to the point of death. He asks no less from us. "If anyone would come after me, he must deny himself and take up his cross and follow me. For whoever wants to save his life will lose it, but whoever loses his life for me will find it. What good will it be for a man if he gains the whole world, yet forfeits his soul? Or what can a man give in exchange for his soul? For the Son of Man is going to come in his Father's glory with his angels, and then he will reward each person according to what he has done" (Matt. 16:24–27). In modern parlance Jesus asked us to drape a hangman's noose around our neck, to carry bullets for our firing squad, to strap ourselves into the electric chair. If we resolve ahead of time to pay the ultimate price for Jesus and His words, He promises to be proud of us in the hereafter (Mark 8:35–38). Resting in the guarantee of resurrection and reunion, Paul faced wild beasts in the Roman stadium (1 Cor. 15:31–32). Convinced that Good Friday was followed by Easter Sunday, Peter and John weren't intimidated by death threats from the Jewish Supreme Court (Acts 4:13, 18, 21).

Biblical counselors will need to minister to those with a spiritual deficit in cross-bearing, professing Christians who live a hedonistic lifestyle or shrink away from public identification with Christ.

Reaching Out to Children

Jesus became indignant when people put barriers in front of children who wanted to see Him (Mark 10:14). Jesus did more than passively receive them;

He actively recruited them to come (Luke 18:16). "Let the little children come to me," He said, "and do not hinder them, for the kingdom of heaven belongs to such as these" (Matt. 19:14). Believing adults have a generous opportunity to write in the wet cement of children's lives. So compelling is this duty that church leaders are judged by how they have handled their privileged years of child rearing. "An elder must be ... a man whose children believe and are not open to the charge of being wild and disobedient" (Titus 1:6).

Abraham Lincoln said, "He is not poor who has a godly mother." To this biblical counselors would add, "No child is poor who has a godly parent or parent figure." After all, spiritual greatness is not measured by who notices us, but by whom we notice.

Honoring Parents

In Moses' day the Law was clear. "God said, 'Honor your father and mother. ... Anyone who curses his father or mother must be put to death'" (Matt. 15:4). Jesus held that ground and added to it. He pronounced it hypocrisy to pledge money for the temple but to "talk poor mouth" to elderly parents who were truly in need (15:4–7). Care of the elderly is not the responsibility of the Social Security Administration or AARP. As Paul wrote, "If a widow has children or grandchildren, these should learn first of all to put their religion into practice by caring for their own family and so repaying their parents and grandparents, for this is pleasing to God" (1 Tim. 5:3–4). Such obedience is blessed with a promise: "that it may go well with you and that you may enjoy long life on the earth" (Eph. 6:3).

Fearing Only God

The ultimate human fear—the fear of death—is a favorite ploy of those who would intimidate us (Heb. 2:15). But Jesus, who holds the keys to life and death (Rev. 1:18), said, "Do not be afraid of those who kill the body and after that can do no more. ... Fear him who, after the killing of the body, has power to throw you into hell. Yes, I tell you, fear him. Are not five sparrows sold for two pennies? Yet not one of them is forgotten by God. Indeed, the very hairs of your head are all numbered. Don't be afraid;

you are worth more than many sparrows" (Luke 12:4–7). In Jesus' warning to fear only God, He reminded us that hell is not Satan's playhouse; He said it is God's prison house and that God protects those who are His own. So even in the face of Corinthian death threats, the Lord encouraged Paul to stay in that dangerous city for eighteen months, teaching the Word. "Do not be afraid; keep on speaking, do not be silent. For I am with you, and no one is going to attack and harm you, because I have many people in this city" (Acts 18:9–10).

And when the believers in Smyrna were about to be persecuted for their beliefs Jesus comforted them: "Do not be afraid of what you are about to suffer. I tell you, the devil will put some of you in prison to test you, and you will suffer persecution for ten days. Be faithful, even to the point of death, and I will give you the crown of life.... He who overcomes will not be hurt at all by the second death" (Rev. 2:10–11).

Biblical counselors recognize that fear always produces avoidance behaviors. On the positive side, godly fear mobilizes people to avoid sin; on the negative side, ungodly fear controls people, making them avoid what they should face.

Praying

Sometimes a biblical counselor does nothing more than listen and pray, but praying with and for a counselee may make the difference between success and failure (Luke 18:1). Jesus said, "Pray for those who persecute you, that you may be sons of your Father in heaven.... Ask and it will be given to you; seek and you will find; knock and the door will opened to you" (Matt. 5:44–45; 7:7). For counselors who would teach their counselees to pray, the door is wide open to pray about God's character, kingdom, and will, as well as confessing our sins, and praying about our interpersonal conflicts and our temptations (6:9–13). The early church, a mighty force in the world, was described as "constantly in prayer," its annals laced with the words "then they prayed" (Acts 1:14, 24).

Despite all of the unknowns in counseling, we do know that one aspect of God's will for all Christians is that they pray with gratitude for every circumstance of life (1 Thess. 5:17–18).

Avoiding Hypocrisy

The sin of hypocrisy is a big deal to God. On a day when thousands of people herded around him, our Lord didn't mince any words. "Be on your guard against the yeast of the Pharisees, which is hypocrisy. There is nothing concealed that will not be disclosed, or hidden that will not be made known. What you have said in the dark will be heard in the daylight, and what you have whispered in the ear in the inner rooms will be proclaimed from the roofs" (Luke 12:1–3). Jesus was fiercely opposed to chameleon behavior, changing our colors between public and private, spinning different views for different groups. When Peter ordered from the nonkosher menu in Antioch and then did an about-face at the dinner table with James's delegation from Jerusalem, Paul called it what it was. Paul said Peter was clearly in the wrong, for he was "afraid of those who belonged to the circumcision group. The other Jews joined him in his hypocrisy, so that by their hypocrisy even Barnabas was led astray. . . . I do not set aside the grace of God, for if righteousness could be gained through the law, Christ died for nothing!" (Gal. 2:12–13, 21).

In light of Jesus' hatred for hypocrisy biblical counselors need to be ready to point out inconsistencies and to respond to sincere, probing questions by their counselees, making sure they don't word their answers in an effort to ensure political correctness with every audience.

Not Judging Motives

Many of us indulge in a special form of pride: the tendency to think that we know what makes other people tick. Maybe we get there by assuming that we are the standard of normalcy and that we know how we tick, but this is a dangerous assumption (Jer. 17:9; 2 Cor. 10:12). Jesus gave specific instructions: "Do not judge, or you too will be judged. For in the same way you judge others, you will be judged, and with the measure you use, it will be measured to you" (Matt. 7:1–2). Even when we jump to conclusions based on people's apparent social status, we have erred. "Have you not discriminated among yourselves and become judges with evil thoughts?" (James 2:1–4).

When Paul was nearly gang-murdered in Jerusalem on false charges, he was arraigned before the Sanhedrin. When the presiding judge disliked part of Paul's testimony, the judge had a soldier punch Paul in the mouth (Acts 22:30–23:2). Wiping blood from his mouth, Paul redressed the bench with legal argument. "You sit there to judge me according to the law, yet you yourself violate the law by commanding that I be struck!" (23:3). Just short of judging the high priest's motives, Paul used the written word to indict one of his specific behaviors. This illustrates the apostle's own caution light regarding the judgment of motives. "Therefore judge nothing before the appointed time; wait till the Lord comes. He will bring to light what is hidden in darkness and will expose the motives of men's hearts. At that time each will receive his praise from God" (1 Cor. 4:5).

As biblical counselors we will be tempted to judge motives. As counselees, many who are dysfunctional will thrive on their alleged ability to mind-read. Rather than having us judge motives, we believe the Word of God judges specific behaviors.

Not Opposing Fellow Believers

The master Designer of "one Lord, one faith, one baptism" (Eph. 4:5) certainly loves unity (Ps. 133:1) and hates divisiveness (Prov. 6:19). But some Christians, some churches, and some parachurch organizations thrive on proud, exclusive relationships. Even Jesus' disciples had to wrestle with the problem of divisiveness. When John saw a stranger successfully performing exorcisms in Jesus' name, John told him to quit; but Jesus corrected John. "Do not stop him. . . . No one who does a miracle in my name can in the next moment say anything bad about me, for whoever is not against us is for us" (Mark 9:38–40).

When we observe a so-called Christian behaving in a way that is chronically divisive, we are under command to name the behavior for what it is, namely, malicious gossip (3 John 9–10). After one or two warnings, if factious people won't repent, we should stand clear of them (Titus 3:10–11).

In counseling, as in any private conversation, there is a risk that speakers might engage in gossip or slander toward people who are not present, while listeners may naively believe everything they hear (Prov. 1:22; 20:19). A discerning listener will always keep reported behavior in quotes ("he said . . . she said") and challenge counselees to confront their alleged offenders in a godly way.

Confronting Specific Behaviors

In the interpersonally rich world of New Testament relationships, believers typically "admonish one another" (Col. 3:16). But how? First, the ball begins rolling when a "brother (or sister) sins" against us (Matt. 18:15). Admonition does not necessarily occur with people outside the faith, nor for issues that are not biblically labeled as "sin."

Second, the ball keeps rolling as the "offended" person initiates a private face-to-face meeting with the "offender" in hopes of restoring the relationship (18:15). Except in the rarest of circumstances (such as an allegedly abused child trying to confront an allegedly abusive adult), admonition does not proceed if the "offended" one is unwilling or unable to execute the private confrontation. When offended people will not confront, the biblical counselor may focus on the offended one's unwillingness to confront. In no case is the offended person permitted the luxury of harboring bitterness or sowing gossip and slander to others.

Third, if the first meeting occurs and fails, the offended individual is instructed to bring one or two others along for a second meeting (18:16). So long as these others are true witnesses (that is, first hand observers of the fault; Deut. 19:15). If there are not witnesses, the unreconciled relationship is simply submitted to prayer, trusting God to bring to light the hidden things of darkness (1 Cor. 4:5).

Fourth, if the second-round meeting fails, the offended one and the witnesses report the evidence to the leaders of the church (Matt. 18:17). If the leaders judge the behavior to be sin, they seek to repair the relationship. But if the offender is still unrepentant after these personal, plural, and public rebukes, the leaders conclude that sinful actions speak louder than professing words. The offender is relegated to the status of an outsider by the whole assembly; insider privileges are suspended until further notice (18:17). This procedure, though compressed, appears in force with the admonition of elders (1 Tim. 5:1, 19–20), individuals (1 Cor. 5:1–13), and families (Acts 5:1–11).

Remembering the Lord's Death

When our Lord spoke of His coming death, He said, "Take and eat. . . . Drink from it, all of you" (Matt. 26:26–27). In the days following the Resurrection, believers reenacted that meal on the first day of the week (Acts 20:7, 11). Indeed, Paul described it as a universal custom throughout the Christian age. "I received from the Lord what I also passed on to you. . . . This is my body. . . . Do this in remembrance of me. . . . This cup is the new covenant in my blood; do this, whenever you drink it, in remembrance of me. For whenever you eat this bread and drink this cup, you proclaim the Lord's death until he comes" (see 1 Cor. 11:17–34).

A biblical counselor may engage a counselee to practice the Lord's Supper in a doctrinally discerning way. If the counselee lacks personal faith, church membership, or a well-ordered life, these gaps may create an agenda for ongoing counseling sessions.

Being Ready for the Lord's Return

The consummate Christian experience is to stand face to face with Christ (John 14:3; 2 Cor. 5:8; 1 John 3:2), an imminent possibility. Jesus warned, "Be on guard! Be alert! You do not know when that time will come. . . . Therefore keep watch because you do not know when the owner of the house will come back. . . . If he comes suddenly, do not let him find you sleeping. What I say to you, I say to everyone: Watch!" (Mark 13:33–37). Weeks after this warning, Jesus' eleven apostles wondered about His timetable. They asked, "Lord, are you at this time going to restore the kingdom to Israel?" (Acts 1:6). His reply was blunt: "It is not for you to know the times or dates the Father has set by his own authority" (1:7). Even as the New Testament closed, the warning about readiness remained. "Remember, therefore, what you have received and heard; obey it, and repent. But if you do not wake up, I will come like a thief, and you will not know at what time I will come to you. . . . I am coming soon. Hold on to what you have, so that no one will take your crown" (Rev. 3:3, 11).

In the work of biblical counseling, Bible prophecy has little to do with ordering events and much to do with ordering lives.

Obeying the Great Commission

In Jesus' final meetings with His followers, He instructed them to sow the seed of the gospel around the globe. Discipling people from every ethnic group, the disciples would seek to win unbelievers to faith in Christ and to strengthen believers in their faith. In Galilee Jesus said, "All authority in heaven and on earth has been given to me. Therefore go and make disciples of all nations, baptizing them in the name of the Father and of the Son and of the Holy Spirit, and teaching them to obey everything I have commanded you. . . . Go into all the world and preach the good news to all creation" (Matt. 28:18–20; Mark 16:15). They obeyed, in crowded cities (Acts 14:21–22) and in quiet households (2 Tim 1:5; 3:14–17). To do less today would be to fall short as a biblical counselor or counselee.

WINNING THE WAR

World War II cost humanity more than any other war in history. In the half-dozen years which marked that conflict nearly forty-five million souls—military and civilian—were propelled into eternity and more than a trillion dollars was consumed by weaponry and property damage. Without adequate leadership and a coordinated battle strategy, the Allies might still be fighting—or enduring the chaos of defeat. But victory over Germany and Japan came on May 8 and September 2, 1945, respectively.

What did it take to achieve these victories? It took vision and viability. But America had to overcome her isolation. Lending and leasing the tools of war to her allies could never achieve the kind of victories that were needed. It took Pearl Harbor, even more than the rumor of death camps, to turn this nation's indecision into all-out resolution.

Vision, Viability, and Victory

For those in the battle for souls, isolation and indecision will never achieve the greatest of victories. For those Christians who only want to engage in the prevention of problems, isolation may make sense. They may enjoy teaching and training but not rebuking and correcting (1 Tim. 4:13, 16; 2 Tim. 3:16).

But the Pearl Harbors of life and the holocaust of our nation's families call other Christians to engage in massive intervention and postvention. Merely lending a few religious values to secular counselors or leasing wholesale approaches from nonbiblical therapists risks a dismal defeat born of indecision. Christian discernment requires an orthodox reaction to Christ (Matt. 16:13–20), and Christian maturity requires a deliberate focus on everything He has commanded us to do.

The vision in biblical counseling must portray what Jesus saw—obedient disciples multiplying through obedient congregations. Such a vision has the spiritual magnetism to sustain us through the hard work of viable plans. After all, we "can do everything [*which is in the will of God*] through him who gives us strength [*to do those things that are His will*]" (Phil. 4:13, italics added). Although we can't leap tall buildings in a single bound, nor run faster than a speeding locomotive, we can count on the fact, as J. Hudson Taylor said, that God's work done in God's way will never lack God's supply.

If the first skill in biblical counseling requires readers to remember polar bears and icebergs, the second and third skills require them to remember vision, viability, and victory. When we have the ability to help people tell their story (skill 1), we owe it to them to point toward some mountain peak that can orient their first steps toward change (skill 2). When we assist people in unraveling their story—perhaps initially in an open-ended one- to two-hour block, we are wise to conclude with prayer, sharing some of Christ's goals for His followers. While we pay attention to our counselee's verbal and nonverbal disclosures, we do well to wrap up the first session with an assignment: (1) to read slowly the list of Christ's goals for seven straight days, (2) to pray daily for Christ's help in relating one or more of His goals to the problem at hand, (3) to commit to scheduling a second session with the counselor after the first two parts of the assignment have been completed, and (4) to recruit a partner who will pray during the second session, ideally a mature person with whom the counselee might be willing to disclose the problem and their sense of Christ's leading with it.

Biblical counseling needn't be fancy to be powerful. In human terms it may even seem simplistic. But by patiently learning someone's story and lovingly lifting their eyes toward the far horizon of Christ's vision for them, we may get the opportunity to taste the joy of viably shepherding a soul toward change (step 3, discussed in the next chapter).

Vision, Viability, and Victory on Death Row

Imagine yourself as a biblical counselor, dressed as a modestly paid security officer in a Texas penitentiary. Pretend you drew the duty to guard "the morgue." The man living inside is Clyde Thompson.[3] Over time you learn his story, partly through what he says, partly through what he shows, and partly by the reports of other people. Your main role in the storytelling process is an attentive physical presence every day and an open posture toward a violent and bitter man.

Clyde was put on death row because he killed four hunters he had come across one Sunday in the woods, a place he habited out of hatred for his father's church. How he came to hate all things Christian, you'll never know. Then, after killing four inmates while he was on death row, he was placed in "the morgue." Locked in prison in Huntsville, Texas, he lived alone, looking for chances to spit at prison staff through his four-inch-square window.

Imagine yourself having the loving courage to do what that believing prison guard did. He said, "Clyde, you don't have anything to read in there. I will bring you a Bible if you promise not to tear it up." Having learned Clyde's story, this guard was challenging him toward one of Jesus' goals: listening to the Word. Clyde promised not to tear it up.

During the six hours of daylight which passed through the little window, Clyde would read. During the total darkness, he would try to remember what he had read. Without knowing it and at times due to sheer boredom, Clyde began meditating on God's truth.

Eventually God enlightened him through the power of the gospel. Over time, his behavior changed. Later, after he was returned to death row, he evangelized sixteen cellmates. As public cynicism melted, Clyde grew into the prison chaplain's assistant, eventually earning a parole. But on the day of his parole he reported immediately to the Lubbock County Jail, where he ministered until his death in 1979.

Although the commands of Christ are not necessarily linear nor mutually exclusive, they do provide a sense of direction for the biblical counselor and biblical counselee. The security officer was used by God to direct a hardhearted counselee to begin listening to the Word. Eventually the counselee believed the gospel. Over time, by God's grace many of Christ's commands for Clyde became Clyde's goals for himself. Would that have ever happened if the guard never imagined any of Christ's goals for Clyde? Ultimately the biblical counselor—lay, pastoral, or professional—is a disciple-maker, seeking to win unbelievers to faith in Christ and to strengthen believers in faith. When successful, the biblical counselor assists the counselee to so love Christ that all other loves, including the love of disobedience, pale in comparison (Mark 8:34; Luke 9:23; 14:26–27).

CHAPTER SIX

Helping People Practice Change

As the drill whirred into its high-pitch scream, bits of saliva and enamel flew everywhere. There I was again, in the dentist's chair.

It seemed like I had been there my whole life, at neat six-month intervals. I never remember not going. Like clockwork, my mother had taken all three of us children to Dr. Dubin twice a year. As the consummate elementary-school secretary, Mom always scheduled the next appointment around a foreseeable school holiday or break. We never missed. There were the occasional cavities, braces, and pulled teeth. But our family dental record was entirely average.

Then came my twenties, thirties, and forties. Mom no longer scheduled the appointments, no longer paid the bills. But I still went every six months, usually. And I was diligent to do what I had always done: a fast brush every morning on the ridges and outsides of my teeth.

But everything was *not* the same. Dentists and hygienists started asking annoying questions: "Mr. Watson, how often do you brush? Do you brush the insides of your teeth? How do you feel about flossing? Ever heard of gingivitis?"

For a while I was able to fend off these prying questions, usually with some half-witted excuse. "Once a day keeps the dentist away!" "How do you get to the insides of your teeth?" "I don't floss—it's against my religion; besides, they didn't have floss when I was a kid and I don't know how." "Of course, everybody's heard of gingivitis. Do I have it, yes or no?"

Since my insurance had changed a half-dozen times, bouncing me from one dentist to another, I was surprised that the people with their fingers in my mouth kept having the same questions. They were learning my story. Unwilling to do my six-month checkup by phone or mail, each practice required my being present in the dentist's chair. Hovering over me and staring into my mouth, they would occasionally furl their brow toward my chart. They knew me better than I wished. Their questions were a way of trying to spark change. A few times this or that hygienist even gave me a lesson on flossing, as if I were really interested. With insincere "thanks" on my lips, I would always deposit the free sample beside my wife's floss arsenal, where I felt it would do some good.

One day things changed. At the age of forty-three, my body was arching like a murderer in an electric chair. No matter how much Novocaine they gave me, my nerves always stayed live. I had what felt like two baked potatoes in my cheeks, but it still felt like they were drilling for black gold.

"Four cavities this time, Mr. Watson. Two on the upper left, one on the lower left, and one on the upper right. We're going to go down to the pulp cap this time."

As hard as it was to get time off from work, I said, "Do 'em all." Two hours later I was ready to change. That occasional cavity now-and-again had become routine cavities again-and-again. After buying a yacht for one orthodontist and putting another's firstborn through college, I determined that I was not going to let a third mouth in our family—mine—send us to the poorhouse.

In graduate school they used to joke, "How many social workers does it take to change a light bulb?" Their satirical answer would resound, "Five. One to hold the light bulb and four to turn the ladder; but the light bulb has *to want to* change!" Well, this light bulb finally wanted to change.

It was awkward to bend my arm that way, brushing the sides of my teeth that faced my tongue, especially the fronts and the uppers. It took forethought to brush every night, knocking those chunks of potato chips out before they settled in for a long winter's nap. And terrified by the ghost of mealtimes yet to come—my gums full of imaginary stitches and bandaids—I knew my Pearl Harbor had come. Indecision and isolation was over. Now I had an all-out resolution: I was going to beat the rap.

Never again would the warden send me to the electric chair! Each evening, ramming those little wooden picks between my teeth, I began to shove the gums down, scraping the plaque away. My floss would break two or three times a session, but I still determined to get it between every pair of crowded teeth every day. And if I were going to quit, I would have done it on day one, when my maiden voyage in flossing sank an old filling to the floor of the ocean, landing a small avalanche of silver debris in my mouth.

Stories get told and goals get set. But what principles help explain the process of change? Why does a lazy brusher become an ardent brusher, picker, and flosser? How do people and groups go from point A to point B? If the apostles and prophets were used as video clips from the film library of Scripture, what would they teach us about viable plans for facilitating change?

PRINCIPLES OF CHANGE

Though there are countless principles that seek to demystify the mysteries of change, a few stand out.

- Acknowledging God
- Embracing suffering
- Focusing on the future
- Surpassing information
- Emphasizing attitudes
- Overcoming barriers
- Building habits
- Balancing control

Acknowledging God

God never changes, yet He offers us the possibility of change, this side of eternity. James, a half-brother of our Lord, wrote, "Don't be deceived. . . . Every good and perfect gift is from above, coming down from the Father of the heavenly lights, *who does not change* like shifting shadows. He chose to give us birth through the word of truth, that we might be a kind of firstfruits of all he created" (James 1:16–18, italics added).

Although God Himself never changes (the doctrine of divine immutability), God *could change* anyone (the doctrine of divine omnipotence); yet God *will change* only those who desire change by His means of grace (the doctrine of divine salvation). Remember the Sunday schooler's question, "If God can do anything, can He make a stone so large that He can't lift it?" Though God *could* make a stone of infinite size, He *can't* do anything contrary to His nature; so He *can't* make a stone that is more powerful than His all-powerful self. Similarly God is too just to send someone to hell who isn't a sinner (Matt. 25:41; Rom. 3:10, 23; 6:23) or send someone to heaven who isn't justified by faith in the divine Substitute (4:4–5; 5:1; 2 Cor. 5:21). God will not altogether override the sinner's choice (for example, "but you would have none of it," Isa. 30:15; "but you were not willing," Matt. 23:37).

Imagine growing up in the home of a house builder, a blue-collar dad with callused hands. James knew what that was like. One of seven children (Matt. 13:55–56; Mark 6:3), he probably knew about his older brother's "illegitimate" conception (Matt. 1:18–19). His parents were adamant; this was a foreordained miracle! Some neighbors had another explanation.

James's father, Joseph, was a good man, a salt-of-the-earth type, but he probably didn't live long enough to see all his children reach adulthood. Although he was still living when Jesus was twelve years old (Luke 2:42), Joseph seems to have disappeared before Jesus stepped into the limelight of public debate. By the time Jesus hit His early thirties, the famed brother had probably already donated the family business to the four younger brothers and left home with His controversial teaching, "I am he!" (see Matt. 27:43; John 4:25–26; 7:29; 8:23–28; 9:9; 13:19).

James didn't believe his brother was the Messiah (John 7:5). If C. S. Lewis's trilogy of appraisals is right—that is, Jesus was either Lord, liar, or lunatic—James had scratched the "Lord" option off his checklist. Either his big brother was lying and knew it or was too crazy to know the difference. What a conclusion! And when James showed up with his mother and siblings at one of Jesus' rallies, Jesus implied, "They're not my family, really" (Matt. 12:46–50). What a put-down!

But the relationship between Jesus and James changed, and not because of some guy sporting horn-rimmed glasses and a goatee. The living Lord confronted a doubting man, his half-brother. Days after Mary saw Jesus executed before her very eyes, James met his brother, alive again

(1 Cor. 15:7). Erasing his presumptuous conclusion from the messianic checklist, James became Jesus' true kin, a prayerful partner with the pre-Pentecost enclave in an upper room (Acts 1:14). Knowing how he had changed, James could interview and confirm another new brother, Paul, who had made his own 180-degree change (Gal. 1:19). Together they would endorse missionary work, sending out preachers to trigger and discover more repentance-based turnabouts (2:9).

In time James would become the recognized leader of the Jerusalem church. His open letter would be richly practical, emphasizing an action-oriented faith (James 1:22, 26–27; 2:14–26), similar in ways to the Book of Proverbs. Writing about himself and every true convert, James celebrated the way a changeless God could bring genuine change through the gospel (1:16–18). For those readers who were farther out or drifting away, James offered the invitation, "Resist the devil, and he will flee from you. Come near to God and he will come near to you" (4:7–8). In James's view there was no good reason not to change; God was entirely adequate to initiate and sustain change.

Even today God changes people without necessarily deferring to any human agency. It's almost as if we could adapt the classic salvation text to read, "For it is by grace you have been *changed*, through faith—and this not from yourselves, it is the gift of God—not by *the* works *of your therapist*, so that no one can boast. For we—*both counselor and counselee*—are God's workmanship, created in Christ Jesus to do good works, which God prepared in advanced for us to do" (Eph. 2:8–10, italics added).

Howard Storm, a professor at North Kentucky University, describes his own Damascus Road conversion.[1] A longtime cynic, Storm was in Paris conducting his European summer tour for art students. As a self-confessed control freak, this secularist hated anything he couldn't prove or control.

On the next-to-last day of his tour, Storm crumpled to the floor with shocking abdominal pain. Rushed to the hospital, he was soon told that the cause was a perforated intestine. With emergency surgery scheduled for the morning, Storm gave into mushrooming pain and surrendered himself to impending death. In a split second the professor-turned-patient slipped from paralyzing pain and profanity to feeling as if he were floating pain-free at the top of his hospital room.

Almost immediately, he testifies, a voice spoke: "Howard, come here."

Staring toward a dim and distant doorway, he began to hear multiple voices, urging him to follow. Hustling toward the door and questioning the murky silhouettes, Storm kept trying to figure out if they were doctors or nurses. Their answers evaded his inquiries.

Progressing deeper into the timeless fog, Storm tried to stop; he insisted he would go no farther. But the beings became more aggressive toward him with their verbal threats . . . pushing . . . clawing and biting . . . profound loneliness.

Although he hadn't prayed since childhood, he felt he heard one other voice say, "Pray to God." Confused and reluctant, he started the twenty-third psalm: "The Lord is my shepherd. . . ." The words threw the creatures into a frenzy, arousing a torrent of verbal humiliation back at him. So he prayed more, and they backed farther away. Reaching way back into his childhood, Storm began to sing a children's hymn: "Jesus loves me . . . this I know . . . for the Bible tells me so." Unleashing his will to sing, Storm sensed an incredible desire to believe those lyrics. Screaming, "Jesus, please just save me," he spotted a tiny light which came to him like a comet. Radiant, gentle, and delicious with color, the light induced him to profound weeping and brokenness. Reviewing his life, he recognized the emptiness of his many achievements and felt regret for his sinful behaviors. He discovered that the most important work of life was to know God. Then, as if assigned to a mission, he was sent back to his body. Deeply changed, he survived the surgery and entered seminary. The former agnostic now serves as a pastor, not a university professor.

Whether we analyze the conversion of James, Jesus' brother, or Howard Storm, we know that God is the Author of good gifts, including every example of enduring, constructive change (James 1:16–18). So we can trust God who is sufficient for these things (2 Cor. 3:5; 9:8). We can trust God who needn't defer to people or methods to facilitate such changes.

Embracing Suffering

When counselees and counselors feel duty-bound or supercompetent to fix a problem, they risk inviting God to step out of the helping picture. After all, as James reminded us, "God opposes the proud," yet He "gives grace to the humble" (James 4:6). Prayerfully trusting God—the Author of all worthwhile change—is the starting point in counseling.

But how do counselors and counselees learn to trust? Often through suffering, through having what they do not want or wanting what they do not have. In deep suffering they can discover an opportunity in disguise, the opportunity to know that they can't handle life and that only God can. This is why James wrote, "Consider it pure joy . . . whenever you face trials of many kinds" (1:2).

Deep suffering, as well as daily hassles, can be the greenhouse for character change. And we can learn to bless our suffering for this positive potential. Indeed, James instructed us to look to Job as an example of incredible patience, a sufferer who was blessed in the end (4:11).

Job was profiled in heaven's job bank as a solid example of integrity (Job 1:1, 8), but his integrity made him a candidate for a once-in-a-lifetime mission. The devil, convinced that even the deepest loyalties could be bought and sold, was going to be taught a lesson (1:6–12), and Job would be the unwitting case study.

Wealthy and influential, Job loved his family. More than just a great businessman, Job also served as chaplain to his ten children (1:2–5). Yet when God allowed a tornado of trouble to sweep up from the abyss, Job's character was about to face its ultimate test.

How can we truly imagine the terror of Job's lot? Ten children, countless employees, and an entire business fortune, all up in smoke in a matter of days; the headlines blamed terrorists and "natural" disasters. In the second wave of persecution, Job began to drown in a sea of pain and chronic illness. Worse, his best friends and wisest advisers publicly ridiculed him; then Job's wife, plunging the final knife in his back, nagged him to blame God and die (2:9). The same man who had privately worried that his children might silently curse God (1:5), smelled the sulfuric breath of the devil in his wife's wicked words (2:9).

Yet Job never cursed God (1:22). In the midst of suffering he blessed the Lord and prayed for those hurtful friends. In the end the suffering sage was humbly outmatched by God in His sovereignty (42:1–6). And when the Lord restored his business and gave him new children (42:10, 12–13, 16), Job showed us that even the best of sufferers still have room to learn. The storm clouds of suffering always contain the potential silver lining of new learning.

As an avid student of suffering, I had always felt that my most perverse pain would erupt if one of my children died from an entirely preventable cause, one that was within my control. Hoping never to writhe in such torture, I purposed to be a safety-conscious dad.

It was Christmas time; my nose confirmed the season. As I entered the kitchen from the garage, braided Christmas breads were rising amidst delicious aromas from the oven. Before I could even set down my brief-case, I spotted a huge serrated knife resting along the edge of the kitchen counter. It was perfect for separating the fragile loaves from their heated baking sheets; but as the father of a four-year-old, I knew that Steven's little hands could innocently roam the inviting counter top that loomed over his head. So I did my part. I moved the knife to the center of the counter space, well out of preschool reach.

In one of those hustle-bustle minutes of family traffic, Nancy hurried her last loaves out of the oven, nodded toward the living room where she said a string of Christmas lights was out, and announced that she was off with Ryan, our nine-year-old, for basketball practice. Strolling into the liv-ing room, I saw what she meant—a whole string was dark. Still in my suit jacket, I lowered my briefcase onto the carpet and parked my keys on its lid.

Shadowed by my blond look-alike, I pulled a spare bulb out of the Tupperware bowl in Nancy's dry sink. Gently pinching the glass section of the good bulb between my lips, I used my free hands to begin pulling and replacing bulbs one at a time. As each culprit came out, the rotating spare went in. I was always careful, mind you, to keep the base of the bulb dry. And by using both hands, I ensured that the electric candle would not be separated from its wire-and-plastic base.

When finally the string came to life, I invented a little job that would fit my four-year-old elf. "Steven, take this and throw it away." Pointing toward the little trash can under the computer, I expected him to run the blackened bulb to the other corner of the living room. But instead, he turned on his heel and made a beeline for the kitchen. "Stop, Steven. Use that one." Wagging his head left to right, he pointed yonder and said, "That one!" I shrugged my shoulders. What did it matter? I was just try-ing to save him some steps. But it did matter.

No more than a minute later as I loosened my tie and thought through the evening's responsibilities, I was stunned—stunned by what I saw and heard. Steven, bloodied from his scalp line to his chin, ran staggering into the living room. Deep gurgling sounds bubbled from his throat as a steady stream of bloody saliva poured from his gaping mouth.

I winced with rapid-fire logic. I assumed he had cut himself deep in the throat, trying to lick the thing! In one motion I snatched him and my keys and sprinted for the car. The bleeding is bad, I thought, but the air passage is worse. I can get him to the fire station before a 911 emergency vehicle can get to me!

As if I was in a dark dream, that mile and a half seemed to take forever. Chest-to-chest on my lap, Steven rested his head on my right shoulder, gurgling blood onto my shirt. Between the awful sounds, he pleaded, "Daddy, am I going to die?"

In a frenzy I was soon trapped behind the only neighbor in town who followed the posted twenty-five-mile-per-hour speed limit. After flashing my high beams and laying on the horn, I swerved around my indifferent roadblock, endangering the life I was trying to save. Had we been in an accident, no one would have had a clue what Steven's real problem was.

As we screeched to a stop in front of the parked fire trucks, Steven swallowed hard one last time. With a deep "gulp" like a bullfrog, he inhaled a huge breath and sat straight up on my lap. "Daddy! I can breathe!"

Amid a flurry of paramedic attention and a lightning dash to the nearest emergency room, the true story began to come out. All the bleeding had come from glass cuts in his mouth; he had gone out of sight to do what he thought daddy was doing, that is, chewing up a brightly colored Christmas tree bulb! As soon as the glass shards had begun to shred his lips, tongue, and throat, he had grabbed the washcloth from the kitchen spigot. In sheer panic he had apparently alternated between trying to dam up his mouth and pulling the cloth away to see if the bleeding had stopped; the bloody cloth—found later by my wife in our empty, lighted house, the front door wide open—had successively patted blood back onto his face. The "gulp" had occurred when the base of the bulb, wedged in his windpipe, had finally passed.

Time would heal all wounds. Nighttime whimpers and fatherly self-humiliation would give way to peace. We would eventually embrace this ordeal. More powerful than any Father's Day sermon, this daddy would learn that a parent's example—more than mere words—could prove to be life-giving or life-ending. And had the outcome been more dire, it would still have been included by the "all things" orchestrated for our eternal good (Rom. 8:28). These joy-worthy "things" (James 1:2) would have passed through the hands of an all-wise, all-kind God (Jer. 29:11–13). And had the suffering been prolonged, the discipline to pray "not my will but yours" (see Matt. 26:39) would have created an openness to divergent outcomes. With such grace in prayer, our plans for the future could have become more evidently humble: "If the Lord wills, we will live and do this or that" (James 4:15).

Focusing on the Future

When trusting God for personal change, perhaps change triggered in the crucible of suffering, we must learn to focus on the future. Staring at the past, we can all become victims of regret, pride, or blame; we can't change the past. But concerning the future the whole realm of choice and opportunity is virgin. Unable to run much of a race facing backwards, we intentionally pivot and run steady for the new finish line (Heb. 12:1–3). As counselors, we resist the counselee's pressure to help them return to life as it was before. Instead, we purpose to accompany the counselee toward life as God would have it become.

When Hannah and Elkanah reminisced about their life (1 Sam. 1–2), they could have easily overdosed on the past. Hannah had a lot of misery to contend with. In a polygamous world, which judged a woman's worth by her ability to deliver children, Hannah was sadly barren (1:2). Worse, Elkanah's second wife was abundantly fertile, but vicious toward Hannah (1:6). At times Hannah was clinically depressed (1:7). In utter irony, when Hannah prayed for God's help at the tabernacle in Shiloh, the high priest mistakenly scolded her for drunkenness (1:12–13). If this woman were going to give up, she had every reason to quit on God, on family, and on ministers.

But this family didn't quit. They focused on what they could do and on the possibilities of the future. Elkanah showed special love to his wife

Hannah (1:5) and tried his best to encourage her (1:8). Hannah intensified her prayer life, vowing that her firstborn son—if God would be so kind—would become a Nazirite (1:9–11). Even when the priest berated her, she spoke up firmly but respectfully, eventually gaining his blessing (1:15–18). The family continued to worship God and Elkanah continued to love Hannah (1:19). And in His own time God gave them Samuel (1:20).

Now if it was ever tempting to go back on her word, Hannah must have felt it as she nursed her newborn son. But Hannah honored her vow, putting Samuel into a year-round apprenticeship with the high priest as soon as he was weaned (1:21–28). By doing so, she knew she would see him only once a year during their family pilgrimage to Shiloh (2:11, 18–21). Just as Hannah and Elkanah learned to focus on the future, their young son learned to face straight ahead in life too. When God began speaking audibly to Samuel, the lad discovered how to abandon the past. He realized this wasn't Eli who was calling him in the night. So Samuel ventured out and began to dialogue with God directly (3:1–21). Samuel was changing; now he knew God, and he came to know he would be representing God nationally as Eli's family was removed in judgment (2:12–17, 22–25, 27–36; 4:1–5:12). Such disciplinary suffering, God said, would have a hidden blessing. "Although good will be done to Israel, in your [Eli's] family line there will never be an old man" (2:32). And later, when Samuel became elderly and his adult sons were discovered to be corrupt, his forward momentum protected him from getting lost in the nostalgia trap. He supported their removal and the nation's transition to kingship (8:1–22).

This emphasis on the future defies some of the traditions of behavioral science. Certain approaches to psychology and psychiatry have gluttonized on the past, hoping to harvest sufficient "insight" that desirable personal or relational change happens almost automatically. Often, however, insight alone does not produce change, and other times the change it produces is not desirable.

Even Christians can get so caught up in remembering the past that they fail to "press on" to a divinely purposeful future (Phil. 3:13–21). One counselee, for instance, using the principles of recovery from Alcoholics Anonymous, became adept at analyzing his family of origin as "dysfunctional" and himself as "an adult child of a problem parent." Much of the analysis fit. But little of the problem behaviors changed. While his self-help approach only sought to explain his behavior, he often felt it helped justify his behavior. Not until he grappled with two of Christ's goals for him—*fearing only God* (Luke 12:5–7) and *avoiding greed* (Matt. 6:19–21; Luke 12:15)—did he see his compulsive work habits as a spiritual problem. While the seedbed for this problem was laid in childhood, the tall oaks of disobedience were still thriving in middle adulthood. With the help of three prayer partners, this man began to face a new future through repentance, accountability, and clarified vision.

Surpassing Information by Emphasizing Attitudes

Helping strategies are misguided when they employ simple, one-dimensional emphases on information. For example, one exercise-equipment company markets a machine to target spot reduction for people who feel they have oversized posteriors. The machine, as demonstrated in the cable-channel commercials, places the client on a platform with a vibrating belt around his or her spandex-clad southern exposure. Rapid right-left alternations of the belt promise "to burn calories." As pictured, people can reduce their unwanted fat while watching television or reading the paper. Indeed, science has proven that the machine does burn calories; that much information is correct. But it only burns 1/2000th of a calorie per minute.[2] At that rate, someone would have to be on the machine for eight days nonstop in order to burn off one Big Mac! Many sales approaches prey on the naiveté of potential customers, linking a thimble-full of information with a first-order behavioral solution: "Just pick up the phone . . . and you can look like this."

In the New Testament the Corinthian church had an overemphasis on information. In Paul's first epistle to them, when the spiritual condition of the congregation seemed profoundly shallow, the apostle used verbs and nouns associated with "knowledge" dozens of times. He admitted, "We all possess knowledge. Knowledge puffs up, but love builds up. The man who thinks he knows something does not yet know as he ought to know" (1 Cor. 8:1–2). In other words Paul felt that a little knowledge was a dangerous thing, but that constructive other-oriented attitudes (for example, love and trust) were stronger fibers in the fabric of life.

Throughout 1 Corinthians, Paul reminded the church that so-called knowledge can be destructive (8:11) and that it is transient (13:2, 8). While he respected certain pieces of knowledge, such as the knowledge of Christ (1:5) and of liberty (8:7), he frequently underscored how little he knew (1:16; 2:2). Furthermore as a brilliant apostle Paul challenged his superficial readers with how little they knew (3:16; 5:6; 6:2–3, 9, 15–16, 19; 9:13, 24). As a bottom line, he credited them with knowing only a few things: who the first converts were (16:15) and how valuable their ministry for the Lord was (15:58).

Behavioral research suggests that there is only a 5 percent (or less) correlation between information and health behavior.[3] In other words, if twenty typical smokers were told, "Smoking is the leading cause of lung cancer," only one smoker would likely change his or her behavior for three months or more. Thus people-helpers need to be careful not merely to provide information as if it were a silver bullet, whether that information is transmitted in a Sunday-school class, small-group studies, books, one-on-one mentoring, sermons, or therapy sessions.

To have a stronger punch, people-helpers and behavioral-change programs need to go deeper than raw data, facts, and figures. They need to touch on people's attitudes, including feelings, beliefs, values, and relationships. The same research is much more optimistic about attitudes. The considerable literature of measurement studies suggests that there is a correlation from 5 to 30 percent between attitudes and health behavior.[4] So, if a smoking-cessation program were offered to twenty typical smokers, it would have a greater likelihood of touching between one and six participants if it stirred them in some of the following ways:

- *Feelings*: "Yuck, look at those color photographs: the heart, lung, and brain of healthy nonsmokers versus lifelong, pack-a-day smokers at the time of their death!"
- *Beliefs*: "Smoking is wrong; God created your body and you will answer for the way you have treated it."
- *Values*: "If you keep smoking like that, you'll probably never cash your first Social Security check. Did you know smokers are keeping

the Social Security fund afloat? They put in dollars for lots of years, but then they do us a favor by dying young."

- *Values:* "Our company will help you quit smoking by giving you good health-insurance coverage and providing a worksite gym."
- *Relationships:* "Honey, I've never really said this to you, but smoking is a definite turnoff: yellow teeth . . . the smell in your clothes and hair . . . $150 a month . . . ashes in the car . . . your getting up and leaving during a concert to light up."
- *Relationships:* "Daddy, I don't want you to die. The kids on my school bus call those 'cancer sticks.' And I don't want to get sick because I breathed your smoke all my life."
- *Relationships:* "If you keep smoking like that, you'll never play basketball with your grandchildren. Even if you are alive, you won't be able to keep up."

Paul put it correctly when he wrote, "Knowledge puffs up, but love builds up" (1 Cor. 8:1–2). Somebody else said, "No one cares how much you know [about smoking or anything else] until they know how much you care!" Engaging both sides of the brain—with information *and* attitudes—increases the likelihood of change.

Overcoming Barriers and Building Habits

Habits are a good thing, despite Protestant objections to so-called legalism and our national obsession with individual freedom. Every time a mom hugs her child who's coming through the front door after school or a dad sleeps through the night in his own bed, we know that a habit is a good thing *so long as it serves a good purpose.*

To build good habits we often have to overcome barriers. For instance, the mom who is available to hug her child every day after school may have had to overcome the habit of telling herself that self-respecting women always hold down full-time jobs in the labor force. She may also have had to break the habit of buying whatever she wanted with credit cards. The dad who is consistently faithful to his marriage vows may have had to conquer the common lie that every husband cheats on his wife. He may also have had to break the habit of pornography.

In the Jerusalem church Jesus' followers had to overcome barriers (old habits) and develop new habits. Some of the new believers had grown up with a heritage that routinized ceremonial washings (Mark 7:3) and extreme interpretations of Sabbath rest (Luke 13:14). Others had nourished habitual hostility toward Jesus and His followers (John 9:22; Acts 22:19; 26:11). These habits had to be broken by the grace of God, and new rhythms established.

For His followers Jesus modeled purposeful habit. Having been raised to follow Jewish custom (Luke 2:27, 42; 4:16), Jesus honored the temple by teaching there daily during Passion week (Matt. 26:55; Luke 19:47). And, though the Savior was the essence of creativity, He practiced praying in customary places (John 18:1–2). When He flew in the face of tradition, He did so purposefully. "Then John's disciples came and asked him, 'How is it that we and the Pharisees fast, but your disciples do not fast?' Jesus answered, 'How can the guests of the bridegroom mourn while he is with them? The time will come when the bridegroom will be taken from them; then they will fast' " (Matt. 9:14–15). When some of his contemporaries wanted to focus on dietary choices, Jesus redirected them to examine the moral choices that emanated from their hearts (15:17–20; Mark 7:18–23; see also Acts 10:9–16).

The Jerusalem church developed new, intentional habits. "They devoted themselves to the apostles' teaching and to the fellowship, to the breaking of bread and to prayer. . . . All the believers were together and had everything in common. Selling their possessions and goods, they gave to anyone as he had need. Every day they continued to meet together in the temple courts. They broke bread in their homes and ate together with glad and sincere hearts, praising God" (2:42–47).

Over time the temple became less a place for spiritual nurture and more a place for public prayer (3:1–26) and outreach (5:12–42). Other spiritual disciplines emerged, such as gathering on "the first day of the week" (John 20:1, 19) for preaching and for financial donations (Acts 20:7; 1 Cor. 16:2). Often the early Christians engaged in the Lord's Supper (11:25), Bible study (Acts 17:11), mentoring (19:9), hospitality (6:1), witnessing (5:42), and mutual encouragement (Heb. 3:13). Even when the Holy Spirit signaled who should go to the mission field and when (Acts 13:1–3), the missionaries themselves seemed to prioritize the major cities of the Asia Minor postal route. And though the missionaries were open to unforeseen guidance (16:9–10), they strategically targeted the Jewish synagogue first in each major city (see, for example, Acts 13:14; 14:1). By the grace of God the early church overcame old barriers and developed new disciplines.

Beyond information and attitudes, health psychologists estimate stronger behavioral correlations with barriers (between 30 and 40 percent) and habits (between 40 and 50 percent).[5] For example, if a smoker could develop effective strategies for overcoming specific barriers and actually go three months without lighting up, the chances of remaining tobacco-free would be much higher. A particular smoker might have to overcome two key barriers before he could truly stop smoking: (a) learning how to handle the jittery nicotine cravings without a lot of nervous overeating and consequent weight gain, and (b) conquering the doubt that he can't quit, since he has quit before and has gone back to the habit. If the counselor and the counselee can anticipate those weak spots (the barriers), they may be able to build in gum-chewing as an alternative for the nicotine jitters and to rehearse the reality that most smokers "quit" several times before successfully stopping. Indeed, practicing a new behavior consistently for thirty days often builds a psychological habit; practicing it for ninety days creates a physical habit. In building healthy habits, failures for more than any two consecutive days require the thirty-day and ninety-day clocks to begin anew.

Balancing Control

Although a counselor wants to be an optimistic person—a person who "always protects ... trusts ... hopes ... and perseveres" (see 1 Cor. 13:7)—they want to have both feet on the ground, facilitating realistic-to-optimistic appraisals. They can't condone faithless *cynicism,* which says, "No one can get there" (that is, to the goal). They shouldn't tolerate doubtful *pessimism,* which predicts, "You probably won't get there." Instead, they begin with stark *realism*—helping people tell their story—so that together counselor and counselee can say, "This is where we are." But seeking to move beyond the present scenario, they identify Christ's goals (for example, spiritual *idealism:* "This is where we could be"—what may be called vision) and try to move in that direction with relational *optimism* ("We can head there together"—what we might call victory) without getting trapped in self-defeating *perfectionism*. ("This is the way it must be or it is a total failure"—legalism, dysfunction, all-or-nothing logic, the lack of viability.) This progression may be seen as a continuum:

Cynicism   Pessimism   Realism   Optimism   Idealism   Perfectionism

To grasp the realistic-to-optimistic part of this continuum, three things must be noted: the rest of the research story, the locus of control, and the biblical balance (Phil. 2:12–13).

First, the rest of the research story suggests that about half of our health outcomes are *not* related to health behavior. That is, they are *not* related to lifestyle choices, such as gathering *information* plus changing *attitudes* plus overcoming *barriers* plus building *habits* concerning smoking cessation. Instead, about half of our health outcomes relate to variables outside of our control, such as *heredity, environment,* and *healthcare access.*[6] For instance, if a child is born with cystic fibrosis *(heredity),* grows up in a house where both parents smoke a pack a day indoors *(environment),* and does not have the regular care of a good doctor, hospital, and pharmacy *(healthcare access),* that child is more likely to suffer death, disability, or disease associated with respiratory distress triggered by tobacco smoke. Although we yearn to influence the volitional half of the equation, we would be fools as counselors and counselees to ignore the other half, the half that requires us to learn to play the hand we're dealt.

Health Outcomes	*Behavioral Correlations*
Beyond our control (50%)	
Heredity (20%)	
Environment (20%)	
Health care (10%)	
Within our control (50%)	
Information	0–5%
Attitudes	6–30%
Barriers	31–40%
Habits	41–50%

Although the research on healthcare outcomes and health behavior is very global,[7] it suggests that about half of the undesirable outcomes in life are beyond our control. The other half can be influenced by choices, especially long-term choices. There are no guarantees that we will not die from a drunk-driving accident. But we can make that outcome far less likely if we (a) choose to avoid alcohol altogether, (b) refuse rides with drivers who are under the influence, and (c) stay off the road between midnight and 6:00 A.M., when many inebriated drivers are on the highway. Although we respect the role of choice—our choices and the choices of others—we know that all variables, outcomes, conditions, and choices mysteriously coexist under the umbrella of God's sovereignty.

Second, "locus of control" is another factor to note. This describes the degree of control people perceive themselves to have in life. For instance, people with a highly external locus of control find it easy to believe that they actually influence very few things in life; their potential death through drunk driving is merely a matter of chance, luck, fate, and the behaviors or policies of others. It's easy to blame people or forces outside themselves—including God—and to take no responsibility for their drinking behavior, nor their choices about those with whom they ride, and when they use the highways. They would never consider it their mission to lobby for a new law on mandatory punishments for driving while intoxicated. On the other hand, people with a highly internal locus of control find it easy to feel responsible for life. The mother whose daughter is killed on her way to the grocery store can blame herself for planning a birthday party. "After all," the mother can reason, "if it wasn't for my birthday party tonight, my daughter wouldn't have been going to the store when that drunk driver came through the red light." People with extreme internal loci of control wrestle with an above-average degree of perfectionism, guilt, and depression. Sometimes the innocent person with a highly internal locus of control feels more guilt than the actual drunk driver, who has a highly external locus of control. We should pray, "Lord, give me the serenity to accept the things I did not cause, the courage to admit the things I did, and the wisdom to know the difference."

Third, we seek biblical balance. In distinguishing between elements that are within our control and those that are not, we should strive to understand the divine-human partnership. Paul instructed the Philippian church in this delicate cooperation: "Continue to *work out* your salvation with fear and trembling, for it is God who works in you to will and to act according to his good purpose" (Phil. 2:12–13, italics added). Some might nod knowingly, "God commands us to work because faith without works is dead" (see James 2:17). Others might object, "No, it is 'not of works, lest anyone should boast'" (Eph. 2:9, KJV). In reality, both are true: God works salvation *in us* and we work salvation *out of us*. God helps us want to do the right thing and to be effective in doing the right thing, but we have to work at it. Indeed, the very word for "working out" our salvation (see Phil. 2:12) was used in the ancient world for mining silver. Although miners can't take credit for creating the silver, they can harvest the silver from the earth and make beautiful objects with it. So it is with the Christian life. God puts the treasure of Jesus Christ in the believer's heart (2 Cor. 4:7; Col. 1:27), but the believer must work out the likeness of Christ through obedience and discipline.

BIBLICAL COUNSELING IN THE WOODS

It was a first-time experience. The church youth group was camped out in southern Maryland. One of the high schoolers, excited about camping in the woods, had hired a substitute to deliver his *Washington Post* papers so he could go away. Accustomed to rising early, he was wide awake when his camp counselor, an Air Force man, unzipped the tent door just before dawn.

"Where are you going?" the boy asked.

"To have my quiet time," the counselor replied.

"Can I go?" the boy asked.

"No," the counselor said promptly. Turning toward the footpath, he took one step and then paused. Looking back to the puzzled youth, he asked, "Do you know what a quiet time is?"

"No."

"Hmm. I'll be back in fifteen to thirty minutes. I'll teach you." So began the journey of the lad's private disciplines in prayer and Bible study.

When the counselor returned, he started simply. He knew the younger guy was a believer, but a shallow one. "It's a beautiful thing every day to spend at least a little time reading the Bible and praying. It's my favorite time of the day. Pick a book of the Bible, anywhere, and read a chapter a day. It could be morning or evening. When you're done, write down any questions you have in a notebook. Then pray. Just try it for a month and let me know how it goes."

What was going on? One brother was counseling another . . . in the woods. The more mature brother had grasped several of Christ's goals. He was reaching out to a young person, discipling him in the art of prayer and Scripture meditation. In essence, the older brother was loving his campsite neighbor and fellow believer. Humbly serving the teen, the teacher didn't judge motives; after all, he had been strung out on drugs when he was the boy's age. Teaching what he knew, he refused to exaggerate his own expertise. Over time he would add new techniques to the boy's growing skill: comparing translations, handwriting a passage, memorizing key verses, color-coding the text. He would even see to it that his disciple anticipated boredom, interruptions, and inconsistencies in his newfound habit.

The change lasted. Instead of *giving* the boy a fish, he *taught him* to fish for himself. Having prayed for the teen in the woods, the mentor had acknowledged his need for God. Shaking off the momentary adversity of the boy nearly invading his private time, he focused on the future and established a training pattern. Besides giving him information, the Navigator sought to stir his attitudes. By targeting certain barriers, the veteran began to help the novice start building beautiful habits.

The older man would go on to train for the ministry once his Air Force tour of duty was up. The younger man would follow suit, attending the same school and engaging in the same ministry. Eventually the younger man would teach many others what he had begun to learn in the woods. You see, he had learned the value of a good example. He had learned that motivation gets us going, but habits get us there. He had been lovingly provoked to believe that eternity gives nothing back to us that we don't include in our minutes. The boy had learned that just as a NASA shuttle will expend most of its fuel when breaking out of the earth's gravity, so overcoming spiritual inertia is always the first giant step toward change. After that, the momentum of good habits can carry us nearly to the moon.

PART THREE

Models of Biblical Counseling

CHAPTER SEVEN

Biblical Counseling by Lay Christians:
Spiritual Credibility

IN MODERN AMERICA who would want to be a spiritual leader? Satirized by cynics and embarrassed by scandals, would-be Timothys often balk at the mountain of unwelcome stress. But "if anyone sets his heart on being an overseer, he desires a noble task" (1 Tim. 3:1). When we have a spiritual "want to lead" and we sense that God gave us that desire (Acts 20:22), we stand up straight and look around for confirmation. Does the Word of God certify our readiness to lead? Do the people of God affirm their willingness to follow our lead?

THE CREDIBILITY PYRAMID

Just as airline passengers are trained that in an emergency they are to don their own oxygen masks before helping those around them, biblical counselors are urged to cultivate their own character before trying to help those around them. In the pursuit of solid character, aspiring biblical counselors can visualize a five-tier pyramid, ranging from billions of people (bottom tier) to thousands of people (next to the top tier). And by learning how to migrate up the pyramid, would-be counselors can discover how to gain credibility in the eyes of the average person who is seeking biblical counseling.

The Credibility Pyramid

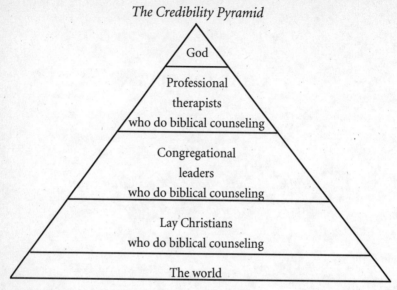

At birth everyone is on the bottom tier of this pyramid and no one has any credibility to speak for God (2 Cor. 3:5). As we grow up, we are prone to use ourselves or our culture as the standard of normalcy. As such, we are like unanchored ships, souls adrift on the sea of moral foolishness (10:12).

Some of us, however, gain character ballast for our ships, learning to navigate life by the map of Scripture. By the grace of God, we begin to drink from the fresh water of divine character and catch the wind of the Holy Spirit in our sails. Over time we develop spiritual credibility for influencing people through biblical relationships. This fourth tier (lay Christians), though smaller than the lowest, is filled regularly with godly Sunday-school teachers, group leaders, and Spirit-filled deacons around the world.

For some, spiritual credibility blossoms at the fourth tier. Yet an up-ward mobility beckons beyond to tier three. Like their colleagues on the fourth tier, citizens of tier three know the Bible. But with the added graces of temperament or giftedness or experience, they have the opportunity to go beyond the beautiful realm of holy friendships and helpful pro-gram relationships. Eventually the men and women of the third tier develop a reputation that besides knowing the Bible they know people. Social qualities and special discernment grant this narrowing band a wid-ening circle of influence. Whereas lay Christians with spiritual credibility (tier four) seem to excel in the skill of biblical goal-setting (see chapter 5), the subset of brothers and sisters on tier three seems to also excel in listening (see chapter 6). This secures a far wider base of opportunity to goal-set with folks who are interested in change. Typically the men and women of tier three become congregational leaders: pastors, elders, and parachurch specialists.

By helping us *to know Scripture* and allowing it to shape our character, God lifts us from the fifth (bottom) tier to the fourth (that is, spiritual credibility). By helping us *to know people* and granting us the daily wisdom to relate to people, God draws many from the level of lay ministers to church leaders (that is, social credibility, discussed in chapter 8). By helping some of us *to know culture* and drawing us through some legal, medical, and social education (tier two), God draws some of us to work as trained therapists (that is, professional credibility, discussed in chapter 9). At every level, the requisite knowledge can be abused, becoming a tool for the advancement of self or the harm of counselees (1 Cor. 8:1). Conversely God can baptize our spiritual, social, and professional knowledge, transforming it with His edifying love. As brilliant as God is, His knowledge does not corrupt Him. As loving as God is, His knowledge always becomes a means to fulfill beautiful ends.

THE SEVENTEEN-FACETED DIAMOND

For those who desire to participate in spiritual leadership (1 Tim. 3:1), God describes a seventeen-faceted diamond of Christian character (3:2–7; Titus 1:6–9). The biblical counselor, like an elder, pursues being characterized by the seventeen qualities listed below and on the following page:

Attributes of an Effective Counselor
- Above reproach and blameless
- The husband of one wife (marital fidelity)
- Temperate
- Self-controlled and disciplined
- Respectable
- Hospitable
- Able to teach

- Not given to drunkenness
- Gentle
- Not a lover of money
- A manager of his own family, with children who believe and behave (household order)
- Not a recent convert
- Of good reputation with outsiders
- Not overbearing, quarrelsome, quick-tempered, or violent
- A lover of the good
- Upright
- Holy

Since interpersonal trust is highly spiritual by nature, the seventeen foregoing attributes are highly relevant to lay, pastoral, and professional counseling. In particular, these attributes address character in reference to the counselor's spiritual status, competencies, attitudes, behaviors, and integrity. These personal qualities serve as basic building blocks for developing spiritually credible helping relationships, thus becoming a biblical counselor at least on the lay level. Such character beckons the would-be counselee to grant trust to the biblical counselor.

The Status of the Counselor

Ideally biblical counselors have (1) *maturity* ("must not be a recent convert," 1 Tim. 3:6); (2) *a positive reputation* ("have a good reputation with outsiders," 3:7); and (3) *a track record for sexual purity and marital loyalty* ("the husband of but one wife," 1 Tim. 3:2; Titus 1:6). Counselors like this are more likely to resist the pride that comes with novelty (1 Cor. 8:1; Gal. 6:1; 1 Tim. 3:6) and to draw on "wisdom that comes from heaven" (James 3:17).

The Competence of the Counselor

Biblical counselors, filled by the Holy Spirit, will demonstrate (4) *clear thinking* ("temperate," 1 Tim. 3:2); (5) *a great capacity for truth* ("able to teach," 3:2; see Titus 1:9); and (6) *the ability to manage a well-ordered home* ("manage his own family well ... whose children believe," 1 Tim. 3:4–5; Titus 1:6).

With growing masteries like these, biblical counselors are less prone to deception (Eph. 5:6) and more prone to deliver teaching through the twin strengths of example and conversation (1 Tim. 4:11–16).

The Attitude of the Counselor

Great counselors (7) *look for the true good in every person and in every situation* ("loves what is good," Titus 1:8), and (8) *avoids the* (temptation toward) *selfish gain* they could achieve through a counseling relationship ("not a lover of money," 1 Tim. 3:3; see Titus 1:7).

Though life hurts, God helps (Gen. 50:20; Rom. 8:18–28). Thus, disciplined to dwell on the things that are true, noble, right, pure, lovely, admirable, excellent, and praiseworthy (Phil. 4:8), biblical counselors invite the God of peace to reign over troubled lives (4:4–7, 9). The biblical counselor seeks to live an other-oriented life, free of greed and materialism (Acts 20:33–35).

The Behavior of the Counselor

Counselors who are ready to partner with God are (9) *sober* ("not given to drunkenness," 1 Tim. 3:3; Titus 1:7). Besides being free from any chemical addiction, spiritually credible counselors (10) *don't overdose on self or rage* (not overbearing . . . not quarrelsome . . . not quick-tempered . . . not violent, see 1 Tim. 3:3; Titus 1:7), and they are (11) *steady under stress*, resisting sudden impulses ("self-controlled . . . disciplined," 1 Tim. 3:2; Titus 1:8). Instead, they take the long view of helping people. They are (12) *generous with their time and resources* ("hospitable," 1 Tim. 3:2; Titus 1:8).

The Integrity of the Counselor

Biblical counselors seek to build lives of spiritual integrity with (13) *devotion to God* ("holy," Titus 1:8); (14) *moral decency* ("respectable," 1 Tim. 3:2); (15) *interpersonal gentleness* ("gentle," 3:3); (16) *impartiality* ("upright," Titus 1:8); and (17) *blamelessness* ("above reproach . . . blameless," 1 Tim. 3:2; Titus 1:6–7).

In addition to surveying the criteria for spiritual credibility this chapter now seeks to illustrate the ministry of lay Christians who are obeying Christ's goal of sexual purity (Matt. 5:29–30; Mark 9:43–47) through prevention, intervention, and postvention. Chapter 8 describes the social maturity of church leaders, and chapter 9 considers the professional preparation of trained Christian therapists.

BIBLICAL COUNSELING BY LAY CHRISTIANS: A CASE STUDY IN PREVENTION

In the early hours before that June dawn, thousands of men began scribbling farewell notes to sleeping wives and children. Soon these sojourners would be joined by other men clustering around train stations, bus stops, and parking lots. As dawn journeyed toward dusk, interstate arteries jammed with men gazing through windshields at the Indianapolis skyline.

Why? These men were not craving the squeak of NBA sneakers at Market Square Arena nor the thunder of stock cars at the Brickyard 500. These men were assembling as one of the largest nonmilitary, all-male gatherings in the history of the world. They would soon participate in one of the grandest examples of prevention-oriented biblical counseling in America—laymen serving laymen through biblical counseling.

In the years leading up to these two days God had redeemed a champion football coach. Delivered from an idolatry toward alcohol, work, and daily Mass, this layman had surrendered the zeal of a pro athlete at the foot of the Cross. Resurrecting that zeal, God had called a new play in the huddle. This coach would help teach a nation of men how to make and keep promises. On that weekend, using a day and a half to cover seven promises, Coach Bill McCartney and six other speakers would each tackle a different promise. Addressing sixty-two thousand men under the billowed roof of the Hoosier Dome, the coach and his team would seek to convert, train, and inspire "point men," laymen who would cultivate cell groups for prayer and accountability back in their communities and churches. Although the speakers' platform and the audience included a few clergy and some trained counselors, these stadium events and their spiritual ripple effects were primarily movements "of the people and for the people."

On Saturday afternoon a Wesleyan clergyman from San Diego stepped up to the mike. Married twenty-five years and the father of two, his task was noble: to lift high the biblical standard for sexual purity. In his down-to-earth style John Maxwell provided a laymen's primer on sexual purity. Recounting how his adolescent son and daughter had laid hands on him, praying that their dad would be God's instrument for that hour, Maxwell clarified his purpose. "I don't talk to you as an authority . . . not even as a pastor today. I talk to you as a man. . . . I don't come to you as some guy laying down the law but as brother to brother."[1] Interlacing Scripture with practical anecdotes, this man, whose father and grandfather were ministers, detailed ten guidelines for resisting sexual temptation.

- *Run from sexual temptation.* "Flee the evil desires of youth" (2 Tim. 2:22).
- *Accept the responsibility of your choices.* "I have set before you life and death, blessings and curses. Now choose life" (Deut. 30:19).
- *Be accountable to other godly men.* "Therefore confess your sins to each other and pray for each other" (James 5:16).
- *Listen to your wife.* "Submit to one another out of reverence for Christ" (Eph. 5:21).
- *Be on guard.* "Keep watch over yourselves" (Acts 20:28).
- *Determine to live a pure life today.* "Do not conform any longer to the pattern of this world, but be transformed by the renewing of your mind" (Rom. 12:2).
- *Realize that sexual sin assaults the lordship of Christ in your life.* "Do you not know that your body is a temple of the Holy Spirit? . . . You are not your own" (1 Cor. 6:19).
- *Recognize the consequences of sexual sin.* "But a man who commits adultery . . . destroys himself" (Prov. 6:32).
- *Think about your children.* "The prostitute reduces you to a loaf of bread" (Prov. 6:26).
- *Get a new definition of success.* "Far be it from me that I should sin against the LORD by failing to pray for you. And I will teach you the way that is good and right" (1 Sam. 12:23).

Although *Sports Illustrated* would describe Bill McCartney's decision to resign from coaching football as "un-American," he recognized his newer call to model and coach character. Through stadium events and local cell groups, through tapes, books, and rebroadcasts of sermons like Maxwell's, the coach would deliver preventive wisdom to millions of men in the locker rooms of life.

BIBLICAL COUNSELING BY LAY CHRISTIANS: A CASE STUDY IN INTERVENTION

While many Christians, like Bill McCartney and John Maxwell, have seen God use them to prevent spiritual failures, they and others have also been blessed to step right into the middle of a mess to do godly intervention. Publishing her story under the pen name of Laurie Hall and with the permission of her now-recovering husband, a laywoman engaged in years of biblical counseling; her ministry was an individual intervention in the battle for her husband's sexual purity.[2]

Laurie's husband—we'll call him Jack—had seemed like an ideal mate. He was a son of Third-World missionaries, a Vietnam War veteran, an engineer with distinguished achievements, and a staff member serving a fruitful southern church. But these phrases only painted a certain portrait: the "public Jack."

The "private Jack" was silhouetted in shades of gray on another canvas, one hidden from view. He had tasted profound loneliness, feeling abandoned by his parents as they lifted off for a new term in Africa following his high-school graduation. Trying to earn his way through college, Jack had encountered a job that let him taste the fleeting sweetness of soft-core pornography. As financial hardships wore him down in college, his planned reprieve of "one semester off" turned into a draft summons for the Mekong Delta. Once in that country, Jack's hard-driving unit began to view soft-core as if it were barbershop wallpaper. Eventually this lonely yet gifted young man was hooked on imaginary companionships, racing blindly down a one-way alley littered by two-dimensional lovers.

Though the postwar years would finesse the outer canvas with White House security clearances, marriage, and churchman status, the "private Jack" was becoming increasingly soiled. A career change, filled with demanding business travel, would rob Jack of the lion's share of his public accountability. The stranger in the business suit could easily ring home at

10 P.M. "Good night" to Laurie could seem like "good night" to Jack's day. But the R- and X-rated movies nightly begged him to indulge in their pretend affections after hanging up the phone. In time the hotel "escort services" could make his imaginations into a toy reality, all on the bed paid for by the corporate credit card. Like a thirsty man drinking salt water, strip joints and bar mates expanded Jack's appetite, an appetite to use and to be used. At his lowest point, Jack locked his five-year-old daughter in a rental car, while he tried to fill an inner vacuum in some urban red-light district. This "business trip with daddy" had been promised to the kindergartner. The strange men knocking on the windows forced her to huddle on the floor, audibly rehearsing Daddy's excuse for leaving her curbside: "He needs to buy a toothbrush."

Laurie eventually began to catch on. A bag of magazines at the bedside, followed by a rash of lies. Money borrowed, but not returned. Deviant pressures, answered by emotional coldness and conjugal boredom. Blocks of unaccounted-for time. A job termination. Threats from creditors.

For eight years Laurie contended for the soul of the man she loved. She begged God to give her victory and to reveal the invisible stronghold that held her husband. Prayer, fasting, and Bible study garnered her power. Empirical studies on sexual addiction prepared her to think with razor-sharp discernment. Though God chose to humble Jack in stages, nothing humbled him as much as when his own son confronted him in the spirit of Matthew 18. Nine months after the onion began to peel, a full confession emerged. Anchored in "a living hope" (1 Pet. 1:3), Laurie helped Jack taste the pure love of God (1 John 1:9), the same God who is now restoring "the years the locusts have eaten" (Joel 2:25).

BIBLICAL COUNSELING BY LAY CHRISTIANS: A CASE STUDY IN POSTVENTION

Sexual purity has always been God's will (Lev. 11:45; 18:1–30; 1 Thess. 4:3–7) for believers—for lay Christians, church leaders, and credentialed therapists. While God leads many biblical counselors to invest preventive and interventive energy toward helping counselees reach this goal, God also calls some to participate in serious postvention. The story of Janice

McBride is a classic example of biblical counseling delivered after the fact, an example of postventive ministry for those who have been victimized by childhood sexual abuse.[3]

Born on the eve of World War II near Scotland's great shipbuilding yards, Janice McBride recalls Luftwaffe bombings, air-raid shelters, and gas masks as if it were yesterday. Tragically, her personal war was filled with a more enduring terror.

As the first of several out-of-wedlock children, Janice grew up battling to survive her mother's acute schizophrenia and live-in boyfriends. While all the children in this home suffered from chokings, burnings, and beatings, only Janice was raped by the live-in "fathers." Apparently stuck in cycles of rage, Janice's mother could never find the "off switch" for her tirades, typically pounding her daughter's head against the wall or floor until someone pulled her away. With deadly effect a story was rehearsed again and again about a nurse at the hospital who had wanted to adopt Janice at birth. Instead, Janice's mother kept her because Janice was her "sin" and "the cross" she had to bear.

Throughout her school years Janice missed weeks and months of classes. After one pummeling, she spent more than a year in a wheelchair. Nearly blinded by one of her "fathers" ramming a turpentine-doused paintbrush into her eyes, Janice feared that she'd never be able to see again. Cast headfirst into a live coal fire, she lost all her hair and gained a lifelong scar.

Janice felt doubly victimized: She underwent incredible violence, but she felt stigmatized away from telling anyone about it. Threatened with the idea that speaking up would destroy the family and splinter the children into abusive orphanages, Janice learned to lie and cover up. Though her mother knew about the sexual abuse and certain neighbors knew about the physical abuse, no one acted to stop it.

At sixteen, Janice walked out. Slamming the door on her family of origin, she tried to deny that she had loved ones and that she had suffered miserably at their hands. In and out of a short marriage, Janice ran from her past. Filled with bitterness and hatred, she was unable to sustain loving relationships. At the first sign of relational strain, she would protect herself and bail out.

Years later in another marriage Janice met the Lord. Watching the *700 Club*, she was converted to Christ at age thirty-eight. Throughout the next two years she devoured the Scriptures. Haunted by an avalanche of memories, Janice made Herculean choices every day to keep on forgiving her abusers. Discovering that her heritage was "common" (1 Cor. 10:13), she refused the pride that would have made her a self-proclaimed "victim." Though she had suffered unwanted and uncontrollable abuse, she recognized that she was also a sinner, unable to rationalize away her own sinful choices. While psychology offered her a "head knowledge," she felt Christ offered her a "heart knowledge." By confessing her own sins and by repeatedly forgiving those who had sinned against her, she turned bitter memories into intercession. Praying again and again for her mother, for the abusing boyfriends, for the conspirators, Janice gradually received "beauty instead of ashes" (Isa. 61:3). She was now concerned for the abused women and children of the world.

By the age of forty Janice found her mother and offered her more than forgiveness. She offered her honest love. And in the decade that followed, Janice's mother and Janice's past were redeemed, granting her the grace to teach weekly "Life Messages" in home study groups.

Wrapped in the velvet of past sufferings, Janice has freedom to present her biblical message in prisons, military bases, and retreat centers. In her recovery principles Janice shows respect for professional counselors. Beyond that, however, she offers hope to those who haven't found godly counselors or feel they can't afford them. Rather than sending her disciples on a solitary trek toward self-esteem, she inspires them to pursue "Christ esteem." Rather than majoring on "who they are in Christ," she helps them discover "who Christ is in them." Rather than using projective techniques to coach people in remembering their past, she suggests that adult children allow the Holy Spirit to bring back the memories God chooses to use. For Janice, a sovereign God can use the old things for new purposes (Gen. 50:20; 2 Cor. 5:17).

BIBLICAL COUNSELING AND THE BUMBLE BEE

It may seem unbelievable that an all-or-nothing gridiron coach, a Vietnam vet's wife, and an incest survivor could become God's special gloves through whom he would reach down to touch groups, families, and individuals for purity. But God has done stranger things before. Remember the bumble bee? On paper it is aerodynamically unsound. Its body is too large in proportion to its wings; it has hair instead of feathers. But happily ignorant that it has been pronounced "unfit to fly," it lifts itself airborne from flower to flower, buzzing merrily through life each day. So it is with laymen, laywomen, and children who are in an all-out pursuit of excellent Christian character. The clergy may be doubtful and therapists downright suspicious, but throughout history God has used more lay Christians to do His work than He has used the ordained and the licensed. Like Ignace Jan Paderewski reaching around a child on the piano bench, God can graciously transform our simple "Twinkle, Twinkle, Little Star" into a symphony of effective biblical counseling.

CHAPTER EIGHT

Biblical Counseling by Congregational Leaders:
Social Credibility

FROM THE BOWERY TO THE SUBURBS, Mickey had come a long way. Born again out of the urban jungle of New York City, this athlete-turned-actor was now being discipled in a suburban Bible college.

It wasn't long before Mickey discovered that there was a third layer of life in the United States. Beyond urban and suburban, there was rural. "Let's go to Harper's Ferry, West Virginia," he suggested to his roommate, Alan. "I hear it's great—the Civil War and the Blue Ridge Mountains. Do you have a tent we can use?"

When the designated weekend finally arrived, the two guys got themselves to a campsite by Friday sundown. Besides overreacting to the night sounds in the woods, Mickey managed to play along as if he belonged. But by Saturday it was obvious that his life experience was as far away from the Appalachian foothills as Mars.

Following a Ranger's recommendation, the two students began to hike a blue-blazed trail on Saturday morning. The trail would pass a Civil War fort and culminate, according to the Ranger, in a breathtaking view of the Shenandoah and the Potomac rivers converging.

The twosome trudged the moderate incline, studying trees and rock formations. One renamed his familiar sights; the other stared like a kid on his first field trip to the zoo.

"Halt!" Mickey grunted from the front. Glancing back over his shoulder with eyes squinted, he pointed stealthily up the path.

Immediately flexing at the knees, Alan, the more seasoned camper, peered around his scout. Expecting to see a moose or a skunk, or maybe a tribe of Sioux warriors, Alan swallowed his laughter when he finally zeroed in on their "intruder"—a box turtle lumbering across the hiking path. Mickey had obviously never seen one in real life.

Walking briskly around the city boy, Alan picked up the turtle, causing it to immediately retract its head and limbs. Alan pointed out the colorations on the shell and estimated the turtle's age. Together they peered into the narrow openings of the contractible bunker, noting how the little reptile peered back at them, intimidated.

The duo then put the turtle back on the ground and headed farther toward the summit. Obviously moved by his little encounter, Mickey kept chattering about the box turtle as they walked. "Don't you think we should go back and capture it again? I wonder if the people in the town have ever seen a box turtle? Do you think they'd pay us a bounty for it?"

What was going on here? Was one man more intelligent than the other? Or more spiritual? No. If the tables were turned and the two were trekking through Harlem, Mickey would have been the teacher and Alan the apprentice.

Their difference was a difference in experience. Alan, who had camped a hundred times and made friends of a dozen box turtles, basically knew turtles. He knew that turtles were so slow and so dull of hearing that hikers needn't break into a stalking mode to catch them. He knew that their turtle was neither dangerous or valuable. Familiar with its frequency in the wild, the boy with more outdoor experience knew the animal was virtually worthless to poachers or collectors.

LAY CHRISTIANS VERSUS CONGREGATIONAL LEADERS

In a way the difference between these two hikers is similar to the difference between lay Christians and congregational leaders. One pool is rarely more intelligent than the other. But experience, relatively speaking, sets them apart. While biblical counseling done by lay Christians can have tremendous value, biblical counseling done by congregational leaders—pastors, elders, missionaries, and others—often has the advantage of greater experience. Having helped, not dozens of people, but hundreds, congregational leaders have an experiential edge and usually have a broader perspective.

If someone comes to his or her pastor for biblical counseling with the problem of worry (Luke 12:32–33), the average clergyman is more likely than the average layperson to discern the variety of this problem. To do so, the church leader seeks to compare the frequency, intensity, and duration of the worrying to the many others who have talked to him about the same issue. Besides investigating the object of the fear, the behavioral exploration focuses on these issues: *How often* does worry affect you (frequency)? *How severely* does it affect you (intensity)? *How long* do the episodes affect you (duration)?

The counselee who gets nervous before a quarterly performance appraisal at work is worlds apart from the counselee who daily experiences apparently untriggered panic attacks that last ten minutes or more and leave such a legacy of dread that the sufferer refuses to venture outside except on rare occasions. While the average lay Christian is strong at goal-setting (for example, to live above worry and fear), the average church leader adds to that skill a greater repertoire for helping the counselee tell the full story (for example, distinguishing it from run-of-the-mill worry).

In the last chapter we encouraged anyone who is committed to the work of biblical counseling to engage in an all-out, ardent pursuit of exemplary character. At a minimum this lifts a person from tier five to tier four on the credibility pyramid for biblical counseling. In this chapter we encourage those who lead—or who seek to lead—whole congregations to add greater social maturity to their character base. This maturity is otherwise known in the counseling profession as facilitativeness. While beautiful character and a love for Scripture often hasten the skill of goal-setting, deeper empathy skills hasten the quality of disclosure and bonding between counselor and counselee. And after exploring process skills in this chapter, we will also survey the most common settings where biblical counseling is practiced by congregational leaders. In closing, we will illustrate the work of three church leaders who engaged Christ's goal for financial integrity (Luke 12:15; 16:9; Matt. 6:19–21; 22:15–22) through preventive, interventive, and postventive counseling.

FACILITATIVENESS IN BIBLICAL COUNSELING

Imagine yourself as a pastor, sitting in the quietude of your study when the phone rings. On the phone is Dr. Somebody, who wants to recruit you for an experimental study. Would you do it?

The researcher promises that your name will be kept out of any ensuing report. In theory the goal is to discover what counseling methods pastors find to be effective in working with their parishioners. Later, when the report does come out,[1] you learn that 105 Protestant pastors were randomly selected from two telephone books. Thirty-nine said no right away, while sixty-six were willing to hear more. Of those who listened to the protocol, twelve more declined.

Now imagine that you were one of the fifty-four bold souls. What had you gotten yourself into? First, you have a choice of locations. You can undergo a brief, experimental interview in your home or at the church office. Second, two requirements are put in front of you: answering a questionnaire in writing and interacting with ten minutes of audiotape.

The writing is much easier than the taping, because sitting in front of you is a perfect stranger with two little cassette recorders. With his right hand he plays snippets of dialogue from an imaginary counselee, who, according to the script, is a leading member of your church. With their left hand, they tell the little machine to record you whenever it's your turn to talk. Later your responses are evaluated by five raters according to a graded scale.[2]

Once the results are out, you learn that the study reports four findings. First, none of the pastors reached minimally facilitative scores (that is, the ability to build interpersonal trust and rapport quickly, to make two-way communication *facile* or "easy"). Second, although there were differences in age and experience among the pastors, these differences did not affect their facilitativeness profile. Third, although everyone fell short, the more conservative ministers fell further short. Fourth, although each of the pastors had completed a formal theological education, those with fewer pastoral counseling courses fell even further short.

Although the report says nothing about the counseling methods the pastors had found to be effective in their work with parishioners, it does recommend that pastoral-training schools include more coursework in the process skills of respect, empathy, genuineness, immediacy, and concreteness. While this recommendation seems entirely reasonable, the study fails to report its own glaring limitation, namely, a highly impersonal and artificial method was used to measure personal sincerity and interpersonal maturity. If the raters had used authentic pastor-parishioner audiotapes or videotapes, their results might have jibed more closely with reality.

However, just as lay Christians were encouraged to pursue the seventeen-faceted diamond (chapter 7) to grow from tier five to tier four, congregational leaders are encouraged to master the pentagon of facilitativeness (respect, empathy, genuineness, immediacy, and concreteness.) This enables them to move from tier four to tier three. While the foregoing study suggests that pastors are often laymen in terms of social maturity, I suggest that congregational leaders must increasingly know people if they are to excel in their ministry of the Word. They must go beyond just knowing *product* (right beliefs, right behaviors, and so forth) and pursue equal mastery of *process* (how to help people tell their story, set goals, and practice change). While God deserves the credit for causing spiritual growth, we must learn to plant and water the seeds of change in ministerial relationships (1 Cor. 3:6–7). But no one should ever expect the average church leader to function as a trained therapist (see chapter 9). Those who feel led to pursue a career of therapy can rightfully spend years perfecting their process skills as they pursue the experiential components that lead to licensure, accreditation, or certification. Yet no one should confuse the legitimate and different roles played by congregational leaders and trained therapists.[3]

Respect

When Paul counseled Philemon, the apostle showed him utmost respect. Philemon, a victim of grand theft, was still smarting. One of his slaves—Onesimus—had stolen himself by running away (Philem. 15–16). This no doubt had brought Philemon considerable grief: the loss of property, labor, and pride. But in God's sovereign plan, Onesimus had ended up in jail where Paul could evangelize him (v. 10) and apprentice him as a partner in the ministry (Col. 4:9). Rather than scolding Philemon or bossing him around, Paul appealed to him gently. "I always thank my God . . . because I hear about . . . your love for all the saints. . . . Although in Christ I could be bold and order you to do what you ought to do, yet I appeal to you on the basis of love. . . . I did not want to do anything without your consent, so that any favor you do will be spontaneous and not forced. . . . If . . . he owes you anything, charge it to me" (Philem. 4–5, 8–9, 14, 18).

In biblical counseling the counselor may have strong feelings about the obvious responsibilities of the counselee. Yet the counselor seeks to communicate respect and acceptance of the person who must do the choosing.

Empathy

When the prophet Jeremiah counseled the nation, he showed that he cared. Although his ministry announced judgment throughout the land, he came to be known as the weeping prophet. Though his message was a hard word, he had anything but a hard heart: "Oh, that my head were a spring of water and my eyes a fountain of tears! I would weep day and night for the slain of my people" (Jer. 9:1; see also 13:17; 14:17). In his preaching he portrayed God weeping for Israel and other nations (9:10; 48:31). In hope, he yearned to hear the nation weep in repentance and joy (31:9; 50:4).

In biblical counseling the counselor learns to mirror what the counselee is feeling (basic accurate empathy) and to anticipate cautiously those feelings the counselee has not yet revealed (advanced accurate empathy). The effective counselor refuses to be negative (antipathetic or hostile), neutral (apathetic), or identical (sympathetic) with the counselee. Instead, the mature counselor is willing to be moved and stirred by the counselee's plight (empathetic), and yet remains an observer with a larger perspective.

Genuineness

When Moses and Jesus counseled people, their meekness was evident (Num. 12:3; Matt. 11:29); they communicated with simple candor and trustworthiness. While hypocrisy presents mixed motivations, sincerity models singular motivation. When Moses stood before Pharoah, with his life on the line, Moses spoke single-mindedly, using the same script he had rehearsed in private: "Let my people go!" (Exod. 5:1; 7:16; 8:1, 20; 9:1, 13; 10:3). When Jesus was under the threat of death in His arrest and trial, His message was genuine and unwavering: "I am he" (John 18:5, 8; see also 8:24, 28; 13:19; Luke 22:70).

In the ancient world old cracked pottery was sometimes pieced back together using melted wax as if it were glue; once the pot was repainted, it sold like new. But when the pot was placed in direct sunlight or was expected to hold boiling liquid, its "hypocrisy" showed; it leaked and sometimes injured those nearby. Unlike these "hypocritical" pots, biblical counselors seek to be simple, meek, and genuine, without the dangerous hypocrisy of mixed motivations and hidden agendas.

Immediacy

When General Joshua counseled the post-Moses generation, one of the favorite phrases on his lips was "this day"—used about forty times in the Book of Joshua. As a godly leader, he didn't get swamped with theory and nostalgia. He was in the business of helping people make right choices in the immediate. As a younger man, he had seen the danger of procrastination and excuse-making (see, for example, Num. 13–14). So as the new generation faced the raging Jordan River and the Canaanite cities, God challenged Joshua and his troops and civilians to meditate on "this Book" (Josh. 1:8). On the eve of the miraculous crossing of the Jordan, Joshua instructed his people with these words: "Consecrate yourselves, for tomorrow the LORD will do amazing things" (3:5). Once across, he set up memorial stones (4:9), and on investigation, he requested an on-the-spot confession from a thief (7:19). Although Joshua was not an impatient man, he refused to wander in disobedience to God. Decisive and present-oriented, Joshua appointed the Gibeonites as woodsmen (9:27) and confronted the eastern tribes with their apparent defection from the Lord (22:18). As death neared, he didn't hide it (23:14). He imitated his mentor in challenging the people, "Choose for yourselves this day whom you will serve" (24:15; see Deut. 30:19).

Biblical counselors, using the skill of immediacy, will always attend to what is happening right in front of them. In hopes of making an eternal difference, biblical counselors will look for legitimate leverage in the here-and-now.

Concreteness

When Epaphroditus visited Paul in prison, he brought a concrete gift, perhaps money, clothing, or food (Phil. 2:25; 4:18). Rather than merely mailing a letter, Epaphroditus nearly gave his life (2:27, 30). His ministry was practical and tangible. Similarly, Western missiologists have begun studying the largest and fastest-growing churches in the world, trying to understand their principles for success. One church in Korea had a surprisingly simple strategy. For years their pastor had taught his members a three-step lifestyle. First, pay attention to the people the Lord has placed around you (immediacy); whenever you hear that someone has encountered a loss (empathy), visit them with a gift of fruit or flowers (concreteness). Second, visit them a week later and tell them that you're praying for them (genuineness). Do not witness to them (respect). Third, visit them a week later and present the gospel. Such an approach, whether used by pastors, missionaries, or biblical counselors, helps believers become "fishers of men" (Matt. 4:19; Mark 1:17), not mere keepers of the aquarium.

Biblical counselors, practicing the five interpersonal courtesies of respect, empathy, genuineness, immediacy, and concreteness, become cross-cultural specialists. By learning about their counselees, they can invite them to walk a relational bridge toward the counselor and toward greater Christlikeness.

COMMON SETTINGS FOR BIBLICAL COUNSELING

Labels abound for church leaders. When Paul summoned the Ephesian "elders," he reminded them that the Holy Spirit had made them "overseers" who were to "shepherd" the church of God (Acts 20:17, 28). In some circles these leaders are strictly nonsalaried; in others, the leaders draw bivocational incomes or receive their total earnings through the congregation, denomination, or parachurch organization. Regardless of one's pay status, those who lead whole congregations or who oversee major components of church life often do biblical counseling from a larger viewpoint; they often recognize not only the needs of individuals but also the needs of whole groups of individuals.

While nonsalaried church leaders tend to carry out their biblical counseling work within their own congregation or in closely affiliated sister congregations, salaried pastors sometimes serve a broader field of counselees through various professional settings. According to Carr, Hinkle, and Moss,[4] the following are the ten most common contexts:

- parish staff counselor
- parish-based pastoral counseling service
- community-based pastoral counseling center
- pastoral counseling group practice
- satellite pastoral counseling office
- seminary, university, hospital, or Armed Forces counseling service
- hospital outpatient pastoral care
- judicatory counseling department
- denominational social service agency
- pastoral counselor in church information centers.

Parish staff counselor. A pastor on a church staff draws a salary from the church and provides counseling to members of the congregation. These counselees either refer themselves to the counselor or are referred by other congregants or staff members. In certain circumstances the pastor-as-counselor will refer specific cases to a trained therapist. This is the most common model for biblical counseling as practiced by professional congregational leaders.

Parish-based pastoral counseling service. This model imitates the above design. However, the pastor also extends his counseling efforts to people in the surrounding community. Since professional care is now being extended beyond the church, a special committee or board may be organized to collaborate on the parameters of this service.

Community-based pastoral counseling center. An individual counselor offers pastoral counseling to multiple churches and the surrounding community, hosting the service in an office that is separate from any of the constituent churches. Because this service probably includes some advertising costs, a receptionist's salary, and lease expenses, the ministry is usually incorporated under a nonprofit board and follows a budget. Overall funding comes either from the counselees (by fees or donations) or from churches providing support to the counselor, much as they would do for missionaries.

Pastoral counseling group practice. This model duplicates the preceding design. However, the practice includes two or more counselors.

Satellite pastoral counseling office. One or more counselors contract with specific churches to do counseling sessions on certain days or evenings of the week at the site of the host church. The church provides the office space, sets up the appointments, and donates whatever internal publicity is needed to create referrals. As before, the funding comes either directly from the counselee or from supporting churches.

Seminary, university, hospital, or Armed Forces counseling service. The school, hospital, or military base salaries a chaplain who primarily serves the students, patients, or military personnel. As he or she has time, the chaplain may also provide additional counseling services to the faculty, staff, civilians, and family members of their target population. This service is usually bundled with other services that are ultimately paid for by fees (student or patient fees) or public funds (taxes).

Hospital outpatient pastoral care. Copying the foregoing design, some hospital chaplains extend their pastoral counseling services to former patients who have been discharged to the community. Similarly some schools might offer care to their alumni and some base chapel programs might include retired military in the area.

Judicatory counseling department. Some denominations or associations of churches provide pastoral counseling to professional religious workers and their families. Unless disciplinary actions are involved, religious workers usually seek out this service on their own. Denominational income typically offsets these costs.

Denominational social service agency. Similar to the judicatory design, some denominations extend their pastoral counseling services to the public who learn of the service by word of mouth or advertising. Examples include the Salvation Army and Lutheran Welfare.

Pastoral counselor in church information centers. Some denominations are large enough to host a headquarters or a tourist center, and they place a pastoral counselor on site. This placement capitalizes on the awareness that a certain percentage of the public who visit the site are in search of spiritual guidance. An example is the Mennonite Information Center in Lancaster, Pennsylvania. Generally, these costs are absorbed in the overall operational budget for the center.

Would-be biblical counselors who feel called to work in one of these ten contexts will often need to secure specialized seminary (or post-seminary) training in counseling and/or business administration. Many will join the American Association of Pastoral Counselors or the American Association of Clinical Pastoral Education. And with the explosive growth in pastoral counseling since the 1960s and the high percentage—43 percent—of people turning first to clergy when they need counseling,[5] frontline ministers report interest in becoming proficient in people skills as well as biblical studies.

BIBLICAL COUNSELING BY CONGREGATIONAL LEADERS: A CASE STUDY IN PREVENTION

In the late 1980s a modest congregation in the Washington, D.C., suburbs drew me and two other men into their leadership circle. According to church stationery, we held different titles—senior pastor, associate pastor, and elder—but scripturally we all held the same office (Acts 20:17, 28). Similar in age, we were each married with children and had earned a Bible college degree in years past. Different in temperament and graduate specialties, we each had developed a unique leadership role in the church.

As the church grew, the average-sized facility began to host four preaching services each Sunday: 8:00, 9:30, and 11:00 A.M., and 6:00 P.M. Typically my ministry as senior pastor focused on clarifying truth: preaching to the larger audiences at 9:30 and 11:00 and providing brief pastoral counseling to people who were struggling with issues in their lives. Jeff Carroll, the associate pastor, served as a spark plug for outreach. Whereas the larger services followed a traditional format, he began pioneering a seeker-oriented style in the 8:00 and 6:00 services, as well as hosting "fishing-pond" seminars at local colleges with a discussion panel of creation scientists or a workshop on Christian abuse-recovery principles. Steve Henry, the elder, gifted at asking "the hard questions" about leadership and finance, taught Sunday school and AWANA and helped another pastor oversee a subset of the congregation.

As 1990 approached, Grace Bible Church planned to begin a daughter congregation in a nearby town. Prayerfully recruiting a core of fifty men, women, and children, Associate Pastor Carroll began to cultivate a strategy. Drawing on lessons from the three previous generations of church planting that had led to the Grace congregation, Carroll studied, prayed, and planned. Chief among his priorities was a five-month leadership module. Before the first public service could take place in rented quarters, the core group would become specially grounded in cardinal doctrines, spiritual gifts, and certain ministry skills. What would begin as training and accountability in January 1990 would culminate in their missionary commissioning the following November.

In order to illustrate biblical counseling as practiced in preventive, interventive, and postventive time frames by church leaders, one component of the core training will be profiled. Anchored by Jesus' commands about financial integrity [*being stewards of our possessions* (Luke 16:9), *avoiding greed* (Matt. 6:19–21, Luke 12:15), *paying civil taxes* (Matt. 22:15–22], and *keeping promises* like paying off debts (5:33–37)), Carroll huddled with me and Steve Henry to develop a month-long training program in biblical finance. He didn't want to provide some sentimental mishmash about money. He wanted to counsel his church-to-be in financial wisdom to prevent his core families from sliding down the slippery slope of financial foolishness.

As a result of these huddles we three committed to a plan. The Grace Church would purchase a video series by Larry Burkett of Christian Financial Concepts, and Steve, a financial planner, would immerse himself in the videos. Steve would prepare and preach a series of four Sunday-morning sermons to the core group that was destined to become Trinity Community Church. During the same month Steve would provide parallel training at Grace on Sunday evenings (a biblical synopsis, one Burkett video, and a question-and-answer session). Although each of us would be involved in helping people at many levels, Pastor Carroll's role tended to focus on prevention, while Steve and I were more often drawn into intervention and postvention.

Besides sponsoring the original monthlong series, Jeff distilled the teaching into a three-tiered pyramid that he could graph on napkins, flash up on an overhead, or chat about with premarrieds. In the biblical ideal his top tier read "Honoring God." In the middle tier the right and left halves read "Family Provision" and "Debt Elimination." The bottom tier read "Discretionary." He could spend the next decade challenging the congregation and families not to invert the pyramid, that is, not buying what you want before you address family and debt responsibilities, and not simply giving "leftovers" to God.

In the end the prevention-oriented biblical counseling of the Trinity Church shepherd paid off. Year after year, the Lord has allowed Trinity to set and exceed their expanding income budget and each year to spend less than they bring in.

As the church learned these lessons, key families in the church mirrored these lessons at home. Two brothers, one highly successful in supermarket merchandising and the other in electrical engineering, would convert these Sunday lessons into a lifestyle. With generous salaries, stock options, and company bonuses, these thirty-something brothers could easily have reasoned, "We'll earn it and give it to ministries." But God had more for them. They both downsized their standards of living, eliminated debt, completed seminary training, and entered vocational service. One brother, having dramatically reduced his home mortgage and his expense budget over time, was financially free to accept a 70 percent pay cut to take on his first pastorate in Iowa. The other brother, having successfully managed a satellite-Internet market for Southeast Asia, gave up his job and moved his family into an unreached people group for the gospel. Because these men and their wives had gained a victory over greed and had achieved excellence in paying off financial obligations, they were financially free to say yes to ministry opportunities. Having become faithful stewards in smaller things, they were entrusted with greater things (Luke 16:10).

BIBLICAL COUNSELING BY CONGREGATIONAL LEADERS: A CASE STUDY IN INTERVENTION

While Associate Pastor Carroll continued to lay the bricks of preventive wisdom on the path of the new church, Grace Church was at a different stage. As an older congregation Grace had more members spanning a wider variety of ages. As the financial training unfolded, various members found their way to my office to react. Some in their senior years felt the series was unnecessary. They had learned these lessons long ago or were frustrated by the idea of long-term planning.

Fortunately the series revealed to a number of individuals and couples that they were standing on the edge of a financial cliff. Discovering the way interest works for you in savings or against you in debt, they recognized that money could be either a useful tool or a terrible master.

One couple made an appointment with me, and in the session they announced, "We think we might have a money problem!" In a matter of minutes it was clear they did. Tens of thousands of dollars in consumer debt loomed like a dark cloud over their marriage and their future. With neither children or a mortgage, they had felt that they had more money than they needed; they were right. But by continually spending more money than they earned, they were wrong.

Through a series of candid meetings both husband and wife came to realize that their marriage could be in jeopardy, if things didn't change. So they committed to freeze all borrowing, to control all spending, and to sustain all income. Honoring their courage and discipline, the Lord helped this couple wade through the harvest of weeds that had sprouted from years of sowing bad seed.

By learning how to sow wise seeds with biblical wisdom, this couple eventually became free of consumer debt and learned how to honor God and to save. After several years of maturing, this couple later owned a home and had children. And because of their financial strength they could consider the pros and cons of the wife staying home with the children without any sense of panic or dread.

BIBLICAL COUNSELING BY CONGREGATIONAL LEADERS: A CASE STUDY IN POSTVENTION

With Associate Pastor Carroll focusing on the prevention of financial crises and me trying to turn around problems that were already somewhat underway, Steve specialized in serious postvention. As a financial counselor this elder offered private sessions with anyone in either congregation who attended the public training. If someone attended three public sessions, he would give them three private sessions in Christian financial counseling. His work was truly the most complex. Problems that had been years in the making were not going to yield to an overnight solution. The long path of disobedience would require a long return trek toward financial integrity.

At the outset of Steve's private work it seemed that the counselor and the counselees always had the same goal (*being good stewards of material possessions*, Luke 16:9). The first session always focused on the same assignment: "Bring a complete record of all your income and all your expenses. It can be a list or a box full of receipts." This assignment would begin the long process of helping counselees tell their financial story.

As the tip of the iceberg was explored, more of the story would come out. Sometimes the numbers would just not add up. Fifty dollars here and a hundred dollars there were unaccounted for. Steve would make it clear: "Either someone is stealing from you or lying to me or sabotaging this process."

The hard questions were like picking at a scab. Hidden habits surfaced again and again: cigarettes, pornography, eating out, alcohol, compulsive clothes-shopping, and so forth. At times the counselees resisted Steve's probing, but he always offered constructive accountability. The apparent goal of good stewardship was too often replaced with the goal of getting a financial monkey off someone's back without them really changing.

At times desperate counselees turned to bankruptcy; others pursued the privacy of the Consumer Credit Counseling Service. Without doubt, Steve's greatest delights came with individuals, couples, and families who just began to plod in the right direction. Rather than looking for a silver bullet, they swallowed hard and bit the bullet. By learning to distinguish between needs and wants, they could say no to McDonald's and cable TV; and by saying no to self, they could begin to say yes to a simpler lifestyle. By practicing the lordship of Christ over their pocketbook and wallet, counselees could honor God first and not pour money into a bag with holes (Hag. 1:6).

No congregational leader is perfect, whether practicing preventive, interventive, or postventive biblical counseling. Those who have leaped into church leadership based on personality rather than character are at grave risk in the work of counseling.

Church leaders must be mature in character and accountable in their relationships. In addition to striving for exemplary character (1 Tim. 3:2–7; Titus 1:5–9), congregational leaders should also seek to model respect, empathy, genuiness, immediacy, and concreteness in their ministries of biblical counseling.

CHAPTER Nine

Biblical Counseling by Trained Therapists:
Professional Credibility

PROFESSIONALISM AND THE BIBLE

fROM TIME TO TIME I ENCOUNTER CHRISTIANS who have a bias against education or money. To some, it seems obviously nobler to live near poverty or to work with their hands. Granted, James rebuked the arrogant businessman (James 4:13–5:6) and Agur commended a moderate lifestyle (Prov. 30:8). Yet Jesus allowed people to minister material goods and finances to Him (Mark 15:40–41; Luke 8:3), and He called some—"not many" (1 Cor. 1:26)—to minister *in His strength* with backgrounds of affluence or erudition. Abraham and Job were super rich (Gen. 12:5; 13:2; Job 1:3; 42:12). Moses and Paul graduated from the best schools in the world (Acts 7:22; 22:3; Phil. 3:4–6). Joseph, Nehemiah, and Daniel served in the highest echelons of human power (Gen. 41:39–46; Neh. 1:11; Dan. 1:3–6). At least one physician, Luke, had the skill and passion to scrutinize myriad eyewitness accounts of Jesus (Luke 1:1–4; Acts 1:1–2) and to accompany Paul's front-line missionary team (see "we" in 16:10–17; 20:5–21:18; 27:1–28:16). In the end it was a highly educated and wealthy duo, Joseph and Nicodemus, who handled all of Jesus' burial arrangements (John 3:1; 19:38–42).

If God could speak through Balaam's donkey (Num. 22:28–30), He can certainly speak through a well-educated, relatively affluent mental-health professional. In fact, when a Christian youth attempts suicide, the hospital usually requires a credentialed therapist to evaluate the underlying cause(s) or to take responsibility for the ensuing outpatient care. Why? Because it could be deadly to trivialize the young patient's problems and to send him or her out of the frying pan (the hospital) and into the fire (a troubled home or poor peer relationships). And when a man has been arrested for conduct on the highway or beyond, the court positions itself to examine "expert testimony" from police officers, attorneys, physicians, therapists, and others. Good intentions just will not do when the culture requires caregivers with specific training in law, medicine, or behavioral science.

This chapter describes the preparation needed by trained therapists who offer biblical counseling in their professional practice, and illustrate how three of these counselors have utilized preventive, interventive, and postventive strategies for pursuing Christ's goal for family unity (*keeping marital promises,* Matt. 5:33–37; *practicing sexual purity,* 5:29–30; Mark 9:43–47; *children honoring parents,* Matt. 15:4–7; and *loved ones managing conflict,* 5:23–24, 38–42; Luke 17:3–4).

PROFESSIONALISM IN THE CULTURE

When the typical American family builds an addition on their house, they want to know if the guy stringing electrical wire is going to put a fire hazard in the wall. When they send their child to public school, they want to know if the teacher knows her subject and has been taught how to teach it. When grandpa is about to undergo heart surgery, they want to know if the surgeon is licensed to practice medicine and board-certified to do a coronary bypass.

In general, governments issue licenses, whereas human-service organizations provide certifications or accreditations. These professional standards, though far from perfect,[1] seek to guarantee a measure of quality assurance to consumers.

Historically the modern era of licensure began when Frederick II instituted a law to combat the problem of witches practicing medicine among the people throughout the Holy Roman Empire. The new law excluded everyone but university-trained physicians from the profession.[2] Since then, the qualifications for various occupations in the United States have been introduced in many state codes (for example, psychologist, 1946; guidance counselor, 1972; marriage and family therapist, 1978; rehabilitation counselor, 1979).

In recent years workshops about licensure and certification have played to standing-room-only crowds. Counselors, psychologists, and graduate students have been trying to get the straight scoop from licensing agencies, certifying bodies, and knowledgeable professionals in the field. Part of the confusion has arisen from laws that vary from state to state (for example, a licensed psychologist can accept a new job in a new state, only to learn that she is unlicensable in that state after she moves). More confusion comes from the proliferation of professional organizations (for example, the American Psychological Association and the American Personnel and Guidance Association have a combined membership of over 100,000, but do not include many local pastors or school counselors). Bruce Fretz and David Mills suggest that the members of licensing boards and committees are typically overworked, underpaid bureaucrats caught up in a no-win situation. If they flexibly apply the criteria, they make applicants (from whose application fees they derive much of their budget) happy. The same decision makes professional colleagues unhappy with the swelling tide of heterogeneous competitors.[3]

Although there are over twenty-eight hundred occupational statutes nationwide and various exceptions to these rules, four general observations may be noted. First, only a psychiatrist (M.D.) has been to medical school; thus only a psychiatrist can prescribe medications and give medical advice. Second, only psychiatrists (with an M.D. degree), psychologists (with a Ph.D., Psy.D., or Ed.D. degree), and licensed, master's-level social workers (with an M.S.W. degree) can psychodiagnose and bill insurance companies. Third, other master's-level counselors or therapists (those with M.A., M.S., M.Ed., M.Div., or other degrees) should proceed cautiously when discussing medical or mental-health affairs with counselees and when collecting a fee (the host state and/or the sponsoring organization should advise accordingly). Fourth, no one should expect to do fee-based counseling with only a bachelor's degree.

Whether one is a counselee in search of an appropriately trained therapist or one is a counselor in search of a trained therapist for referral purposes, one can always ask for full, voluntary disclosure from the prospective provider (for example, education, license, certification/ accreditation, religious membership). Based on this disclosure, a background check could verify the credentials. While the laws can't prohibit pastors, priests, and rabbis from providing spiritual counseling, biblical counselors should venture out into psychosocial nomenclature and practice only *if* they have the appropriate credentials to occupy that broader vocational niche.

BIBLICAL COUNSELING BY TRAINED THERAPISTS: A CASE STUDY IN PREVENTION

The Word of God is "living and active" (Heb. 4:12), whether wielded by lay Christians, church leaders, or credentialed therapists. This "sword of the Spirit" (Eph. 6:17), ministered often since Pentecost, has shown the world its kaleidoscopic potential to prevent, interrupt, and repair spiritual problems. Thus in light of God's norm for family unity (Gen. 2:24; Matt. 19:6), many Christian therapists have used their skills to withstand the ungodly drift toward family divisiveness.

One counselor who has used many of his professional energies to try to prevent fractures in the family is James Dobson. Raised in a solid, middle-American home, this son of a Nazarene minister accepted his vocation from God and eventually earned a Ph.D. in child development from the University of Southern California. As a licensed psychologist, Dr. Dobson's early expertise focused on the varieties of mental retardation and on the coping repertoire of parents with mentally disabled children.

Building on nearly two decades of work as an assistant professor of clinical pediatrics at the USC School of Medicine and as part of the attending staff at the Children's Hospital of Los Angeles, Dobson's love for children demanded that he do more. Knowing that his work at the university and the hospital mattered, Dobson longed to touch more families in their churches and homes. With his groundbreaking book in 1970, *Dare to Discipline*,[4] the young West Coast psychologist rocked the politically correct world. For many social scientists and Baby Boomers who had accepted the foregone conclusion that spanking was immoral and abusive, Dobson gave them a reason to rethink the issue. Catapulted into the public eye, this communicator began to utilize video, radio, and print media to serve American families. Eventually heard on more than thirteen hundred radio stations in twenty-five countries, Dobson counseled in the kitchens and commuter cars of the nation and even advised presidents and senators. Although frequently slandered for his opposition to abortion, pornography, and gambling, he has continued to sow the biblical seeds of prevention in the soil of avid listeners.

Although hundreds of examples could be given, only one is necessary to illustrate that James Dobson is a biblical counselor with a heart focused on prevention. In an effort to encourage pastors, counselors, courting couples, and the nation itself, Dobson commissioned his Focus on the Family staff to conduct a broad-based survey of existing research concerning marital status. "From a social science perspective," he asked, "is it a good thing to be married? Or is marriage just a piece of paper, as many family cynics have suggested?"

What resulted was a thirty-six-page summary of seventy-two research studies,[5] mostly secular, which clearly showed the advantage, for the average person, of being married. Comparing traditional populations (married couples and children living with married birth parents) to other populations (never-married singles, cohabiting couples, separated/divorced individuals, blended stepfamilies, and others) across a number of variables (income, physical and mental health, lifestyle habits), the report argued that marriage is a definite "plus" for both adult spouses and dependent children.

Based on this paper and the spin-off broadcasts and articles it inspired, Sunday-school teachers could say to teenagers, "Did you know that 90 percent of cohabiting couples *plan* to get married someday, but 40 percent break up before they say 'I do'? And did you know that those who live together before they get married are nearly *twice as likely* to get a divorce afterward, compared to couples who never played house? In fact, the longer a couple lives together before marriage, the *more likely* they are to get a divorce afterward!" Based on this study, pastors could illustrate their sermons. "The Bible says it's not good for man to be alone (Gen. 2:18, 24), nor for humans *not* to live in family relationships. Did you know that 84 percent of all documented child abuse occurs in single-parent homes, with half of those instances occurring at the hands of boyfriends? Did you know that a pregnant woman is four times more likely to be beaten by her boyfriend than by her husband?" Even therapists, gaining leverage from the report, would encourage couples to stay together. "Some people will tell you that divorce is the answer ... that it's a brief crisis and your kids will get over it. But the research suggests that children of divorce are far more likely to end up as adults with poorer incomes, weaker emotional adjustments, and less stable marriages." Though God's delightful grace has given many of us membership in Paul's "such were some of you" (1 Cor. 6:9–11, KJV), the power of Dobson's prevention-oriented biblical counseling shows up every time one of his listeners successfully vows, "Forsaking all others ... till death do us part."

BIBLICAL COUNSELING BY TRAINED THERAPISTS: A CASE STUDY IN INTERVENTION

Professional therapists familiar with Scripture know that God designed marriage to be monogamous (Gen. 2:24), heterosexual (1 Cor. 6:9), and permanent (Mark 10:9)—one man and one woman for a lifetime. God bluntly banned incest, homosexual acts, plural partners, and bestiality (Lev. 18). Thus the New Testament sets the marital high bar with its timeless standard. "Marriage should be honored by all and the marriage bed kept pure, for God will judge the adulterer and all the sexually immoral" (Heb. 13:4). Unfortunately modern culture is rolling the dice with family unity and sanctified sexuality by its undiscerning embrace of the homosexual movement.

One counselor, biblical in his outlook, has committed himself to intervention. Growing out of his respect for the godly goals of family unity and sexual purity, Jeffrey Satinover, M.D., has entered the battle against homosexual disinformation and for the souls of men and women who are ensnared by same-sex habits. Tragically, some who are ensnared have been abusing the Bible to rationalize their bondage and to market their lifestyle. They have alleged that the Bible endorses homosexual love affairs (for example, David and Jonathan, 2 Sam. 1:26) and that the Bible merely forbids lustful love (Matt. 5:28) and anything contrary to one's inherited sexual nature (Rom. 1:26).

As a graduate of Harvard University and M.I.T., Dr. Satinover brings more than twenty years of psychiatric experience into every therapeutic conversation. As a former Child Psychiatry Fellow from Yale University and a Harvard University lecturer in psychology and religion, Satinover has carefully measured the issues of normal development and ethical boundaries.

In *Homosexuality and the Politics of Truth*[6]—hailed by the *Congressional Record* as "the best book on homosexuality written in our lifetime"—Satinover supports a sixfold intervention strategy.

- *First, tell the truth.* These are some facts that need to be communicated. Scientists have not discovered a homosexual gene. No one is born homosexual. Only 2.8 percent of males and 1.4 percent of females practice the homosexual lifestyle.[7] Because men have such extensive neocortexes, sexual variability among men is extraordinary. While the majority of heterosexuals are monogamous and avoid anal intercourse, the majority of homosexuals are promiscuous and practice anal intercourse.[8]
- *Second, warn about the dangers.* For example, anal intercourse is not safe, even with a condom.
- *Third, compassionately indict the behavior.* For example, homosexuality is sin. A modern type of paganism, homosexuality is a form of "soul sickness." Homosexuality is highly correlated with childhood sexual abuse, emotional rejection by the same-sex parent, and widespread unhappiness in many aspects of life.[9]
- *Fourth, emphasize choice.* While a heritable gene may predispose a carrier toward physical height, heredity does not require anyone to play for the National Basketball Association. Stated differently, even though a person may be born with a vulnerability toward manic depression or alcoholism, one's personal outcomes can be modified by choice and by experience. If a boy with a sensitive disposition is marked as "different" by his father and is subsequently rejected by male authority figures, peers, and potential heterosexual partners, he may experiment with the temporary anesthesia of homosexual companions. What starts out as a relatively "free" act can become less so over time because of the biological power of repetition.
- *Fifth, offer hope.* Homosexuality can be changed. The vast majority

of young people who adopt homosexuality eventually give it up.[10] An overview of secular therapies suggests an approximately 50 percent success rate, with Masters and Johnson reporting 65 percent in a five-year follow-up.[11] Successful approaches focus on treating social anxieties rooted in father-to-son gender-identity injuries[12] and on encouraging Christian forms of abstinence, self-discipline, and mutual accountability.[13]

- *Sixth, predict realistic treatment scenarios.* The brain has chemical-release mechanisms associated with pleasure centers. The experience of pleasure creates powerful, behavior-shaping incentives.[14] Unregulated sexual tendencies become habits, then compulsions, and finally something barely distinguishable from addictions. Sexual fantasies may not be entirely erasable, but new, acceptable fantasies can be learned in place of the older ones. New behaviors can become more gratifying than the old ones; the power of the old behaviors can weaken and wither, although during stress old patterns are more easily provoked.

With a prescription for biblical intervention Satinover recommends that Christian therapists and support groups provide patient, loving, sexually clear relationships in which a repentant homosexual can experience grace while practicing change. At times the recovery process may feel like the painful process Jacob experienced in wrestling with the angel (Gen. 32). But the process, like Jacob's, can result in blessing.

BIBLICAL COUNSELING BY TRAINED THERAPISTS: A CASE STUDY IN POSTVENTION

Judging from Jesus' last-minute promise of paradise (Luke 23:42–43), it is never too late to start doing what's right. It's never too late to offer or receive biblical counseling. Imagine a dying counselor (Isa. 9:6) caring for a dying counselee. For biblical counselors involved in major postventive work, God's mercies are "new" every day (Lam. 3:23).

For Clyde Narramore, postventive biblical counseling has become a trademark. He is burdened for people recovering from past adversities and chronic stress, including members of missionary families. As a licensed school psychologist for the Los Angeles public school system for many years, Narramore learned to weigh skillfully the impact of past hardships on young lives. Biblically committed to the ideal of family unity between the generations (Exod. 20:12; Eph. 5:22–6:4), Narramore and his wife pioneered an array of ministries, many of which targeted the parent-child bond among Christ's frontline soldiers—career missionaries. Blending the professional expertise of Clyde's Ed.D. degree from Columbia University with Ruth's experiential expertise from the mission field, the two were a perfect pair to pioneer their ministry.

Through the Narramore Christian Foundation the couple began to offer biblically based psychological services to North America and beyond. With the popularity of Narramore's *Encyclopedia of Psychological Problems*[15] and his "Psychology for Living" radio program, many people began to think about their problems in his characteristic three-dimensioned way: physiological, spiritual, and psychological. With a professional staff to handle the volume of ensuing phone calls, referral requests, and the need for various booklets, Narramore emerged as "the first dean of Christian psychology." Eventually he cofounded the Rosemead School of Psychology (now at Biola University), one of the few evangelical graduate schools recognized by the American Psychological Association.

To illustrate the strength of Narramore's postventive approach for missionary families, a few of his ministries can be profitably profiled. Since many missionaries serve in some of the most hostile and stressful regions of the world, Narramore began to send trauma teams to conduct emergency field consultations. Their goal was to promote spiritual and emotional healing in the missionary family and team. For example, his trauma team would conduct an on-site workshop on "Dealing with Depression and Anger," while providing private consultation for the particular crisis that triggered the postvention.

As another example of the Narramore ministry, missionary children are invited to a twelve-day "MK Re-entry Seminar" during the summer after high-school graduation. Debriefing on their past and preparing for their future, these children of missionaries are taught to understand themselves and to anticipate culture shock, and are given psychological and vocational testing. Starting with a five-hour testing appointment, these young people are coached on career profiles and personality issues. Licensed personnel schedule follow-up appointments, offering individual and group counseling where needed.

At a stage in life when many people are focusing on the leisure of retirement, Narramore continues to speak to families about excellent parent-child practices.[16] Now well into his eighties, Narramore continues to imitate Jesus' outreach to the end, "making the most of every opportunity" in postventive biblical counseling, knowing "the days are evil" (Eph. 5:16).

SOUND BYTES AND SHIPS

How often have we heard it said that "power corrupts and absolute power corrupts absolutely"? The line seems to fit so perfectly into sermons, especially fresh on the heels of some new presidential scandal. How about the equation, "Justice delayed is justice denied"? Doesn't that say it well after another felon has gotten a mere criminal-justice rap on the knuckles, only to commit a crime far worse? But the impassioned logic is slippery, because both, though neither of these sound bytes is entirely true. If they were they would indict God of corruption and injustice.

In the professional realms of medicine, law, and behavioral science, there are many slippery "truths." Because of this danger, many people try to avoid doctors, lawyers, and shrinks altogether. The same could be said about the slippery "truths" in religion, driving many to avoid the clergy of all sorts. But avoiding these helpers may be like forbidding trans-oceanic travel after the *Titanic* disaster.

Granted, the ocean is dangerous and human beings are fragile, so no one should take a transatlantic voyage lightly. But there was much that was right about the *Titanic*. It was just two flaws that did her in: pride and lack of accountability. In pride, the shipbuilders stowed only enough life-boats for one-third of the passengers. "We'll never sink," they thought. And when the wireless operators received repeated warnings of icebergs in their vicinity, they and Captain Smith ignored the warnings. They were single-minded about setting a speed record from Southampton to New York. Worse yet, they had become too busy on the wireless, arranging ticker-tape parades and celebration parties at home.

At 11:00 P.M. a stunned crew recognized that they were on a collision course with a frozen mountain. Steering sharply to the left, they hoped they could dodge the floating glacier. Tragically, the right side of the ship scraped the iceberg, opening a slice three hundred feet long. The slice, not even a half-inch wide, begged the black ocean to fill the "water-tight" compartments below deck, and so, more than fifteen hundred souls sank to their grave.

Like the *Titanic*, there is much that is right about professional people-helping. Though it should never replace voluntary helping (that is, lay counseling) or church-based helping (that is, pastoral counseling), it can be a godsend when practiced with the humility and accountability required by the institutions of our culture. Whether one reads books on theology or psychology, biblical counselors must compare slippery "truths" to the full knowledge of Christ. By mutual submission, counselors and counselees can remain accountable to their spouses, their peers, their parents, and their spiritual leaders (Eph. 5:21; Col. 3:18; Heb. 13:17; 1 Pet. 2:13; 5:5). Had the *Titanic* practiced equivalent precautions, she might still be afloat today.

CHAPTER TEN

Conclusion

WHEN THE DEVIL QUOTED WORDS from the Bible to Jesus, he was not offering biblical counsel. When he baited the Lord to turn bricks into bread, to free-fall from the high Jerusalem wall, and to kiss the ring of evil, he was not engaged in the art of biblical counseling *even though Psalm 91 was on his lips* (Matt. 4:6). When David Koresh haunted his Branch Davidians with twisted Scripture, he was not functioning as a biblical counselor. When he suggested that Jesus' "first coming in purity" implied a "second coming in impurity" (that is, Koresh's own incestuous lifestyle as an alleged reincarnation of Jesus), his words smelled of sulphur.

Genuine biblical counseling is any form of intentional, interpersonal influence characterized by the true meaning of Scripture. As this book has sought to show through exposition, illustration, and explanation, genuine biblical counseling occurs whenever men, women, or children seek to influence individuals, families, or groups to follow God's biblical standards. Whether in an office or an informal setting, lay, ordained, and licensed Christians provide biblical counseling every day. By learning how to help fellow pilgrims tell their spiritual story, to set Christian goals, and to practice elements of change, biblical counselors assist their counselees in identifying areas of moral delinquence. As they walk together, the counselor assists the counselee—by the grace of God—to restore moral innocence and build moral competence. By prayerfully hungering and thirsting for exemplary character, biblical counselors can be increasingly filled with the Spirit of Christ. By further acquiring interpersonal skills, some biblical counselors also inherit shepherding responsibilities for whole groups of Christians. Though much fewer in number, some biblical counselors even go beyond the trademark qualifications for lay and pastoral counseling to obtain a government-sanctioned, professional identity.

In the field of biblical counseling some practitioners have written from the lay perspective. At times their goal-setting has been caricatured as stern and simplistic. Other authorities have written from the therapist's perspective. Their patience-with-change and their integration of Scripture with legitimate therapy has sometimes left them burned in effigy as psychoheretics. Those with a pastor's perspective have sometimes been lampooned, as if they were merely indulging in mutual storytelling around some office "campfire."

But the kingdom of God is big enough to include lay Christians, church leaders, and professional therapists in the sincere, though differing, work of biblical counseling. Imagine a parody on Gettysburg's battlefield. How foolish would be the Union generals if they commanded the right flank not to fire because they weren't educated or patient enough! How questionable would be the judgment of General George Meade if he told those on the left end of the line to avoid engaging the enemy because of the complexities of Devil's Den, the Peach Orchard, and Little Round Top! Worse yet, would God forgive the twenty-first-century church if she forgot how to love, if she turned her weapons against her own soldiers and fought over the best ways to love counselees?

When Cora walked into Fellowship Chapel, she seemed mature. Having come to know the Lord through a college church on the Gulf Coast, she arrived ready to worship and ready to serve. As a single woman, her schedule could flex with the rhythms of the ministry, and she soon became endeared to the youth director and his wife. The three of them became fast friends, with Cora a virtual fixture in the youth activities.

But something was not quite right. Although Cora took a great interest in who was dating whom, she never dated. Although she spoke of marriage in idyllic terms, she acted like a deer caught in the headlights whenever a man expressed interest in her. The youth director and his wife were concerned. As a Christian, Cora had become an excellent example of reaching out to young people and of maintaining moral purity. Yet she did not accept her singleness as God-given. Although she was "devoted to the Lord in both body and spirit" (1 Cor. 7:34), she yearned for physical and emotional companionship. Although she prayed for a mate, her overt behavior seemed hypocritically disinterested. After consistently failing to match-make for their friend, the youth director and his wife asked Cora to talk to the pastor about her romantic tugs of war. Reluctantly, she went.

As difficult as it was for Cora to tell her story, the pastor proved to be a good listener. In time, both of them concluded that her romantic life was full of avoidance. Worries had kept her from dating and fear had kept her from marrying. "How can I go out with him? What if *abc* happens?" she had obsessed. "And I want to get married, but I don't want *xyz*." Perhaps her comfort level with high schoolers was a clue about her developmental stage of life. It didn't take a rocket scientist to know that a hard question had to be asked. Yes, there had been sexual abuse in the past—in the family. Now it made sense. The fear was reality-based.

Although Cora and the pastor agreed that she needed to work on forgiving those who had wronged her and on trying to reconcile the relationships, this was going to be tricky. The journey would take time and expertise. The necessary candor might create a period of emotional rawness, the kind of rawness that might make it difficult for Cora every week when she heard the pastor speak. At times it might seem like he was talking about her.

Together, they selected a Christian psychiatrist to take over the case, a woman with a proven reputation for practical Christian intervention. This therapist could give Cora the privacy she needed, while identifying with the womanliness of her concerns.

This doctor was the right choice. As an undergraduate years ago, this woman had heard God's call on her life. Her Bible professor had challenged the class. "Students, critics of the Bible have arisen from the fields of history, archaeology, and geography. But credentialed apologists have arisen to the occasion. But who will answer Freud? Who will address the objections from the realm of psychology?" Silently, she had committed herself to that battle. After medical school and a practice in pediatrics, she had retrained in psychiatry at a notable university. Now in practice again, she had an excellent reputation for minimal medications and maximal Christianity. She served on the board of her own church and actively sought to be an encouragement to the master's-level Christian counselors in her area.

When Cora arrived for their first meeting, she was nervous about a hundred things. When she left, only one remained: money. Now that Cora knew the psychiatrist's rate, her assignment was threefold: find out what percentage her insurance would pay, what percentage her budget could allow, and what remainder the church might need to provide.

By the second session Cora was confident. Fellowship Chapel had written a benevolent check to the doctor for the church's share of ten sessions. It had only one request: "Provide care as long as progress is being made. If it takes less than ten sessions, refund the difference. If it takes more than ten sessions, notify the referring pastor for additional funds."

The therapy succeeded, and it signaled a two-way partnership. At times during the therapy, the counselor asked Cora to hold conversations with her pastor, her friends, and various members of her family. These assignments were a part of testing perceptions and healing. When the last session was over, the psychiatrist sent a supergenerous gift to the church's benevolent fund. The attached note read, "If your church cares this much about its members, I want to help your benevolent fund to assist more people."

What a shame it would have been if the lay youth workers hadn't trusted their pastor enough to make the first referral or the pastor hadn't trusted the medical doctor with the second referral. Far from being passed off by inept or unwilling helpers, this young woman profited immensely through the youth workers' original strength in goal-setting. Subsequently the pastor had shown an additional strength in diagnostic listening, and the therapist had untied the knot of emotional bondage that had prevented Cora from dating.

Biblical counselors affirm the help-seeking behavior of counselees. After all, "many advisers make victory sure" (Prov. 11:14). But if it is wise for counselees to seek help, is it not also wise for counselors to seek help, to partner with others in the helping process? In building any house—

including the "goodly house" of biblical counseling for Cora—it often takes a partnership from many workmen to deliver a passable, turn-key inspection.

Several years ago in Bruno, Nebraska, I saw the value of a person not attempting to do everything by himself. After massive rains the local creek had overflowed its banks and was continuing to rise. One farmer, with a barn already standing in twenty-nine inches of water, was sure that his prized structure would soon float off of the stone foundation and be destroyed. He came up with a wise plan and asked for help; 343 people showed up, willing to follow the plan. With volunteers standing inside and outside each vertical plank in the barn, each pair was handed a one-foot pipe and told to stick it through the newly drilled one-inch holes in the planks. With one practice lift, the group discovered that together they could lift a 3,700-pound barn. With the right communication and cooperation, this spontaneous team moved that huge barn 143 feet up a slight incline and out of harm's way. In one hour's time the barn was safe from danger and later was lifted onto a new foundation.

The world isn't looking for one or two great counselors any more than that Nebraska farmer was looking for one or two great weightlifters. The world is looking for a loving assortment of lay, pastoral, and professional counselors who have learned to work together for Christ and neighbor. "Lord, may we not lean on our own understanding. May we lean on You, our Source of true wisdom" (see Prov. 3:5; 1 Cor. 1:30).

ENDNOTES

CHAPTER 1—INTRODUCTION

1. Leah Garchik, "How the Shrinks Stand Up in Court," *San Francisco Chronicle*, 31 January 1996, E8.

2. The Holy Spirit indwells every believer from the moment of salvation onward (Acts 10:44; 19:2; Eph. 1:19). However, in the inaugural episode in which salvation was extended to Samaria, God wanted these new Samaritan converts to link their spiritual ancestry to their Jewish heritage in Jerusalem, thereby preventing the development of a rival Samaritan-Christian church. So God did not bestow the Holy Spirit on these new converts until there was an apostolic hand-laying (Charles C. Ryrie, *The Ryrie Study Bible* [Chicago: Moody, 1976], 1553).

3. Mary Vander Goot, "The Shingle and the Manse: Should Pastors Be Counselors?" *Reformed Journal* 33 (September 1983): 15–18; and Richard L. Krebs, "Why Pastors Should Not Be Counselors," *Journal of Pastoral Care* 34 (December 1980): 229–33.

4. Ralph Earle, "2 Timothy," in *The Expositor's Bible Commentary* (Grand Rapids: Zondervan, 1978), 11:410–11.

CHAPTER 2—BIBLICAL COUNSELING: WHAT IT ISN'T

1. Jimmy Carter, *Living Faith* (Toronto: Random House, 1996), 187.

2. Dietrich Bonhoeffer, *The Cost of Discipleship* (New York: Harper & Row, 1959), 3.

3. Charles R. Swindoll, *The Grace Awakening* (Dallas: Word, 1990), 62.

4. M. Scott Peck, *The Road Less Traveled* (New York: Touchstone, 1988), 99.

5. Charles H. Gabriel, "My Savior's Love," in *Praise! Our Songs and Hymns* (Grand Rapids: Zondervan, 1979).

6. Gerald Egan, *The Skilled Helper* (Belmont, Calif.: Wadsworth, 1986), 75–82.

7. Gene Edward Veith, "Academic Respectability," *World*, 28 June 1997, 26.

8. American Psychiatric Association staff, eds., *Diagnostic and Statistical Manual of Mental Disorders*, 4th ed. (Washington, D.C.: American Psychiatric Association), 1994.

9. Matthew P. Dumont, "A Diagnostic Parable," *Readings: A Journal of Reviews and Commentary in Mental Health* 2 (1987): 9–12.

10. Herb Kutchins and Stuart A. Kirk, "The Business of Diagnosis," *Social Work* 33 (1988): 215–19.

11. G. Brock Chisholm, "The Reestablishment of Peacetime Society: The Responsibility of Psychiatry," *Psychiatry: Journal of Biology and Pathology of Interpersonal Relations* 9 (February 1946): 7–9.

CHAPTER 3—BIBLICAL COUNSELING: WHAT IT IS

1. Jeffrey A. Watson, "The Flower Fadeth: A Pastoral Care Curriculum for Biblical Death Education in the Church," in *The Pastoral Role in Caring for the Dying and Bereaved*, ed. Brian P. O'Connor et al. (New York: Praeger, 1986), 32.

2. See Thomas L. Campbell, "Physical Illness," in *Families and Change: Coping with Stressful Events*, ed. P. C. McKenny and S. J. Price (Thousand Oaks, Calif.: Sage, 1994): 126–51; G. L. Engel, "The Need for a New Medical Model: A Challenge for Biomedicine," *Science* 196 (1977): 129–36; G. L. Engel, "The Clinical Application of the Biopsychosocial Model," *American Journal of Psychiatry* 137 (1980): 535–44; R. Ader, ed., *Psychoneuroimmunology* (New York: Academic,

1981); and Norman Cousins, *Head First: The Biology of Hope* (New York: Dutton, 1989).

3. Walter Bauer, William F. Arndt, F. Wilbur Gingrich, *A Greek-English Lexicon of the New Testament and Other Early Christian Literature*, 2d ed., rev. F. Wilbur Gingrich and Frederick W. Danker (Chicago: University of Chicago Press, 1979), 298.

4. James Epperly, "The Cell and the Celestial: Spiritual Needs of Cancer Patients," *Journal of the Medical Association of Georgia* 72 (1983): 374.

5. M. W. Lusk, "The Psychosocial Evaluation of the Hospice Patient," *Health and Social Work* 8 (1983): 210–18; G. G. Merrill, "Religious Values in Treatment," *Maryland State Medical Journal* 31 (1982): 33–34; J. Westermeyer, "Education and Counseling in Hospital Care," *American Journal of Public Health* 72 (1982): 127–28; and J. G. Zimring, "When Is the Physician 'Playing God'?" *Journal of the American Geriatric Society* 28 (1980): 419–21.

6. Judith A. Shelly, "Spiritual Care: Planting Seeds of Hope," *Critical Care Update* 9 (1982): 7–17.

7. Raphael J. Becvar and Dorothy Stroh Becvar, *Systems Theory and Family Therapy* (Lanham, Md.: University Press of America, 1982), 50.

8. R. Dayringer, "The Religious Professionals' Contribution to Health Care," *Surgery Annual* 15 (1983): 113.

9. Howard G. Hendricks, "The Ministry of Presence," in *Pastor to Pastor: Exploring Challenges beyond the Pulpit,* Audiocassette 29 (Colorado Springs: Focus on the Family, 1997).

CHAPTER 4—HELPING PEOPLE TELL THEIR STORIES

1. J. F. Masson, *Against Therapy: Emotional Tyranny and the Myth of Psychological Healing* (New York: Atheneum, 1988).

2. C. Cerf and V. Navasky, *The Experts Speak: The Definitive Compendium of Authoritative Misinformation* (New York: Random House, 1984).

3. American Psychiatric Association Commission on Psychotherapies, *Psychotherapy Research: Methodological and Efficacy Issues* (Washington, D.C.: American Psychiatric Association, 1982); P. London, "Major Issues in Psychotherapy Integration," *International Journal*

of Eclectic Psychotherapy 5 (1986): 211–16; and M. L. Smith, G. V. Glass, and T. I. Miller, *The Benefits of Psychotherapy* (Baltimore: Johns Hopkins University Press, 1980).

4. A. Mehrabian, *Silent Messages* (Belmont, Calif.: Wadsworth, 1971).

5. *Diagnostic and Statistical Manual of Mental Disorders.*

6. Charles Wesley, "Hark, the Herald Angels Sing," in *Living Hymns* (Montrose, Pa.: Encore, 1972), 106.

7. "Last Supper," in *New Encyclopaedia Britannica*, 6:64.

8. For a full analysis of Jesus' questions see Roy B. Zuck, *Teaching as Jesus Taught* (Grand Rapids: Baker, 1995), 235–76.

9. "Icebergs and Pack Ice," in *New Encyclopaedia Britannica*, 9:155.

10. "Polar Bear," in *New Encyclopaedia Britannica*, 8:75; and "Bear," in *Encyclopedia of Knowledge*, 3:20–22.

CHAPTER 5—HELPING PEOPLE CHOOSE THEIR GOALS

1. Richard Leineweber, Jr., "The Commands of Christ" (Limerick Chapel, Limerick, Pa., 1994, photocopy). See also Zuck's list of Jesus' 481 commands in the appendix to his *Teaching as Jesus Taught*, 331–42.

2. A. Cohen, ed., *The Soncino Chumash: The Five Books of Moses* (London: Soncino, 1947), 248, 308; Isidore Epstein, *Hebrew English Edition of the Babylonian Talmud* (London: Soncino, 1936), 483–84; and M. Rosenbaum and A. M. Silberman, *Pentateuch* (New York: Hebrew Publishing, n.d.), 249.

3. American Rehabilitation Ministries, 4 April 1998. "The Terror of Gadara." *Tracts* [On-line]. Available: http://www.arm.org/gadara.htm.

CHAPTER 6—HELPING PEOPLE PRACTICE CHANGE

1. Phillip L. Berman, *The Journey Home: What Near-Death Experiences and Mysticism Teach Us about the Gift of Life* (New York: Pocket, 1996).

2. Jack L. Groppel (lecture presented at the Success Seminar 1998, Baltimore, Md., 13 April 1998).

3. Robert Feldman (lectures on health behavior presented at the University of Maryland, College Park, Md., fall 1995).
4. Ibid.
5. Ibid.
6. Ibid.
7. Ibid.

CHAPTER 7—BIBLICAL COUNSELING BY LAY CHRISTIANS: SPIRITUAL CREDIBILITY

1. John Maxwell, "Becoming a Man of God," Audiocassette CS880/ 13644 (Colorado Springs: Focus on the Family, 1995).
2. Laurie Hall, *An Affair of the Mind* (Colorado Springs: Focus on the Family, 1996).
3. Janice McBride, "Beauty for Ashes," Audiocassette 209.2000000 'MCB'AAA (Florissant, Mo.: Preparing Christ's Bride Ministry, n.d.).

CHAPTER 8—BIBLICAL COUNSELING BY CONGREGATIONAL LEADERS: SOCIAL CREDIBILITY

1. Henry A. Virkler, "The Facilitativeness of Parish Ministers: A Descriptive Study," *Journal of Psychology and Theology* 8 (1980): 140–46.
2. R. R. Carkhuff, *Helping and Human Relations: Practice and Research* II (New York: Holt, Rinehart, & Winston, 1969); C. B. Truax , "A Scale for the Measurement of Accurate Empathy," *University of Wisconsin Psychiatric Institute Bulletin* 1 (1961): 12; C. B. Truax, "A Tentative Scale for the Measurement of Unconditional Positive Regard," *University of Wisconsin Psychiatric Institute Bulletin* 2 (1962):1; C. B. Truax, "A Tentative Scale for the Measurement of Therapist Genuineness or Self-Congruence," *University of Wisconsin Psychiatric Institute Discussion Papers* 2 (1962): 35; C. B. Truax and R. R. Carkhuff, *Toward Effective Counseling and Psychotherapy: Training and Practice* (Chicago: Aldine, 1967); and C. B. Truax and K. M. Mitchell, "Research on Certain Therapist Interpersonal Skills in Relation to Process and Outcome," in *Handbook of Psychotherapy*

and Behavior Change: An Empirical Analysis, ed. A. E. Bergin and S. L. Gerfield (New York: Wiley, 1971).

3. Vander Goot, "The Shingle and the Manse: Should Pastors Be Counselors?" 15–18; and Krebs, "Why Pastors Should Not Be Counselors," 229–33.

4. John C. Carr, John E. Hinkle, and David M. Moss III, *The Organization and Administration of Pastoral Counseling Centers* (Nashville: Abingdon, 1981), 1–200.

5. Ibid., 13.

CHAPTER 9—BIBLICAL COUNSELING BY TRAINED THERAPISTS: PROFESSIONAL CREDIBILITY

1. G. Koocher, "Credentialing in Psychology: Close Encounters with Competence," *American Psychologist* 34 (1979): 698–702; and J. D. Matarazzo, "Higher Education, Professional Accreditation, and Licensure," *American Psychologist* 32 (1977): 856–59.

2. S. J. Gross, "The Myth of Professional Licensing," *American Psychologist* 33 (1978): 1009–16.

3. Bruce R. Fretz and David H. Mills, *Licensing and Certification of Psychologists and Counselors: A Guide to Current Policies, Procedures, and Legislation* (San Francisco: Jossey-Bass, 1980), 50.

4. James Dobson, *Dare to Discipline* (Wheaton, Ill.: Tyndale, 1970); revised under the title *The New Dare to Discipline* (Wheaton, Ill.: Tyndale, 1992).

5. Glenn T. Stanton, *Only a Piece of Paper? The Social Significance of the Marriage License and the Consequences of Cohabitation, Divorce, and Stepfamilies* (Colorado Springs: Focus on the Family, 1995).

6. Jeffrey Satinover, *Homosexuality and the Politics of Truth* (Grand Rapids: Baker, 1996).

7. R. T. Michael et al., *Sex in America: A Definitive Survey* (Boston: Little, Brown, 1994), 134.

8. Ibid.

9. L. S. Doll, "Self-Reported Childhood and Adolescent Sexual Abuse among Adult Homosexual/Bisexual Men," *Child Abuse and Neglect* 16 (1992): 855–64.

10. E. O. Laumann et al., *The Social Organization of Sexuality: Sexual Practices in the United States* (Chicago: University of Chicago Press, 1994), 295.

11. M. F. Schwartz and W. H. Masters, "The Masters and Johnson Treatment Program for Dissatisfied Homosexual Men," *American Journal of Psychiatry* 141 (February 1984): 173–81.

12. Joseph Nicolosi, *Reparative Therapy of Male Homosexuality: A New Clinical Approach* (New York: Jason Aronson, 1991).

13. E. M. Pattison and M. L. Pattison, "Ex-Gays: Religiously Mediated Change in Homosexuals," *American Journal of Psychiatry* 137 (1980): 1553–62.

14. John DeCecco, "Confusing the Actor with the Act: Muddled Notions about Homosexuality," *Archives of Sexual Behavior* 20 (1990): 421–23.

15. Clyde Narramore, *Encyclopedia of Psychological Problems: A Counseling Manual* (Grand Rapids: Zondervan, 1966).

16. Clyde Narramore. *Parents at Their Best* (Nashville: Nelson, 1985).

BIBLIOGRAPHY

Adams, Jay. *Competent to Counsel*. Grand Rapids: Zondervan Publishing House, 1986.

Aden, Leroy, and David Benner, eds. *Counseling and the Human Predicament: A Study of Sin, Guilt, and Forgiveness*. Grand Rapids: Baker Books, 1992.

Beck, James, and David Moore. *Helping Worriers*. Grand Rapids: Baker Books, 1994.

Benner, David. *Strategic Pastoral Counseling: A Short-Term Structured Model*. Grand Rapids: Baker Books, 1992.

———, and Robert Harvey. *Understanding and Facilitating Forgiveness*. Grand Rapids: Baker Books, 1996.

Counseling Insights: A Biblical Perspective on Caring for People. Anaheim, Calif.: Insight for Living, 1998.

Crabb, Lawrence J. *Basic Principles of Biblical Counseling*. Grand Rapids: Zondervan Publishing House, 1991.

Fagerstrom, Douglas L., ed. *Counseling Single Adults: A Handbook of Principles and Advice*. Grand Rapids: Baker Books, 1996.

Harvey, Donald R. *Surviving Betrayal: Counseling an Adulterous Marriage.* Grand Rapids: Baker Books, 1995.

Howe, Leroy T. *The Image of God: A Theology for Pastoral Care and Counseling.* Nashville: Abingdon Press, 1995.

Hurding, Roger F. *The Tree of Healing: Psychological and Biblical Foundations for Counseling and Pastoral Care.* Grand Rapids: Zondervan Publishing House, 1985.

Kirwan, William. *Biblical Concepts for Christian Counseling.* Grand Rapids: Baker Books, 1983.

Kruis, John G. *Quick Scripture Reference for Counseling.* 2d ed. Grand Rapids: Baker Books, 1994.

Luter, A. Boyd, and Kathy McReynolds. *Disciplined Living: What the New Testament Teaches about Recovery and Discipleship.* Grand Rapids: Baker Books, 1996.

Meier, Paul, and Frank Minirth. *Happiness Is a Choice: The Symptoms, Causes, and Cures of Depression.* Grand Rapids: Baker Books, 1994.

Meier, Paul, Frank Minirth, Frank Wichern, and Donald Ratcliff. *Introduction to Psychology and Counseling: Christian Perspectives and Applications.* 2d ed. Grand Rapids: Baker Books, 1991.

Minirth, Frank, and Walter Byrd. *Christian Psychiatry.* 2d ed. Grand Rapids: Baker Books, 1990.

Narramore, Clyde. *The Psychology of Counseling.* Grand Rapids: Zondervan Publishing House, 1980.

Oates, Wayne E. *Behind the Masks: Personality Disorders in Religious Behavior.* Louisville: John Knox Press, 1991.

Oden, Thomas. *Classical Pastoral Care: Pastoral Counsel.* San Francisco: Harper & Row, 1983.

Taylor, Glenn, and Ron Wilson. *Helping Angry People.* Grand Rapids: Baker Books, 1997.

Watson, Jeffrey A. *Courage to Care—Helping the Aging, Grieving, and Dying.* Grand Rapids: Baker Books, 1992.

Welch, Edward T., and Gary S. Shogren. *Addictive Behavior.* Grand Rapids: Baker Books, 1995.

Worthington, Everett L., Jr. *Marriage Counseling: A Christian Approach to Counseling Couples.* Downers Grove, Ill.: InterVarsity Press, 1993.

SCRIPTURE INDEX

SUBJECT INDEX

inappropriate disclosure, 37–40
mind reading, 27–29
"playing doctor," 40–42
political issues, 34–37
value neutrality, 22–24.
    See also Biblical counseling, hallmarks
Biblical counseling, hallmarks
    communication, 55–58
    compassion with integrity, 53–55
    hallmarks, listed, 47
    permeable privacy, 61–65
    persons as interdependent, 58–61
    principled intervention, 51–53
    relational accountability, 73–76
    scriptural process, 48–51
    shepherding souls, 70–73
    spiritual resiliency, 65–67
    transparency, 67–70.
    See also Biblical counseling,
        professional issues
Biblical counseling, professional
    issues, 183–86
    differing emphases, 195–96
    facilitativeness, 169, 170–74
    lay vs. professional counseling,
        160–65
    need for mutual aid, 198–99
    setting, 174–77
    use of trained therapists, 186–92.
    See also Change, as goal of counseling;
    Communication; Confidentiality;
    Congregational leaders, as biblical
    counselors; Counselor, effective
    biblical counselor; Credibility; Jesus
    Christ, as counselor; Lay counseling;
    Nonbiblical counseling; Rebuking
    sin; Success, in counseling; Training
    believers
Bonhoeffer, Dietrich, 24
Boundaries, confidentiality within
    boundaries. 61–65.
    See also Confidentiality
Burkett, Larry, 119, 178–79

—C—

Carr, Hinkle, and Moss, 175
Carroll, Jeff, 177, 178, 179, 180
Celibacy. *See* Singleness
Change, as goal of counseling
    acknowledging God's role, 135–38
    as slow and uncertain, 20–22
    attitude vs. information, 144–46
    balancing control, 148–51
    building habits, 146–48
    focus on future, 142–44
    nonbiblical attitudes, 9–10
    overcoming barriers, 146–48
    principles of change listed, 135
    role of suffering, 138–42
Character, 112, 155. *See also* Credibility
Children, Jesus' view, 121–22
Chisholm, G. Brock, 43
Choices, and outcomes, 150.
    See also Change, as goal of counseling
Christ. *See* Jesus Christ
Christian Financial Concepts, 119
Citizenship issues, 114
Communication
    in difficult situations, 55–58
    two–way communication, 84–86.
    See also Listening
Competence, of counselor, 158–59
Concreteness, in counseling, 174
Confidentiality
    danger of promising secrecy, 32–34
    limits, 22–24
    permeable privacy, 61–65
Confrontation, 126.
    See also Rebuking sin
Congregational leaders, as biblical coun-
    selors, 167–68
    intervention, 180
    postvention, 181–82
    prevention, 177–79
    vs. lay counselors, 168–69.
    See also Lay counseling
Consumer Credit Counseling Service,
    181–82
Control, locus of control, 150

Timothy
  focus on relationships, 12–14
  his family, 3–4
Training believers, 13–14

—U/V/W—

Unprofitable speech, 70
Value neutrality, vs. Biblical
  counseling, 22–24

Values, and behavior change, 145–46
Victim role, of counselee, 55
Vision, as counselor's need, 128–31
Warner, H.M., 81
Watson, Thomas, 81
Word of God. *See* Bible; Jesus Christ
Worry, 119–20

The
Swindoll Leadership Library

ANGELS, SATAN AND DEMONS
Dr. Robert Lightner

The supernatural world gets a lot of attention these days in books, movies, and television series, but what does the Bible say about these other-worldly beings? Dr. Robert Lightner answers these questions with an in-depth look at the world of the "invisible" as expressed in Scripture.

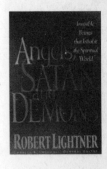

THE CHURCH
Dr. Ed Hayes

In this indispensable guide, Dr. Ed Hayes explores the labyrinths of the church, delving into her history, doctrines, rituals, and resources to find out what it means to be the Body of Christ on earth. Both passionate and precise, this essential volume offers solid insights on worship, persecution, missions, and morality: a bold call to unity and renewal.

COACHING MINISTRY TEAMS
Dr. Kenn Gangel

When it comes to effective discipleship, it takes a discipler, a coach, who is capable of not only leading by example, but also empowering his "players" to stay the course. In fifteen practical chapters, Christian education expert Kenn Gangel examines, among other topics, the attitudes in "The Heart of a Champion," leadership modeling in "Setting the Standard for the Team," and strategic planning in "Looking Down the Field."

COLOR OUTSIDE THE LINES
Dr. Howard G. Hendricks

Just as the apostle Paul prodded early Christians "not to be conformed" to the world, Dr. Howard Hendricks vividly—and unexpectedly—extends that biblical theme and charges us to learn the art of living creatively, reflecting the image of the Creator rather than the culture.

EFFECTIVE CHURCH GROWTH STRATEGIES
Dr. Joseph Wall and Dr. Gene Getz

Effective Church Growth Strategies outlines the biblical foundations necessary fo raising healthy churches. Wall and Getz examine the groundwork essential fo church growth, qualities of biblically healthy churches, methods for planting a ne church, and steps for numerical and spiritual growth. The authors' study Scripture, history, and culture will spark a new vision for today's church leader

EFFECTIVE PASTORING
Dr. Bill Lawrence

In *Effective Pastoring,* Dr. Bill Lawrence examines what it means to be a pastor i the 21st century. Lawrence discusses often overlooked issues, writin transparently about the struggles of the pastor, the purpose and practice servant leadership, and the roles and relationships crucial to pastoring. In doin so, he offers a revealing look beneath the "how to" to the "how to be" for pastor:

EMPOWERED LEADERS
Dr. Hans Finzel

What is leadership really about? The rewards, excitement, and exhilaration? O the responsibilities, frustrations, and exhausting nights? Dr. Hans Finzel take readers on a journey into the lives of the Bible's great leaders, unearthin powerful principles for effective leadership in any situation.

END TIMES
Dr. John F. Walvoord

Long regarded as one of the top prophecy experts, Dr. John F. Walvoord now explores world events in light of biblical prophecy. By examining all of the prophetic passages in the Bible, Walvoord clearly explains the mystery behind confusing verses and conflicting viewpoints. This is the definitive work or prophecy for Bible students.

THE FORGOTTEN BLESSING
Dr. Henry Holloman

For many Christians, the gift of God's grace is central to their faith. But another gift—sanctification—is often overlooked. *The Forgotten Blessing* clarifies this essential doctrine, showing us what it means to be set apart, and how the process of sanctification can forever change our relationship with God.

GOD
Dr. J. Carl Laney

With tenacity and clarity, Dr. J. Carl Laney makes it plain: it's not enough to know *about* God. We can know *God* better. This book presents a practical path to life-changing encounters with the goodness, greatness, and glory of our Creator.

THE HOLY SPIRIT
Dr. Robert Gromacki

In *The Holy Spirit,* Dr. Robert Gromacki examines the personality, deity, symbols, and gifts of the Holy Spirit, while recapping the ministry of the Spirit throughout the Old Testament, the Gospel Era, the life of Christ, the Book of Acts, and the lives of believers.

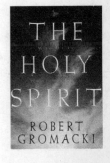

HUMANITY AND SIN
Dr. Robert A. Pyne

Sin may seem like an outdated concept these days, but its consequences remain as destructive as ever. Dr. Robert A. Pyne takes a close look at humankind through the pages of Scripture and the lens of modern culture. As never before, readers will understand sin's overarching effect on creation and our world today.

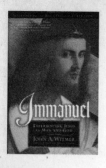

IMMANUEL
Dr. John A. Witmer

Dr. John A. Witmer presents the almighty Son of God as a living, breathing incarnate man. He shows us a full picture of the Christ in four distinct phases: the Son of God before He became man, the divine suffering man on Earth, the glorified and ascended Christ, and the reigning King today.

A LIFE OF PRAYER
Dr. Paul Cedar

Dr. Paul Cedar explores prayer through three primary concepts, showing us how to consider, cultivate, and continue a lifestyle of prayer. This volume helps readers recognize the unlimited potential and the awesome purpose of prayer.

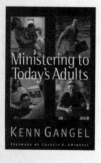

MINISTERING TO TODAY'S ADULTS
Dr. Kenn Gangel

After 40 years of research and experience, Dr. Kenn Gangel knows what it takes to reach adults. In an easy-to-grasp, easy-to-apply style, Gangel offers proven systematic strategies for building dynamic adult ministries.

MORAL DILEMMAS
J. Kerby Anderson

Should biblically informed Christians be for or against capital punishment? How should we as Christians view abortion, euthanasia, genetic engineering, divorce, and technology? In this comprehensive, cutting-edge book, J. Kerby Anderson challenges us to thoughtfully analyze the dividing issues facing our age, while equipping believers to maneuver through the ethical and moral land mines of our times.

The New Testament Explorer
Mark Bailey and Tom Constable

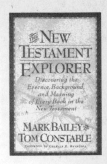

The New Testament Explorer provides a concise, on-target map for traveling through the New Testament. Mark Bailey and Tom Constable guide the reader paragraph by paragraph through the New Testament, providing an up-close-and-to-the-point examination of the leaders behind the page and the theological implications of the truths revealed. A great tool for teachers and pastors alike, this exploration tool comes equipped with outlines for further study, narrative discussion, and applicable truths for teaching and for living.

Salvation
Earl D. Radmacher

God's ultimate gift to His children is salvation. In this volume, Earl Radmacher offers an in-depth look at the most fundamental element of the Christian faith. From defining the essentials of salvation to explaining the result of Christ's sacrifice, this book walks readers through the spiritual meaning, motives, application, and eternal result of God's work of salvation in our lives.

Spirit-Filled Teaching
Dr. Roy B. Zuck

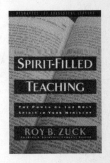

Whether you teach a small Sunday school class or a standing-room-only crowd at a major university, the process of teaching can be demanding and draining. This lively book brings a new understanding of the Holy Spirit's essential role in teaching.

Tale of the Tardy Oxcart and 1501 Other Stories
Dr. Charles R. Swindoll

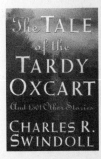

In this rich volume, you'll have access to resourcing Dr. Charles Swindoll's favorite anecdotes on prayer or quotations for grief. In The Tale of the Tardy Oxcart, thousands of illustrations are arranged by subjects alphabetically for quick-and-easy access. A perfect resource for all pastors and speakers.

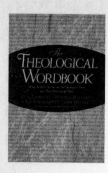

THE THEOLOGICAL WORDBOOK
Campbell, Johnston, Walvoord, Witmer

Compiled by four of today's best theological minds, *The Theological Wordbook* is a valuable, accessible reference guide to the most important theological terms. Definitions, scriptural references, engaging explanations—all in one easy-to-find, applicable resource—for both the lay person and serious Bible student.

WOMEN AND THE CHURCH
Dr. Lucy Mabery-Foster

Women and the Church provides an overview of the historical, biblical, and cultural perspectives on the unique roles and gifts women bring to the church while exploring what it takes to minister to women today. Important insight for any leader seeking to understand how to more effectively minister to women and build women's ministries in the local church.

DATE DUE